Studies in the Economics of Uncertainty

Josef Hadar

Thomas B. Fomby   Tae Kun Seo
Editors

Studies in the Economics of Uncertainty

In Honor of Josef Hadar

With 25 Illustrations

Springer Verlag
New York Berlin Heidelberg
London Paris Tokyo Hong Kong

Thomas B. Fomby
Department of Economics
Southern Methodist University
Dallas, Texas 75275-0496
U.S.A.

Tae Kun Seo
Department of Economics
Southern Methodist University
Dallas, Texas 75275-0496
U.S.A.

Library of Congress Cataloging-in-Publication Data

Studies in the economics of uncertainty in honor of Josef Hadar/
edited by Thomas B. Fomby and Tae Kun Seo.
p. cm.
ISBN-13:978-1-4613-8924-8
1. Uncertainty. 2. Stochastic processes. 3.Hadar, Josef.
I. Hadar, Josef. II. Fomby, Thomas B. III. Seo, Tae Kun.
HB615.S78 1989
330'.01'5192—dc20 89-11343
CIP

Printed on acid-free paper

Camera-ready copy supplied by authors.

9 8 7 6 5 4 3 2 1

ISBN-13:978-1-4613-8924-8 e-ISBN-13:978-1-4613-8922-4
DOI: 10.1007/978-1-4613-8922-4

CONTENTS

CONTRIBUTORS

Marcel Boyer
University of Montreal, Canada

Mary S. Broske
Oklahoma State University

Georges Dionne
University of Montreal, Canada

Peter C. Fishburn
AT&T Bell Laboratories

J. Horen
U.S. Sprint Communications

Takao Itagaki
University of Tsukuba, Japan

Donald W. Katzner
University of Massachusetts, Amherst

Richard Kihlstrom
University of Pennsylvania

Yoram Kroll
Hebrew University, Jerusalem

Haim Levy
Hebrew University and University of Florida

Daniel McFadden
Massachusetts Institute of Technology

Jack Meyer
Michigan State University

John W. Pratt
Harvard University

William R. Russell
Southern Methodist University

Tae Kun Seo
Southern Methodist University

G. Alex Whitmore
McGill University, Canada

Sam Y. Wu
University of Iowa

INTRODUCTION

It is a pleasure to be able to offer the enclosed collection of papers on the economics of uncertainty, all to honor the contributions of Professor Josef Hadar to his profession, students, and colleagues. Among his contributions to the profession, Joe along with Bill Russell, wrote one of the seminal papers on Stochastic Dominance, "Rules for Ordering Uncertain Prospects," *American Economic Review*, 59 (1969), 25–34. Thus it seems quite fitting that the subject of this Festschrift should be "the Economics of Uncertainty." A search of the literature in any number of subject areas (the theory of the firm, international trade, portfolio theory, income distribution theory, on and on) will give a clear indication of the importance of the Stochastic Dominance concept to economics and allied disciplines. The current papers bear strong witness to the maturity of the subject given its beginnings only 20 years ago. One can only guess what researchers will be applying the stochastic dominace principle to in the next 20 years.

Apart from the SD concept, Joe has made contributions in the areas of imperfect competition, diversification, international trade under uncertainty, and the theory of multinational firms. In addition to his advanced research, Joe has made substantial contributions to the lucid exposition of microeconomic theory. Many graduate students have cut their microeconomic teeth on his *Mathematical Theory of Economic Behavior* (Addison-Wesley, 1971) and have come away much the better for it.

Since Joe's arrival at Southern Methodist University in 1972, 16 students have had the distinct honor of writing dissertations under his direction while countless others have benefitted from his counsel though not writing directly under his supervision. In fact, it is easy to spot a Hadar dissertation student. He or she is typically walking out of his office carrying a well marked manuscript that was submitted only the day before. No moss has ever collected on his students' drafts. Quite understandably Hadar students are known for their questioning minds, rigor of thought, and precision of written expression.

The department's faculty has greatly benefitted from Joe's collegiality. Joe has been and continues to be available for consultation on matters involving microeconomics, mathematical economics and the economics of uncertainty. The department's research productivity has directly benefitted as a result. Even outside his fields of expertise Joe serves as an astute sounding board.

If you will indulge an econometrician's story, recently Joe came across a newspaper article on the new statistical technique called bootstrapping. Once the conversation began, a few minutes of probing questions followed. The core of the concept was quickly uncovered. Joe said, "What if you have an atypical sample to begin with." Point made. It has not been uncommon to see the collars of seminar speakers become progessively tighter from a barrage of Hadar questions. All of this was, of course, for the better because the speakers' papers subsequently became much better for it.

On December 28, 1988 a reception was held in Joe's honor in the Petit Trianon room of the New York Hilton during the American Economic Association meetings. Several of the contributors to this Festschrift as well as many of his students and colleagues (past and present) were in attendance. All agreed that the attention Joe drew was well deserved. Joe, this volume's contributors, your students, colleagues, and friends thank you.

The editors would especially like to thank Ms. Gloria Jones for her role in putting together this Festschrift, from being an expert word processor to being a skilled artist.

March 1, 1989

Thomas B. Fomby and Tae Kun Seo
Department of Economics
Southern Methodist University
Dallas, Texas
Editors

PART I
Theory

STOCHASTIC DOMINANCE IN NONLINEAR UTILITY THEORY

P.C. Fishburn
AT&T Bell Laboratories
Murray Hill, NJ 07974

1. Introduction

Stochastic dominance has interested mathematicians for more than half a century (Karamata, 1932; Hardy, Littlewood and Polya, 1934; Sherman, 1951; Lehmann, 1955), and its integration into decision theory began nearly forty years ago (Masse and Morlat, 1953; Allais, 1953a, 1953b; Blackwell and Girshick, 1954; Quirk and Saposnik, 1962; Fishburn, 1964). However, it was not until a cluster of important papers on stochastic dominance appeared around 1969-71 (Hadar and Russell, 1969, 1971; Hanoch and Levy, 1969; Whitmore, 1970; Rothschild and Stiglitz, 1970, 1971) that it emerged as a central topic in economic decision theory. Hundreds of papers as well as a survey book (Whitmore and Findlay, 1978) and an extensive research bibliography (Bawa, 1982) testify to its popularity.

The vast majority of this literature addresses the use of stochastic dominance in expected utility analysis, based on either the von Neumann-Morgenstern (1944) linear utility theory for decision under risk or Savage's (1954) theory of subjective probability and linear utility for decision under uncertainty. Fishburn and Vickson (1978) summarizes the fundamentals of stochastic dominance in the linear utility context.

My purpose here is to discuss the role of stochastic dominance in what I shall refer to as nonlinear utility theories. These theories are based on the same formulations as the linear utility theories of von Neumann-Morgenstern and Savage, but they use different utility models to represent preference between risky prospects or uncertain acts. With the exception of Allais (1953a, 1953b, 1979), most of the nonlinear theories arose around 1980. All of them were motivated by the empirical research of Allais and others, including May (1954), Ellsberg (1961), Tversky (1969), Lichtenstein and Slovic (1971, 1973), MacCrimmon and Larsson (1979), and Kahneman and Tversky (1979), which uncovered systematic violations of the preference axioms that imply the linear models. For the most part, the preference axioms for the nonlinear models are weaker than those for the linear models. Their weaker axioms allow the nonlinear representations to accommodate some preference patterns that are at variance with the theories of von Neumann-Morgenstern and Savage.

The nonlinear utility theories for decision under risk or under uncertainty abandon, or at least weaken, independence axioms that induce the usual expectation operations of the linear theories. Moreover, some of the new theories do not assume that preferences are transitive, while others do not require subjective probabilities to be additive. I shall say more about some of these as we proceed. Readers interested in more thorough reviews and additional references should consult Machina (1987a, 1987b) and Fishburn (1986, 1988).

The next section of the paper recalls standard definitions of stochastic dominance relations and the linear utility models to prepare for ensuing discussion. Section 3 then comments on transitive nonlinear theories for decision under risk that essentially include the first-degree stochastic dominance relation in the decision maker's preference relation. The theories of Allais (1953a, 1953b, 1979), Machina (1982) and Quiggin (1982) are included in this category.

Section 4 examines first, second, and third-degree stochastic dominance in the setting of a general nontransitive and nonlinear utility model for decision under risk. This model, referred to as the nontransitive convex model (Fishburn, 1988), includes the Kreweras (1961)-Fishburn (1982) SSB (skew-symmetric bilinear) model and a transitive weighted linear model (Chew and MacCrimmon, 1979; Chew, 1982, 1983; Fishburn, 1983) as special cases. Despite its substantial weakening of the von Neumann-Morgenstern axioms, the nontransitive convex model has implications for stochastic dominance that are very similar to those of the linear model. For example, if one risky prospect first-degree stochastically dominates a second risky prospect, and if we adopt a version of the assumption that more money is preferred to less in the nontransitive convex setting, then the first risky prospect must be preferred to the second.

Our final section, Section 5, looks at stochastic dominance in Savage's formulation for decision under uncertainty. Given the traditional assumption of additive subjective probability, we consider the principle that first-degree stochastic dominance ought to determine preference between uncertain acts. This principle, which is implied by Savage's model when preference for money or wealth increases in the amount, is also adopted by Allais in his transitive nonlinear theory for the uncertainty setting. An example suggests, however, that some people will violate the principle for defensible reasons. Empirical work related to this point is included in Tversky and Kahneman (1987).

One model that accommodates violations of the first-degree principle for decision under uncertainty has been developed by Loomes and Sugden (1982, 1987), Bell (1982) and Fishburn (1988, 1989). While Bell and Loomes-Sugden interpret this model through notions of regret and rejoicing, Fishburn shows that it follows from a weakening of Savage's axioms whose main thrust is to relax his transitivity assumption. Moreover, if we impose the indifference version of the first-degree principle on this model, to the effect that a decision maker should be indifferent between two acts whose induced probability distributions on outcomes are identical, then the model reduces to Savage's. Thus, in this particular case, agreement with a specialization of first-degree stochastic dominance forces global transitivity.

2. Stochastic Dominance and Linear Utility

We assume throughout that decision outcomes are real numbers $x, y, \ldots$ associated with levels of wealth, monetary payoffs, or increments to present wealth. All possible outcomes are presumed to lie in a closed interval I that is bounded below. With no loss in generality, I can be taken to be either $[0,1]$ or $[0,\infty)$.

Probability measures $p, q, \ldots$ that describe risky prospects are defined at least on the Borel subsets of the reals with $p(I) = 1$ and $p(A) = 0$ whenever $A \cap I = \emptyset$. A measure p is <u>simple</u> if its support is finite, i.e., if the $p(\{x\})$ sum to 1 for a finite number of x, in which case we write $p(x)$ in place of $p(\{x\})$.

The <u>distribution function F</u> of a measure p on the reals is defined by

$$F(x) = p(\{y: y \le x\}) \quad \text{for all real } x.$$

When $I = [0,1]$ or $I = [0,\infty)$, $F(x) = 0$ for all $x < 0$ and, when $I = [0,\infty)$, we assume that $F(x) \to 1$ as $x \to \infty$. Our definition implies that F is nondecreasing and continuous from the right. It has a discontinuity or jump at $x \in I$ if $\lim\{F(y): y \uparrow x\} < F(x)$. The distribution functions of simple measures are step functions with a finite number of steps.

As suggested by our assumptions about outcomes, we consider only univariate stochastic dominance relations. For any distribution function F on the real line $\mathbb{R}$, let $F^1 = F$ and for each $k \ge 1$ let

$$F^{k+1}(x) = \int_{-\infty}^{x} F^k(y)dy \quad \text{for all } x \in \mathbb{R}.$$

This series of successive cumulative functions gives rise to a series of nonstrict ($\geq_k$) and strict ($>_k$) stochastic dominance relations as follows. For any distribution functions F and G on IR and for each $k \in \{1,2,\ldots\}$,

$$F \geq_k G \quad \text{if} \quad F^k(x) \leq G^k(x) \quad \text{for all } x \in IR;$$
$$F >_k G \quad \text{if} \quad F \geq_k G \quad \text{and} \quad F \neq G.$$

It should be noted that these definitions for the nonstrict and strict k^{th}-degree relations involve all of IR and not just I. This distinction is immaterial for first-degree and second-degree stochastic dominance, but it makes a difference for third-degree and beyond (Fishburn, 1976, 1980a) when I is bounded above.

For first-degree stochastic dominance, $F \geq_1 G$ says that $F \leq G$. In other words, for each $x \in IR$, the probability that F yields an outcome greater than x is at least as large as the probability that G yields an outcome greater than x. When $F >_1 G$, G lies strictly above F over some nondegenerate interval of outcomes. Similar remarks apply to F^k versus G^k for $k \geq 2$ in the higher-degree relations.

A form of the von Neumann-Morgenstern linear utility representation that is appropriate for our univariate context says that there is a bounded real valued utility function u on $[0,\infty)$ such that, for all distribution functions F and G that correspond to risky prospects in the situation at hand,

$$F >_0 G \iff \int_I u(x)dF(x) > \int_I u(x)dG(x),$$

where $>_0$ is the decision maker's strict preference relation. We denote the corresponding indifference relation by $\sim_0$, so that $F \sim_0 G$ if and only if neither $F >_0 G$ nor $G >_0 F$. Hence $F \sim_0 G$ if and only if F and G yield the same expected utility.

Standard theories for stochastic dominance in the linear setting for decision under risk identify classes of utility functions whose members all yield the same relation between the expected utilities of F and G when F and G are dominance related. For example, let U_k denote the set of all u on $[0,\infty)$ such that u and its first k derivatives are continuous and bounded and, for all $x > 0$ and all $1 \leq j \leq k$, $(-1)^{j+1}u_j(x) > 0$, where u_j denotes the jth derivative of u. Thus the derivatives of the $u \in U_k$ alternate in sign, with positive first derivative so that u increases in x. Functions in U_2 are increasing and concave, and those in U_3 have convex first derivatives. For U_3, utility increases at a decreasing rate, the absolute value of which becomes smaller as x increases.

The following theorem (Fishburn and Vickson, 1978; Fishburn, 1980a; and earlier papers) is typical.

Theorem 1. Suppose $I = [0,1]$ or $I = [0,\infty)$, and F and G are distribution functions that correspond to probability measures that assign probability 1 to I. Then, for each $k \in \{1,2,3,\ldots\}$,

$$F >_k G \Longleftrightarrow \int_I u(x)dF(x) > \int_I u(x)dG(x) \quad \text{for all } u \in U_k.$$

Section 4 establishes similar results for the first few degrees ($k \leq 3$) when $>_0$ is represented by a much more general utility model that, among other things allows cycles in $>_0$ such as $F >_0 G >_0 H >_0 F$.

The preceding formulation for decision under risk says nothing about the extent to which outcomes for two risky prospects might be correlated. By starting with measures p and q, or distribution functions F and G, it is based on the presupposition that the only thing that matters in the preference comparison between p and q is the probabilities they assign to various outcomes. In other words, it ignores some information on the joint distribution of the two prospects.

On the other hand, Savage's formulation for decision under uncertainty is quite explicit about joint distributions even though his utility representation pays no attention to utility correlations. For Savage (1954), the decision maker's uncertainty concerns which state of a set S of states of the world is the true state, and this uncertainty is encoded by a finitely additive probability measure π on the set 2^S of all subsets of S. For $A \subseteq S$, $\pi(A)$ is the decision maker's subjective probability that some state s in A is the true state.

Savage's theory applies the preference relation $>_0$ and its induced indifference relation $\sim_0$ to a set of acts, f, g, ..., where each act is a function from S into the set of outcomes. In our present setting, f maps S into I. If the decision maker chooses f and state s obtains, or is the true state, then the outcome of his or her decision is f(s) in I. When f and g are compared, their correlation between outcomes is evident: for each s, f yields f(s) and g yields g(s).

Savage's additive probability and linear utility representation for preference between acts is

$$f >_0 g \Longleftrightarrow \int_S u(f(s))d\pi(s) > \int_S u(g(s))d\pi(s),$$

where u is a bounded utility function on $[0,\infty)$ and $\int u(f(s))d\pi(s)$ is the expected utility for act f. Because this representation separates f and g, it ignores utility correlations under the various states. In particular, if we let π_f denote the distribution function on IR induced by π through f, so that

$$\pi_f(x) = \pi(\{s \in S: f(s) \le x\}) \quad \text{for all } x \in \mathbb{R},$$

then Savage's representation implies the reduction principle (Fishburn, 1987, 1988) which says that:

$$\text{if } \pi_f = \pi_h \text{ and } \pi_g = \pi_k, \text{ then } f >_0 g \Longleftrightarrow h >_0 k.$$

In Section 5 we consider an alternative to Savage's representation that does not entail the reduction principle because it does not separate f and g. As noted there, this has important consequences for stochastic dominance.

Our earlier remarks on stochastic dominance for risky prospects apply directly to decision under uncertainty when Savage's model is used. One simply replaces F and G by the induced distribution functions π_f and π_g, noting that

$$\int_S u(f(s))d\pi(s) = \int_I u(x)d\pi_f(x)$$

for increasing and bounded utility functions.

3. Transitive Nonlinear Theories

The principle that first-degree stochastic dominance should determine preference is considered by several writers as essential for rational preference in the risky monetary setting. They have therefore incorporated it either directly or indirectly into transitive nonlinear generalizations of the linear utility representation of von Neumann-Morgenstern. Using distribution functions on $\mathbb{R}$, these generalizations have the basic representation

$$F >_0 G \Longleftrightarrow V(F) > V(G),$$

where V is a real valued function. The differences among generalizations of this form lie in their treatment of V.

Allais (1953a, 1953b, 1979) adopts a notion of riskless intensive utility for outcomes similar to that suggested by Bernoulli (1738) and quite unlike the lottery-based approach of von Neumann and Morgenstern (1944). He also rejects the latter authors' independence axiom, which says that if p, q and r are probability measures on outcomes and $0 < \lambda < 1$, then $\lambda p + (1 - \lambda)r >_0 \lambda q + (1 - \lambda)r$ whenever $p >_0 q$. Besides his contention that the utility for outcomes has a logarithmic form for most people, Allais' only basic requirement for the representation of the preceding paragraph is that it preserve the nonstrict first-degree stochastic dominance relation, so that $V(F) \geq V(G)$ whenever $F \geq_1 G$. He refers to this requirement as the axiom of absolute preference. Additional refinements for V in his theory, which are motivated in part by Hagen (1972), are described in Allais (1979, 1986).

Machina (1982) proposes a nonlinear generalization of linear utility that also rejects the von Neumann-Morgenstern independence axiom but, unlike Allais, does not adopt a riskless intensive view for outcome utility. The distinctive feature of Machina's approach is his assumption that V is "smooth" over the set of distribution functions on $I = [0,1]$. This means that V changes continuously as F varies continuously, and that $V(F)$ is approximately linear in a neighborhood around F. The technical content of smoothness is embodied by Fréchet differentiability, and alternatives to this assumption were subsequently suggested by Allen (1987) and Chew, Karni and Safra (1987).

Machina (1982, p. 296) notes that when his utility function essentially increases in x, then his representation implies that $V(F) > V(G)$ whenever $F >_1 G$. He also describes assumptions for his theory that preserve second-degree stochastic dominance and goes on to explore economic implications of second-degree dominance.

A third version of V that is variously described as anticipated utility, rank-dependent utility, and decumulative utility, involves a transformation of probability. With $1 - F(x)$ the probability that F yields an outcome larger than x, the general form for V in this case is

$$V(F) = \int_I \tau(1 - F(x))du(x),$$

where u is a utility function on outcomes and τ is a probability-transformation function that is continuous and nondecreasing from $[0,1]$ onto $[0,1]$. This representation preserves first-degree stochastic dominance if u is an increasing function. It was first discussed at length by Quiggin (1982). Subsequent contributors include Chew (1984), Segal (1984) and Yaari (1987).

4. Nontransitive Convex Utility

The nontransitive convex representation for a convex set P of probability measures on I consists of a real valued function ϕ on $P \times P$ that satisfies:

$$p >_0 q \iff \phi(p, q) > 0,$$

$$\phi(p, q) > 0 \iff \phi(q, p) < 0,$$

$$\phi(\lambda p + (1 - \lambda)q, r) = \lambda\phi(p, r) + (1 - \lambda)\phi(q, r),$$

for all $p,q,r \in P$ and all $0 \le \lambda \le 1$. In terms of distribution functions, we have

$$F >_0 G \iff \phi(F, G) > 0,$$

$$\phi(F, G) > 0 \iff \phi(G, F) < 0,$$

$$\phi(\lambda F + (1 - \lambda)G, H) = \lambda\phi(F, H) + (1 - \lambda)\phi(G, H),$$

where $\phi(F, G) = \phi(p, q)$ when F and G are the distribution functions for p and q respectively.

The nontransitive convex representation allows preference cycles such as $p >_0 q >_0 r >_0 p$, via $\phi(p, q) > 0$, $\phi(q, r) > 0$, and $\phi(r, p) > 0$. Moreover, its representing functional ϕ is linear in the first argument since $\phi(\lambda p + (1 - \lambda)q, r) = \lambda\phi(p, r) + (1 - \lambda)\phi(q, r)$. As we shall see, this limited degree of linearity allows straightforward connections to stochastic dominance despite the fact that $>_0$ need not be transitive everywhere. If ϕ were also linear in its <u>second</u> argument then the nontransitive convex representation would specialize to the SSB model of Kreweras (1961) and Fishburn (1982). The SSB model in turn specializes to weighted linear utility (Chew, 1982, 1983; Fishburn, 1983) if preference is assumed to be transitive everywhere, and the weighted linear model reduces to the von Neumann-Morgenstern model if independence ($p >_0 q \Rightarrow \lambda p + (1 - \lambda)r >_0 \lambda q + (1 - \lambda)r$) is also imposed. Without these additions, the nontransitive convex representation is based on two axioms as described in Fishburn (1988, Section 3.8). One of these is a continuity condition. The other is a convexity-dominance condition which says, for example, that if each of p and q is preferred to r, then $\lambda p + (1 - \lambda)q$ is preferred to r.

To explicate connections between stochastic dominance and the nontransitive convex representation, we begin with the first-degree and second-degree relations for simple probability measures. Given ϕ for the nontransitive convex representation, we assume that all one-point measures are in the domain of the representation and define $\phi(x, q)$ for outcome x and measure q by

$$\phi(x, q) = \phi(p, q) \quad \text{when} \quad p(x) = 1.$$

<u>Theorem 2. Suppose p and q are simple probability measures on I. If $\phi(x, q)$ increases in x, then</u>

$$p >_1 q \Rightarrow \phi(p, q) > 0.$$

If, in addition, ϕ is concave in x, then

$$p >_2 q \Rightarrow \phi(p, q) > 0.$$

Remarks. $p >_i q$ means the same thing as $F >_i G$ when F and G are the distribution functions of p and q respectively. When $\phi(x, q)$ increases in x, we say that $\phi(x, q)$ is concave in x if, whenever $x > y > z$, $[\phi(y, q) - \phi(z, q)]/(y - z) > [\phi(x, q) - \phi(y, q)]/(x - y)$.

Proof. Given simple p and q let $\{x_1 < x_2 < \ldots < x_n\}$ be their set of support points. Also let $p_i^1 = p(\{x_1,\ldots,x_i\})$ and $q_i^1 = q(\{x_1,\ldots,x_i\})$. Since $\phi(q, q) = 0$ for the nontransitive convex representation, we have

$$\begin{aligned}\phi(p, q) &= \phi(p, q) - \phi(q, q)\\ &= \sum_{i=1}^{n} [p(x_i) - q(x_i)]\phi(x_i, q)\\ &= \sum_{i=1}^{n-1} (q_i^1 - p_i^1)[\phi(x_{i+1}, q) - \phi(x_i, q)],\end{aligned}$$

where the initial summation arises from linearity in the first argument, and the final expression follows from summation by parts.

Suppose $\phi(x, q)$ increases in x, and $p >_1 q$. Then $\phi(x_{i+1}), q) - \phi(x_i, q) > 0$ and $q_i^1 - p_i^1 \geq 0$ for all $i \leq n - 1$, and $q_i^1 - p_i^1 > 0$ for some i. Therefore $\phi(p, q) > 0$. This proves the first part of the theorem.

For the second part let

$$p_{i+1}^2 = \sum_{k=1}^{i} p_k^1(x_{k+1} - x_k),$$

which is the value of p's second cumulative at x_{i+1}. A similar definition applies to q_{i+1}^2, and if $p >_2 q$ then $q_{i+1}^2 - p_{i+1}^2 \geq 0$ for all i from 1 through $n - 1$, with strict inequality for some such i.

Continuing from our preceding expression of $\phi(p, q)$, and using summation by parts to get the double sum, we have

$$\begin{aligned}
(p, q) &= \sum_{i=1}^{n-1} [(q_i^1 - p_i^1)(x_{i+1} - x_i)] \left[\frac{\phi(x_{i+1}, q) - \phi(x_i, q)}{x_{i+1} - x_i}\right] \\
&= \sum_{i=1}^{n-2} \left\{ \sum_{k=1}^{i} (q_k^1 - p_k^1)(x_{k+1} - x_k) \right\} \left[\frac{\phi(x_{i+1}, q) - \phi(x_i, q)}{x_{i+1} - x_i} \right. \\
&\qquad \left. - \frac{\phi(x_{i+2}, q) - \phi(x_{i+1}, q)}{x_{i+2} - x_{i+1}}\right] \\
&\qquad + \sum_{k=1}^{n-1} (q_k^1 - p_k^1)(x_{k+1} - x_k) \left[\frac{\phi(x_n, q) - \phi(x_{n-1}, q)}{x_n - x_{n-1}}\right] \\
&= \sum_{i=1}^{n-2} (q_{i+1}^2 - p_{i+1}^2) \left[\frac{\phi(x_{i+1}, q) - \phi(x_i, q)}{x_{i+1} - x_i} \right. \\
&\qquad \left. - \frac{\phi(x_{i+2}, q) - \phi(x_{i+1}, q)}{x_{i+2} - x_{i+1}}\right] \\
&\qquad + (q_n^2 - p_n^2) \left[\frac{\phi(x_n, q) - \phi(x_{n-1}, q)}{x_n - x_{n-1}}\right] .
\end{aligned}$$

Suppose $\phi(x, q)$ increases and is concave in x, and $p >_2 q$. Then all ϕ differences in brackets are positive, and it follows with $p >_2 q$ that $\phi(p, q) > 0$. ■

The meanings of $\phi(x, q)$ increasing in x and of $\phi(x, q)$ being concave in x will be deferred to the end of the section after we consider another theorem for the first three degrees that mimics theorems for linear stochastic dominance in Fishburn and Vickson (1978).

For the next theorem we use the $\phi(F, G)$ form of the nontransitive convex representation and presume in addition that for all distribution functions F and G on I that

$$\phi(F, G) = \int_I \phi(x, G)dF(x).$$

While this follows immediately from linearity in the first argument if F is simple (a finite-step step function), it entails additional technical assumptions that I shall not go into when F is not simple.

Similar to the U_k classes of utility functions used in Theorem 1, we consider the following classes of ϕ functionals for our new theorem. $\Phi_1(G)$ is the set of all $\phi(x, G)$ for fixed G and $x \in [0,\infty)$ such that the first derivative $\phi_1(x, G)$ with respect to x is continuous and bounded, and positive for $x > 0$. $\Phi_2(G)$ is the subset of $\Phi_1(G)$ for which the second derivative $\phi_2(x, G)$ with respect to x is continuous and bounded, and negative for $x > 0$. And $\Phi_3(G)$ is the subset of $\Phi_2(G)$ for which the third derivative $\phi_3(x, G)$ with respect to x is continuous and bounded, and positive for $x > 0$.

<u>Theorem 3. Suppose $I = [0,1]$ or $I = [0,\infty)$ and F and G are distribution functions that correspond to probability measures that assign probability 1 to I. Then, for each $k \in \{1,2,3\}$,</u>

$$F >_k G \iff \int_I \phi(x, G)dF(x) > 0 \quad \underline{\text{for all}} \quad \phi \in \Phi_k(G).$$

<u>Proof</u>. The proof is analogous to the proofs of Theorems 2.1-2.3 in Fishburn and Vickson (1978) with one change in the third-degree case caused by the particular definition of $>_3$ used in the present paper. We sketch the $\Rightarrow$ proof for $I = [0,1]$.

Given $I = [0,1]$, successive integrations by parts give

$$\begin{aligned}
\phi(F,G) &= \int_0^1 \phi(x,G)dF(x) - \int_0^1 \phi(x,G)dG(x) \\
&= [\phi(1,G) - \int_0^1 F(x)\phi_1(x,G)dx] - [\phi(1,G) - \int_0^1 G(x)\phi_1(x,G)dx] \\
&= \int_0^1 [G(x) - F(x)]\phi_1(x,G)dx \\
&= -\int_0^1 [G^2(x) - F^2(x)]\phi_2(x,G)dx + [G^2(1) - F^2(1)]\phi_1(1,G) \\
&= \int_0^1 [G^3(x) - F^3(x)]\phi_3(x,G)dx - [G^3(1) - F^3(1)]\phi_2(1,G) \\
&\quad + (\mu_F - \mu_G)\phi_1(1,G),
\end{aligned}$$

given the existence of the derivatives. Here μ_F and μ_G are the means of F and G respectively.

The conclusions of Theorem 3 for h = 1,2, and 3 ($\Rightarrow$) follow from the final three expressions for $\phi(F, G)$ in the preceding paragraph. The sign of the derivative $\phi_k(x, G)$ in each case coupled with $F >_k G$ implies that the integral term is strictly positive in that case. Likewise, for k = 2,3, the second terms in the last two expressions are nonnegative. Finally, for third-degree stochastic dominance, our definition for $>_3$ implies that $\mu_F \geq \mu_G$ (Fishburn, 1980b) so that $\phi(F, G) > 0$ when $F >_3 G$ and $\phi \in \Phi_3(G)$.

We now consider the meaning of $\phi(x, q)$ increasing in x for the nontransitive convex model. Given $x > y$, what is needed for $\phi(x, q) > \phi(y, q)$?

If either $x \succsim_0 q >_0 y$ or $x >_0 q \succsim_0 y$, where $\succsim_0$ is the union of $>_0$ and $\sim_0$, then $\phi(x, q) > \phi(y, q)$ follows immediately from the sign requirements of the representation. Suppose then that $x >_0 q$ and

$y >_0 q$. If there is no outcome z less preferred than q, there is a problem in explicating $\phi(x, q) > \phi(y, q)$ as explained in Section 4.3 of Fishburn (1988), and I shall not go into this possibility. Assume henceforth in this paragraph that $q >_0 z$, so that $x >_0 q >_0 z$ and $y >_0 q >_0 z$. Then by the nontransitive convex representation, there are unique α and β strictly between 0 and 1 such that (with x^* the measure assigning probability 1 to x)

$$\alpha x^* + (1 - \alpha)z^* \sim_0 q$$
$$\beta y^* + (1 - \beta)z^* \sim_0 q,$$

and it follows that $\phi(x, q) > \phi(y, q) \iff \alpha < \beta$. To see this, observe that the two preceding $\sim_0$ statements correspond to

$$\alpha\phi(x, q) + (1 - \alpha)\phi(z, q) = 0$$
$$\beta\phi(y, q) + (1 - \beta)\phi(z, q) = 0$$

with $\phi(x, q) > 0$, $\phi(y, q) > 0$ and $\phi(z, q) < 0$. Consequently, $\alpha(1 - \beta)\phi(x, q) = \beta(1 - \alpha)\phi(y, q)$, and it follows that $\phi(x, q) > \phi(y, q) \Longleftrightarrow \beta(1 - \alpha) > \alpha(1 - \beta) \Longleftrightarrow \alpha < \beta$.

Thus, when $x >_0 q >_0 z$ and $y >_0 q >_0 z$, we get $\phi(x, q) > \phi(y, q)$ when the mixing probability α that makes $\alpha x^* + (1 - \alpha)z^*$ indifferent to q is less than the mixing probability β that makes $\beta y^* + (1 - \beta)z^*$ indifferent to q. Although not automatic for the nontransitive convex representation, this is what we would expect when $x > y$.

Similar remarks apply when $q >_0 x$ and $q >_0 y$. Hence $\phi(x, q)$ increasing in x is a fairly natural assumption or expectation in the nontransitive convex setting.

To consider the less natural condition that $\phi(x, q)$ is concave in x, suppose for simplicity that $\phi(x, q)$ is twice differentiable in its first argument with $\phi_1(x, q) > 0$. Then $\phi(x, q)$ is concave if for each x in the interior of I, and for every small positive δ, we have $\phi(x + \delta, q) - \phi(x, q) > \phi(x + 2\delta, q) - \phi(x + \delta, q)$, or

$$2\phi(x + \delta, q) > \phi(x, q) + \phi(x + 2\delta, q).$$

Let r denote the simple measure that assigns probability 1/2 to each of x and $x + 2\delta$. Then, since ϕ is linear in its first argument, the preceding inequality is the same as

$$\phi(x + \delta, q) > \phi(r, q).$$

This is clearly violated if $r \gtrsim_0 q \gtrsim_0 x + \delta$, so a first requirement for concavity is $x + \delta >_0 q$ or $q >_0 r$.

Suppose for definiteness that $x + \delta >_0 q$. If $q \gtrsim_0 r$ also, then $\phi(x + \delta, q) > 0 \geq \phi(r, q)$, so $\phi(x + \delta, q) > \phi(r, q)$. On the other hand, if $r >_0 q$, we proceed as before provided that $q >_0 z$ for some outcome z. Given such a z, let α and β be defined by

$$\alpha(x + \delta)^* + (1 - \alpha)z^* \sim_0 q$$

$$\beta r + (1 - \beta)z^* \sim_0 q.$$

Then $\phi(x + \delta, q) > \phi(r, q) \iff \alpha < \beta$. Although $\alpha < \beta$ may well hold here, it lacks the intuitive appeal of $\alpha < \beta$ for the $x > y$ case described earlier.

5. Decision under Uncertainty

This section first emphasizes the point made by Loomes and Sugden (1982, 1987) and Fishburn (1987) that violations of first-degree stochastic dominance may be quite reasonable in Savage's formulation for decision under uncertainty with additive subjective probabilities over states. We then comment briefly on a version of stochastic dominance for a representation that admits nonadditive probability.

Consider the following four-state payoff matrix for acts f and g, and suppose that the decision maker believes that the states are equally probable:

	1	2	3	4
f	\$40,000	\$30,000	\$20,000	\$10,000
g	\$30,000	\$20,000	\$10,000	\$40,000

Since the induced distribution functions π_f and π_g are identical, Savage's representation requires $f \sim_0 g$. However, it is not obvious, because of the connections between outcomes under each state, that most people will be indifferent between f and g. Some people may prefer f to g because f yields \$10,000 more than g in three out of four cases. Others may prefer g to f because they would hate to end up in the position of having state 4 obtain when f is chosen and lose out on the \$30,000 differential there.

Each of $f >_0 g$ and $g >_0 f$ violates the reduction principle described at the end of Section 2 as well as the nonstrict first-degree stochastic dominance principle. Violations of the strict first-degree principle are suggested by slight modifications in the matrix. For example, if $f >_0 g$, and if h is obtained from f by subtracting \$1 from each outcome in the first row of the payoff matrix, then it seems likely that h will be preferred to g. However, $\pi_g >_1 \pi_h$.

An alternative to Savage's representation for preference between acts that accommodates such violations has the general form

$$f >_0 g \iff \int_S \phi(f(s), g(s))d\pi(s) > 0,$$

in which π is an additive probability measure on 2^S as in Savage's theory, and ϕ is a skew-symmetric $[\phi(y, x) = -\phi(x, y)]$ real valued function on pairs of outcomes. Bell (1982) and Loomes and Sugden (1982, 1987) develop this model with interpretations for ϕ that include notions of regret and rejoicing which are designed to capture the within-state comparisons between outcomes for f and g. For example, a person with $g >_0 f$ in the preceding example may have much stronger regret at losing out on $30,000 than on $10,000.

Fishburn (1988, 1989), who refers to the preceding representation as the SSA (skew-symmetric additive) model, shows that it follows from a subset of Savage's assumptions about preference that exclude his axiom that preference is transitive everywhere. In particular, if full transitivity is added to Fishburn's axioms, then the SSA model reduces to Savage's, with $\phi(x, y) = u(x) - u(y)$. More to the point of the present paper, Fishburn (1987) proves that if the nonstrict principle of first-degree stochastic dominance ($\pi_f \geq_1 \pi_g \Rightarrow f \gtrsim_0 g$) is imposed on the SSA model, then again it reduces to Savage's model.

Thus, despite the fact that adherence to first-degree stochastic dominance and transitivity are very different notions for the nontransitive convex model (or its SSB specialization) discussed in Section 4, adherence to first-degree stochastic dominance and transitivity are essentially equivalent for the SSA model.

We conclude with remarks on a different generalization of Savage's model developed by Schmeidler (1984) and Gilboa (1987). Like Savage, they maintain separation between f and g in their representation, but unlike Savage and the SSA model they do not require additivity for subjective probability. Their representation is

$$f >_0 g \iff \int_S u(f(s))d\sigma(s) > \int_S u(g(s))d\sigma(s),$$

where σ is a <u>monotonic</u> $[A \subset B \Rightarrow \sigma(A) \leq \sigma(B)]$ but not necessarily additive measure on 2^S. Because σ need not be additive, the integral $\int_S w(s)d\sigma(s)$ requires a special definition. They use Choquet (1955) integration, which is based on the order of w values and turns out to have direct connections to stochastic dominance.

To explain this, we assume for simplicity that the set of possible outcomes is finite, say $\{x_1,\ldots,x_n\}$, ordered so that $x_1 > x_2 > \ldots >$

x_n. Also assume that u increases in x, hence $u(x_1) > u(x_2) > \dots > u(x_n)$, and let σ_f^* denote the <u>decumulative</u> distribution function induced by σ through f so that

$$\sigma_f^*(x) = \sigma(\{s: f(s) \geq x\})$$

with $\sigma_f^*(x) = 0$ for $x > x_1$ and $\sigma_f^*(x_n) = 1$. Then, by definition of Choquet integration,

$$\int u(f(s))d\sigma(s) = \sum_{i=1}^{n-1} [u(x_i) - u(x_{i+1})]\sigma_f^*(x_i) + u(x_n).$$

A fairly natural definition of strict first-degree stochastic dominance in this context is

$$\sigma_f^* >^1 \sigma_g^* \quad \text{if} \quad \sigma_f^*(x) \geq \sigma_g^*(x) \quad \text{for all } x, \quad \text{and } \sigma_f^* \neq \sigma_g^*.$$

This is equivalent to our earlier definition of $>_1$ whenever σ is additive. Moreover, since

$$\int_S [u(f(s)) - u(g(s))]d\sigma(s) = \sum_{i=1}^{n-1} [u(x_i) - u(x_{i+1})][\sigma_f^*(x_i) - \sigma_g^*(x_i)],$$

it follows that $f >_0 g$ whenever $\sigma_f^* >^1 \sigma_g^*$. Thus the Schmeidler-Gilboa representation has a natural affinity to a first-degree principle in the monetary setting.

It should be added that $>^1$ is not generally equal to the first-degree relation $>_1$ defined from the <u>cumulative</u> distribution function σ_f, where

$$\sigma_f(x) = \sigma(\{s: f(s) \leq x\})$$

and

$$\sigma_f >_1 \sigma_g \quad \text{if} \quad \sigma_f(x) \leq \sigma_g(x) \quad \text{for all } x, \quad \text{and } \sigma_f \neq \sigma_g.$$

It is true that $\sigma_f^* >^1 \sigma_g^* \iff \sigma_f >_1 \sigma_g$ when σ has the property of <u>complementary additivity</u>, i.e., $\sigma(A) + \sigma(S\backslash A) = 1$ for all $A \subseteq S$, but in general the two relations are not equivalent. Additional remarks on complementary additivity, which make a case for this condition in the Schmeidler-Gilboa context, are included in Gilboa (1985).

<u>References</u>

Allais, M. (1953a), "Le Comportement de l'Homme Rationnel devant le Risque: Critique des Postulats et Axiomes de l'École Américaine," <u>Econometrica</u>, 21: 503-546.

Allais, M. (1953b), "Fondements d'Une Théorie Positive des Choix Comportant un Risque et Critique des Postulats et Axiomes de l'Ecole Américaine," Colloques Internationaux du Centre National de la Recherche Scientifique. XL. Econometrie: 257-332. Translated and augmented as "The Foundations of a Positive Theory of Choice Involving Risk and a Criticism of the Postulates and Axioms of the American School," in Allais and Hagen (1979).

Allais, M. (1979), "The So-Called Allais Paradox and Rational Decisions under Uncertainty," in Allais and Hagen (1979).

Allais, M. (1986), The General Theory of Random Choices in Relation to the Invariant Cardinal Utility Function and the Specific Probability Function. Dordrecht, Holland: Reidel. (In press.)

Allais, M. and O. Hagen (eds.) (1979), Expected Utility Hypotheses and the Allais Paradox. Dordrecht, Holland: Reidel.

Allen, B. (1987), "Smooth Preferences and the Approximate Expected Utility Hypothesis," Journal of Economic Theory, 41: 340-355.

Bawa, V.S. (1982), "Stochastic Dominance: A Research Bibliography," Management Science, 28: 698-712.

Bell, D. (1982), "Regret in Decision Making under Uncertainty," Operations Research, 30:961-981.

Bernoulli, D. (1738), "Specimen Theoriae Novae de Mensura Sortis," Commentarii Academiae Scientiarum Imperialis Petropolitanae, 5: 175-192. Translated by L. Sommer as "Exposition of a New Theory on the Measurement of Risk," Econometrica, 22 (1954): 23-36.

Blackwell, D. and M.A. Girshick (1954), Theory of Games and Statistical Decisions. New York: Wiley.

Chew, S.H. (1982), "A Mixture Set Axiomatization of Weighted Utility Theory," Discussion Paper 82-4, College of Business and Public Administration, University of Arizona.

Chew, S.H. (1983), "A Generalization of the Quasilinear Mean with Applications to the Measurement of Income Inequality and Decision Theory Resolving the Allais Paradox," Econometrica, 51: 1065-1092.

Chew, S.H. (1984), "An Axiomatization of the Rank Dependent Quasilinear Mean Generalizing the Gini Mean and the Quasilinear Mean," mimeographed. Department of Political Economy, Johns Hopkins University.

Chew, S.H., E. Karni and Z. Safra (1987), "Risk Aversion in the Theory of Expected Utility with Rank-Dependent Probabilities," Journal of Economic Theory, 42: 370-381.

Chew, S.H. and K.R. MacCrimmon (1979), "Alpha-Nu Choice Theory: A Generalization of Expected Utility Theory," Working Paper 669, Faculty of Commerce and Business Administration, University of British Columbia.

Choquet, G. (1955), "Theory of Capacities," Annales de l'Institut Fourier, 5: 131-295.

Ellsberg, D. (1961), "Risk, Ambiguity, and the Savage Axioms," Quarterly Journal of Economics, 75: 643-669.

Fishburn, P.C. (1964), Decision and Value Theory. New York: Wiley.

Fishburn, P.C. (1976), "Continua of Stochastic Dominance Relations for Bounded Probability Distributions," Journal of Mathematical Economics, 3: 295-311.

Fishburn, P.C. (1980a), "Continua of Stochastic Dominance Relations for Unbounded Probability Distributions," Journal of Mathematical Economics, 7: 271-285.

Fishburn, P.C. (1980b), "Stochastic Dominance and Moments of Distributions," Mathematics of Operations Research, 5: 94-100.

Fishburn, P.C. (1982), "Nontransitive Measurable Utility," Journal of Mathematical Psychology, 26: 31-67.

Fishburn, P.C. (1983), "Transitive Measurable Utility," Journal of Economic Theory, 31: 293-317.

Fishburn, P.C. (1986), "Alternatives to Expected Utility for Risky Decisions," in L. Samuelson, ed., Microeconomic Theory. Boston: Kluwer-Nijhoff.

Fishburn, P.C. (1987), "Reconsiderations in the Foundations of Decision under Uncertainty," Economic Journal, 97: 825-841.

Fishburn, P.C. (1988), Nonlinear Preference and Utility Theory. Baltimore: Johns Hopkins University Press.

Fishburn, P.C. (1989), "Nontransitive Measurable Utility for Decision under Uncertainty," mimeographed. AT&T Bell Laboratories.

Fishburn, P.C. and R.G. Vickson (1978), "Theoretical Foundations of Stochastic Dominance," in Whitmore and Findlay (1978).

Gilboa, I. (1985), "Duality in Non-Additive Expected Utility Theory," Working Paper 7-85, Foerder Institute for Economic Research, Tel-Aviv University.

Gilboa, I. (1987), "Expected Utility with Purely Subjective Non-Additive Probabilities," Journal of Mathematical Economics, 16: 65-88.

Hadar, J. and W.R. Russell (1969), "Rules for Ordering Uncertain Prospects," American Economic Review, 59: 25-34.

Hadar, J. and W.R. Russell (1971), "Stochastic Dominance and Diversification," Journal of Economic Theory, 3: 288-305.

Hagen, O. (1972), "A New Axiomatization of Utility under Risk," Teorie A Metoda, 4: 55-80.

Hanoch, G. and H. Levy (1969), "The Efficiency Analysis of Choices Involving Risk," Review of Economic Studies, 36: 335-346.

Hardy, G.H., J.E. Littlewood and G. Polya (1934), Inequalities. Cambridge: Cambridge University Press.

Kahneman, D. and A. Tversky (1979), "Prospect Theory: An Analysis of Decision under Risk," Econometrica, 47: 263-291.

Karamata, J. (1932), "Sur Une Inegalité Relative aux Fonctions Convexes," Publications Mathématiques de l'Université de Belgrade, 1: 145-148.

Kreweras, G. (1961), "Sur Une Possibilité de Rationaliser les Intransitivités," La Décision, Colloques Internationaux du Centre National de la Recherche Scientifique: 27-32.

Lehmann, E.L. (1955), "Ordering Families of Distributions," Annals of Mathematical Studies, 26: 399-419.

Lichtenstein, S. and P. Slovic (1971), "Reversals of Preferences between Bids and Choices in Gambling Decisions," Journal of Experimental Psychology, 89: 46-55.

Lichtenstein, S. and P. Slovic (1973), "Response-Induced Reversals of Preferences in Gambling: An Extended Replication in Las Vegas," Journal of Experimental Psychology, 101: 16-20.

Loomes, G. and R. Sugden (1982), "Regret Theory: An Alternative Theory of Rational Choice under Uncertainty," Economic Journal, 92: 805-824.

Loomes, G. and R. Sugden (1987), "Some Implications of a More General Form of Regret Theory," Journal of Economic Theory, 41: 270-287.

MacCrimmon, K.R. and S. Larsson (1979), "Utility Theory: Axioms Versus 'Paradoxes'," in Allais and Hagen (1979).

Machina, M.J. (1982), "'Expected Utility' Analysis Without the Independence Axiom," Econometrica, 50: 277-323.

Machina, M.J. (1987a), "Decision-Making in the Presence of Risk," Science, 236: 537-543.

Machina, M.J. (1987b), "Choice under Uncertainty: Problems Solved and Unsolved," Economic Perspectives, 1: 121-154.

Massé, P. and Morlat (1953), "Sur le Classement Economique des Perspectives Aléatoires," Colloques Internationaux du Centre National de la Recherche Scientifique, 40: 165-199.

May, K.O. (1954), "Intransitivity, Utility, and the Aggregation of Preference Patterns," Econometrica, 22: 1-13.

Quiggin, J. (1982), "A Theory of Anticipated Utility," Journal of Economic Behavior and Organization, 3: 323-343.

Quirk, J.P. and R. Saposnik (1962), "Admissibility and Measurable Utility Functions," Review of Economic Studies, 29: 140-146.

Rothschild, M. and J.E. Stiglitz (1970), "Increasing Risk I: A Definition," Journal of Economic Theory, 2: 225-243.

Rothschild, M. and J.E. Stiglitz (1971), "Increasing Risk II: Its Economic Consequences," Journal of Economic Theory, 3: 66-84.

Savage, L.J. (1954), The Foundations of Statistics. New York: Wiley.

Schmeidler, D. (1984), "Subjective Probability and Expected Utility Without Additivity," Preprint 84, Institute for Mathematics and Its Applications, University of Minnesota.

Segal, U. (1984), "Nonlinear Decision Weights with the Independence Axiom," Working Paper 353, Department of Economics, University of California, Los Angeles.

Sherman, S. (1951), "On a Theorem of Hardy, Littlewood, Polya, and Blackwell," Proceedings of the National Academy of Sciences, 37: 826-831.

Tversky, A. (1969), "Intransitivity of Preferences," Psychological Review, 76: 31-48.

Tversky, A. and D. Kahneman (1987), "Rational Choice and the Framing of Decisions," in R.M. Hogarth and M.W. Reder, eds., Rational Choice. Chicago: University of Chicago Press.

von Neumann, J. and O. Morgenstern (1944), Theory of Games and Economic Behavior. Princeton: Princeton University Press. Second edition, 1947; third edition, 1953.

Whitmore, G.A. (1970), "Third-Degree Stochastic Dominance," American Economic Review, 60: 457-459.

Whitmore, G.A. and M.C. Findlay (eds.) (1978), Stochastic Dominance. Lexington, MA: Heath.

Yaari, M.E. (1987), "The Dual Theory of Choice under Risk," Econometrica, 55: 95-115.

THE "COMPARATIVE STATICS" OF THE SHACKLE-VICKERS APPROACH TO DECISION-MAKING IN IGNORANCE[1]

Donald W. Katzner
University of Massachusetts/Amherst
Amherst, MA 01002

The analysis of decision-making under conditions of ignorance developed by Shackle [8] and Vickers [9], [10] begins with the assumption that the decision-maker is able to describe a potential surprise function defined over the subsets of an incomplete[2] collection of possible outcomes or states of the world.[3] The potential surprise of an outcome-set A is the surprise the decision-maker imagines now that he would experience in the future were A to occur. Let a decision set containing the objects of choice be specified, and suppose that the decision-maker has an ordinal utility function defined over the Cartesian product of the decision set and the incomplete collection of states of the world. For each state of the world, then, the utility function maps objects of choice or elements of the decision set into associated utility values. More importantly, for each object of choice, the utility function also maps states of the world into utility values. Using this latter relation, the potential surprise function can be translated into a potential surprise density (or frequency) function[4] defined over utility values. Thus the original potential surprise function, whose domain is a collection of outcome-sets, becomes a potential surprise density function with a domain consisting of utility magnitudes, or real numbers. Although it has a different significance and meaning, the potential surprise density function is often drawn to look something like an inverted probability density function.

The next step in the Shackle-Vickers approach is to identify, for every object of choice, two pairs, each consisting of a utility value

[1]The author would like to thank Randall Bausor and Douglas Vickers for numerous and helpful suggestions.

[2]The collection is incomplete because not all of the possible outcomes can be known or imagined in advance.

[3]For a more detailed statement of the Shackle-Vickers theory and its potential surprise foundation, see Katzner [5], [6], [7].

[4]Katzner [6], [7].

along with its associated potential surprise from the potential surprise density function. The utility values in these pairs define, respectively, a "favorable" and an "unfavorable" outcome, frequently referred to in the Shackle-Vickers vocabulary as the "focus gain" and the "focus loss." The two pairs themselves are selected so as to maximize the appropriate half of an attractiveness function subject to the potential surprise density function or, in other words, they are picked for their power to attract the attention of the decision-maker. The pairs are then used in constructing a decision function defined over the decision set. In particular, the decision function is built up by assigning a value to the potential surprise numbers and the outcome or utility magnitudes contained in the two pairs that correspond to each object of choice. This function is understood to be ordinal in character; it ranks the objects of choice in the decision set. The object receiving the highest rank, i.e., given the highest value by the decision function, is chosen by the decision-maker.

The purpose of the present paper is to examine several issues concerning the "comparative static" properties of the Shackle-Vickers model. First to be considered is the question of what it means to do comparative statics in the potential surprise context within which the model is set. The second concerns the conditions under which the constrained maxima of the two halves of the attractiveness function may be said to exist. The third, and last, issue is the nature of the comparative statics properties derived from such a maximization. It turns out that a notion of dominance, not unlike those explored by Josef Hadar [2], [3], [4], in whose honor this essay is written, is relevant to these comparative static properties. Two detailed examples are provided to illustrate the ideas.

I

The notion of potential surprise, indeed the entire Shackle-Vickers model, is set in an environment having the property that time is historical. That is, time is thought to flow along a unidirectional and irreversible stream in which each moment is unique. The recurrence of a moment of time that has already gone by cannot happen. Thus phenomena that arise in historical time never repeat themselves in exactly the same way, or in the same ontological and epistemic context, and therefore explanations of them are necessarily different for each manifestation. (The idea that a dynamic model can be restarted over and over again at its initial condition, thereby replicating its behavior, is irrelevant. Even if the model were a "reasonable" approximation of reality at the first time that it was started up, the presumption is that by the time it would be started again, the world would have changed sufficiently so as to require a new model.)

Without the possibility of replication, however, it makes no sense to speak of probability. For the concept of probability, regardless of whether it is interpreted as frequency of appearance or as subjective probability, has no meaning in the absence of the possibility to replicate. Probability is clearly a relevant and useful idea in analyzing, say, the drawing of red and white balls from an urn because one may draw from the urn over and over again, and the mechanism that generates the outcome of each draw has a stable and unchanging structure. But the Shackle-Vickers model applies to situations in which the repetition of identical trials is impossible. Hence the rejection of probability and its replacement by potential surprise.

Another aspect of the environment of the Shackle-Vickers model is that, although information about the past, however imperfect, may be obtained through observation, information about the future is impossible to secure because the future cannot be observed until it is past. Ignorance of, and uncertainty about, the future is a fact of life. In making decisions, then, one might be able to anticipate some possible future consequences or outcomes of a decision, but certainly not all of them. Thus, since not all possible outcomes can be imagined in advance, designation of the potential surprise of all outcomes (probability, as indicated above, is irrelevant) is unattainable. Moreover, the determination of the potential surprise values for the known possible outcomes, although based on what the decision-maker knows or thinks he knows from prior experience, is also confronted by the same ignorance and uncertainty. Under these conditions, then, the decision-maker can only imagine and guess using his imperfect and incomplete information about the past, and hence his potential surprise function is highly personal and subjective. None of this, however, is meant to suggest that the potential surprise function is a shadowy or fuzzy construct. On the contrary, it is assumed to be precisely specified and well-defined. The question of how decisions might be made in such an environment is the main focus of the Shackle-Vickers model.

Some implications of the previous remarks are that in the Shackle-Vickers model the decision-maker's potential surprise function is necessarily unique in time, unique for each decision-maker, unique for each decision, and unique for each object of choice. More generally, the decision-maker enters the moment of decision with a unique history and unique (imperfect) information gleaned from it. This enables him to determine his unique potential surprise functions, each relating to the imagined possible outcomes associated with an object of choice in the decision set. Both the utility function that defines these outcomes as well as the situation in which the decision is made are also unique. Thus the decision opportunity itself is unique and can never reappear in the same form again.

In traditional economic theory, comparative static analysis involves the comparison within a given model of alternative, timeless equilibrium positions based on different parameter values. Often the equilibria are taken to be sufficiently close together to allow the analysis to proceed through the calculation of the signs of derivatives. In any case, comparative static analysis serves two purposes. On the one hand, it leads to a more complete examination, and hence understanding, of the model under consideration. In particular, it forces the implications of assumptions and the interrelations between variables to be more fully worked out. On the other hand, it performs as an aid in the empirical corroboration of the model by providing constraints that can be used either as part of the procedure for estimating the model's functions or as a means for directly verifying the consistency of the model with observed data. For example, in the theory of demand comparative static analysis takes, in part, the form of the derivation of the matrix of Slutsky functions and its properties. This has clearly resulted in a deeper understanding of the theory and its interrelationships; and the properties of the Slutsky functions so obtained have proved significant in many empirical studies of demand behavior.[5]

In the environment of the Shackle-Vickers model, however, the idea of comparative static analysis must assume a different form. First of all, timeless equilibria do not exist. Second, even if one solved the model at each moment to secure a solution for that moment alone, one could still not compare the solutions because the model itself varies from moment to moment. Finally, in the absence of replication and with the unavailability of probability, much of the standard empirical analysis that makes use of the comparative static results would have to be discarded because that analysis rests on probability concepts. Nevertheless, comparative static analysis remains relevant in the Shackle-Vickers model in the sense of asking what would happen if different parameter values were applied to the same moment, and therefore to the same choice-decision nexus, rather than to distinct

[5]See, for example, Deaton and Muellbauer [1].

moments in time. And the two purposes that it serves, as described above, are left intact. Thus comparative static analysis would reduce to the derivation of the implications of assumptions, and the use of the results so derived in empirical work when possible.

II

Much of the discussion of the Shackle-Vickers model that follows is expressed in reference to two examples. Before presenting the examples, however, it is necessary to consider some general ideas and to introduce some notation.

Let X be the decision set and Ψ the collection of utility values over which potential surprise density functions are defined. Let x and ψ be variables ranging over, respectively, X and Ψ. Define a 1-1 correspondence, ξ, between X and a subset B of the real line. Then, for all x in X,

$$b = \xi(x),$$

where b is in B. To keep matters simple, take B to be a closed interval. (Thus B is a continuum and, through ξ, so is X.) The function ξ is an artifice introduced for analytical convenience so that the not-necessarily-quantifiable elements of X can be identified with real (scalar) numbers. (If x already were a real scalar variable, then the transformation ξ would not be needed.) Clearly such an identification, that is ξ, is arbitrary. To ensure that ξ does not itself interfere with the representation of the decision-making process under scrutiny, it is necessary to suppose that ξ is fixed and given for the duration of the analysis and, further, that all conclusions obtained with a particular ξ are independent of that ξ. In terms of subsequent discussion, this latter requirement means that changes in ξ always are accompanied by offsetting alterations in the functions introduced below so that the derived results do not vary. Similar assumptions must be made concerning the particular ordinal utility function that gives rise to the utility values ψ as described at the beginning of this paper.

Suppose for every object of choice the decision-maker specifies a unique potential surprise density function over the possible imagined outcomes or, that is to say, over the utility values in Ψ representing those outcomes. Such a potential surprise density function then exists for each x in X or, equivalently, for corresponding b in B. Let this family of potential surprise density functions be described by the functional relation

$$y = f(\psi, b),$$

where f is defined on $\Psi \times B$, and y represents the potential surprise[6] associated with utility value ψ and object of choice surrogate b. Then each potential surprise density function in the family is a section of f obtained for a fixed b in B. Although the decision-maker is only concerned with the fact that different values of b identify his different potential surprise density functions $f(\psi,b)$, an outside investigator would also be interested in how the potential surprise density functions vary with b. The possible forms that such a potential surprise density function can take on, and the implications of these forms for decision-making, will be examined in the illustrations that follow.

The relationship between $f(\psi,b)$ and individual potential surprise density functions is often clarified by using a symbol, say b°, to denote a given selection of b in B. Then the potential surprise density function determined by that selection is written $f(\psi,b^\circ)$. This emphasizes that the potential surprise density function given b° is a function of the single variable ψ. Such notation also enhances derivations based on $f(\psi,b^\circ)$. For example, associated with $f(\psi,b^\circ)$, and hence with the selection b°, is the collection of utility values N_{b° that are assigned zero potential surprise under $f(\psi,b^\circ)$. That is,

$$N_{b^\circ} = \{\psi\colon f(\psi,b^\circ) = 0\},$$

or in other words, the decision-maker would not be surprised by the occurrence of any of the utility values in N_{b°. It is now obvious that variations in b° modify both $f(\psi,b^\circ)$ and N_{b°. But because notation would become too cumbersome later on, hereafter the superscript "naught" on the b is dropped. The reader may wish to keep in mind, however, that all symbols b appearing subsequently would more properly be written as b°.

For all b in B, assume that N_b is a nonempty, bounded and connected subset of Ψ. Identify some element ψ_b of N_b as the boundary between the "more favorable" and "less favorable" utility values in Ψ. Set

$$\Psi_b^+ = \{\psi\colon \psi \geq \psi_b\},$$

---

[6]By contrast, if f were a family of probability density functions, then except in the discrete case, $y = f(\psi,b)$ could not be interpreted as the probability of ψ given b.

$$\Psi_b^- = \{\psi: \psi \le \psi_b\},$$

so that $\Psi_b^+ \cap \Psi_b^- = \{\psi_b\}$ and $\Psi_b^+ \cup \Psi_b^- = \Psi$. The shape of the potential surprise density function depends on the way in which the decision-maker views the uncertainty of achieving the increasingly more appealing utility values in Ψ_b^+ and the increasingly less appealing utility values in Ψ_b^-.

Recall now that B is the range of the artifice ξ mapping the decision set into the real line, and that Ψ is the collection of all utility values in the domains of the potential surprise density functions. For purposes of the examples and discussion presented here, take Ψ to be the real line and let $B = \{b: \frac{1}{2} \le b \le 1\}$. (Such a characterization of B will prevent negative potential surprise values at certain constrained maxima in the second example.) Given, as indicated earlier, that for each element of the decision set X, values of ψ in Ψ arise from the ordinal utility transformation of outcomes or states of the world, and values of b in B arise from the artifice ξ, the signs and magnitudes of the partial derivatives of the function $f(\psi,b)$, when they exist, can be interpreted with respect to each of its arguments. In particular, the partial derivative with respect to utility magnitudes ψ, denoted by $f_\psi(\psi,b)$, envisages a movement along the graph of the potential surprise density function for fixed b as shown in subsequent diagrams, and the partial derivative with respect to the object of choice surrogate b, written $f_b(\psi,b)$, represents a movement to a different potential surprise density curve at ψ (not shown in any of the diagrams). It should be noted in the latter case that, although the existence of $f_b(\psi',b')$ means that "small" variations in b from b' (with ψ' fixed) induce small and "smooth" changes in y, since ξ is required to be neither differentiable nor continuous, a similar assertion about alterations in y with respect to x, where $b = \xi(x)$, need not hold.

In the first example to be considered here, define for b in B, the potential surprise density function

$$f(\psi,b) = \begin{cases} 1, & b + 1 \le \psi, \\ (\psi - b)^2, & b \le \psi \le b + 1 \\ 0, & -\frac{1}{b} \le \psi \le b, \\ \left(\psi + \frac{1}{b}\right)^2, & -\frac{1}{b} - 1 \le \psi \le -\frac{1}{b}, \\ 1, & \psi \le -\frac{1}{b} - 1. \end{cases} \qquad (1)$$

A picture of the density function for a typical b in B appears as the curve labeled f in Figure 1. Observe that the potential surprise density curve in Figure 1 is defined over the domain Ψ as depicted on the (horizontal) ψ-axis. The b-value in equation (1) and in the diagram serves the purpose, as indicated earlier, of identifying the object of choice (in the decision set X) to which, respectively, the function and curve relate. Again, a change in the value of b would imply a move to a different object of choice and a different associated potential surprise density curve. This fact is highly relevant to the interpretation of the comparative statics properties of the argument that follows.

Moreover, in the formulation of equation (1), the rule that links the domain of f to its range is broken up into subrules, each characterized over a particular interval or subdomain of Ψ. Here the value of b plays two additional roles. On the one hand, it algebraically figures into the determination of the potential surprise values assigned to the utility magnitudes in two subdomains according to the corresponding subrule. On the other, it delimits the subdomains of f over which each subrule is characterized. Observe that as b varies over B, both the two subrules and all of the subdomains are modified. Moreover, these modifications occur in such a way as to preserve the potential surprise function values as numbers between 0 and 1.

Clearly, in this example, $N_b = \{\psi: -\frac{1}{b} \le \psi \le b\}$. Set the boundary between the more favorable and less favorable utility values at $\psi_b = 0$. Then Ψ_b^+ and Ψ_b^- are the nonnegative reals and the nonpositive reals, respectively. The values and signs of the first-order partial derivatives of f, namely $f_\psi(\psi,b)$ and $f_b(\psi,b)$, and the values and signs of the second-order partial derivatives, or $f_{\psi\psi}(\psi,b)$, $f_{bb}(\psi,b)$ and $f_{\psi b}(\psi,b) = f_{b\psi}(\psi,b)$, are indicated in Table 1 for the interior of the sets $[b, b + 1] \times B$ and $[-\frac{1}{b} - 1, -\frac{1}{b}] \times B$, where $[b, b + 1]$ and $[-\frac{1}{b} - 1, -\frac{1}{b}]$ are closed intervals in Ψ. In reference to Figure 1, where the partial derivatives of f exist, $f_\psi(\psi,b)$ describes the slope of the potential surprise density curve at each ψ in Ψ given b, while $f_b(\psi,b)$ indicates how potential surprise values change with b at every ψ. Note that potential surprise increases with ψ at an increasing rate between b and b + 1, and increases at an increasing rate as ψ declines between $-\frac{1}{b}$ and $-\frac{1}{b} - 1$.

TABLE 1

EXAMPLE 1

Derivative	Value and sign over the interior of the set			
	$[b, b+1] \times B$	$[-b^{-1} - 1, -b^{-1}] \times B$	$\Psi_b^+ \times Y$	$\Psi_b^- \times Y$
$f_\psi(\psi,b)$	$2(\psi - b) > 0$	$2(\psi + b^{-1}) < 0$		
$f_b(\psi,b)$	$-2(\psi - b) < 0$	$-2b^{-2}(\psi + b^{-1}) > 0$		
$f_{\psi\psi}(\psi,b)$	$2 > 0$	$2 > 0$		
$f_{bb}(\psi,b)$	$2 > 0$	$-2b^{-3}(2\psi + 3b^{-1}) \gtrless 0$		
$f_{\psi b}(\psi,b)$	$-2 < 0$	$-2b^{-2} < 0$		
$g_\psi(\psi,y,b)$			$\alpha > 0$	$-\alpha < 0$
$g_y(\psi,y,b)$			$-\beta < 0$	$-\beta < 0$
$g_{\psi\psi}(\psi,y,b)$			0	0
$g_{yy}(\psi,y,b)$			0	0
$g_{\psi y}(\psi,y,b)$			0	0

Turning to the second example, leave Ψ as the real line and $B = \{b: \frac{1}{2} \leq b \leq 1\}$. For b in B, define

$$f(\psi,b) = \begin{cases} 1, & b + 1 \leq \psi, \\ \psi - b, & b \leq \psi \leq b + 1, \\ 0, & -\frac{1}{b} \leq \psi \leq b, \\ -\psi - \frac{1}{b}, & -\frac{1}{b} - 1 \leq \psi \leq -\frac{1}{b}, \\ 1, & \psi \leq -\frac{1}{b} - 1. \end{cases} \tag{2}$$

With $\psi_b = 0$, the sets N_b, Ψ_b^+ and Ψ_b^- remain as before. The graph of this potential surprise density function given b is identified as f in Figure 2, and the values and signs of its partial derivatives over the same sets employed in Table 1 are listed in Table 2. Here the rate of change of potential surprise with respect to ψ is constant, although not always the same constant, as ψ varies throughout Ψ.

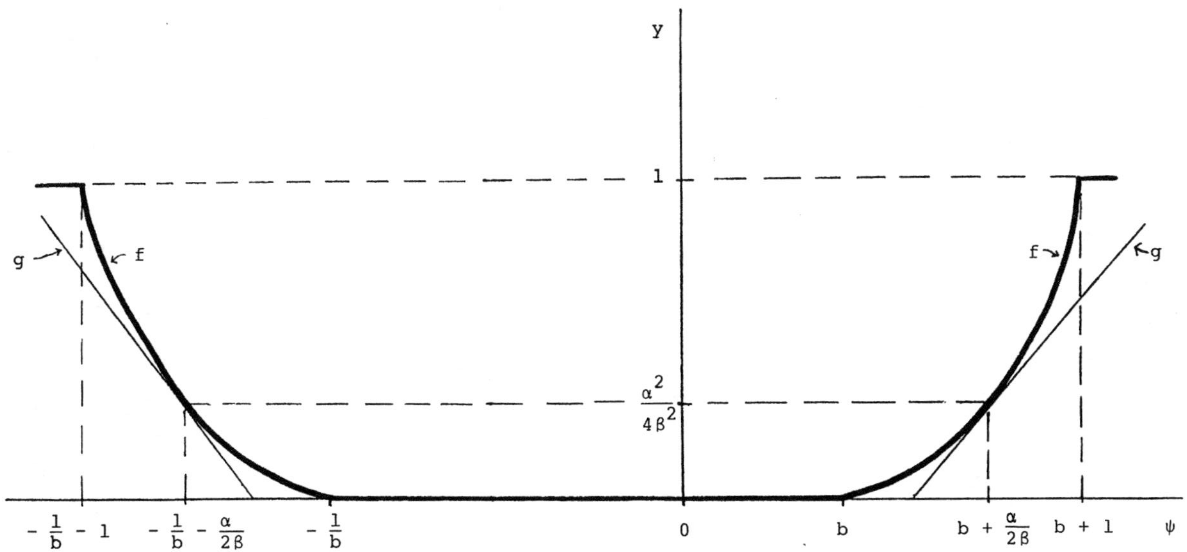

Figure 1: Example 1

TABLE 2

EXAMPLE 2

Derivative	Value and sign over the interior of the set			
	$[b, b + 1] \times B$	$[-b^{-1} - 1, -b^{-1}] \times B$	$\Psi_b^+ \times Y$	$\Psi_b^- \times Y$
$f_\psi(\psi,b)$	$1 > 0$	$-1 < 0$		
$f_b(\psi,b)$	$-1 < 0$	$b^{-2} > 0$		
$f_{\psi\psi}(\psi,b)$	0	0		
$f_{bb}(\psi,b)$	0	$-2b^{-3} < 0$		
$f_{\psi b}(\psi,b)$	0	0		
$g_\psi(\psi,y,b)$			$(1 - y) > 0$	$(y - 2) < 0$
$g_y(\psi,y,b)$			$- < 0$	< 0
$g_{\psi\psi}(\psi,y,b)$			0	0
$g_{yy}(\psi,y,b)$			0	0
$g_{\psi y}(\psi,y,b)$			$-1 < 0$	$1 > 0$

Consider next the second element of the Shackle-Vickers decision apparatus, namely, the so-called "attractiveness" function, defined over the possible utility outcomes and the possible potential surprise magnitudes that can be associated with them. It should be emphasized that the attractiveness function is not another utility function of outcomes but, rather, serves only to describe, given b in B, the ability of the various pairs (ψ,y) to focus the decision-maker's thoughts or, that is, to describe their ability to attract his attention to the pay-off and uncertainty features that are significant in his scrutiny of the objects of choice for decision-making purposes.

The attractiveness function has two independent halves, one defined on $\Psi_b^+ \times Y \times B$, and the other on $\Psi_b^- \times Y \times B$, where Y is the range of the family of potential surprise density functions f. (Frequently as in the previous examples, $Y = \{y: 0 \le y \le 1\}$.) The same symbol, $g(\psi,y,b)$, is used to represent both halves of the attractiveness function. For each b in B, then, $g(\psi,y,b)$ on, say $\Psi_b^+ \times Y$, is an ordinal function that orders the pairs of $\Psi_b^+ \times Y$ according to their power to attract the decision-maker's attention. When they exist, the slopes of the iso-attractiveness contours determined by g in $\Psi_b^+ \times Y$ may

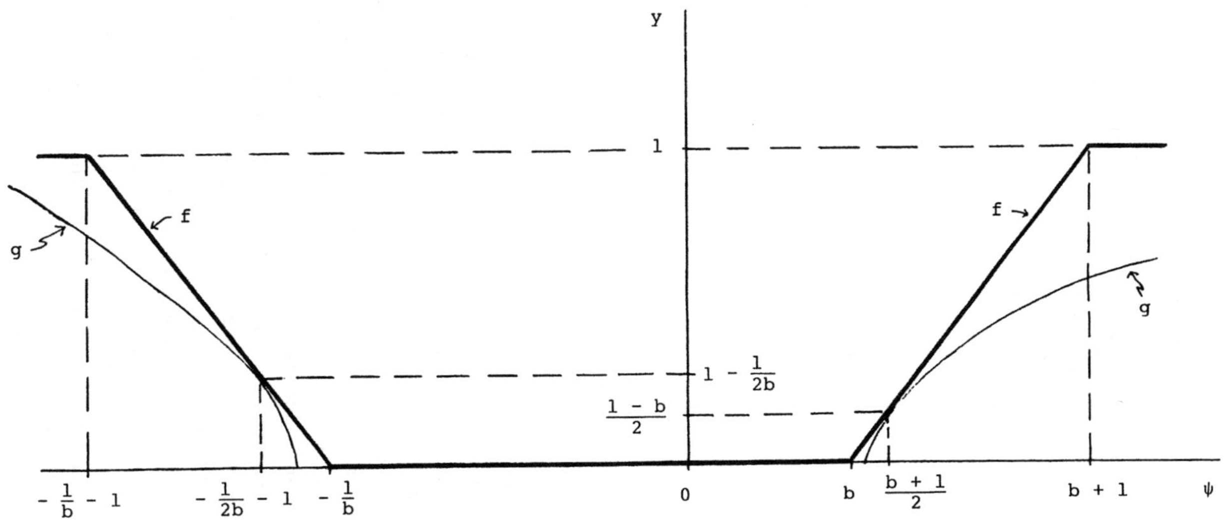

Figure 2: Example 2

interpreted with respect to love of, or aversion to, uncertainty,[7] and the shape of the iso-attractiveness contours characterizes the manner in which these feelings play themselves out as ψ varies. Given b, the decision-maker is assumed to focus his attention on those pairs (ψ_b^+, y_b^+) and (ψ_b^-, y_b^-) that maximize the half of the attractiveness function over, respectively, $\Psi_b^+ \times Y$ and $\Psi_b^- \times Y$. The comparative statics of this maximization are the central concern of subsequent discussion.

It is not difficult to add attractiveness functions to the previous illustrations. In the case of (1), hereafter referred to as Example 1, let the attractiveness function be independent of b and of the form

$$g(\psi, y, b) = \begin{cases} \alpha\psi - \beta y, & \text{on } \Psi_b^+ \times Y, \\ -\alpha\psi - \beta y, & \text{on } \Psi_b^- \times Y, \end{cases}$$

where $\alpha > 0$, $\beta > 0$ and $\alpha < 2\beta$. (The fact that g appears to have two function values when $\psi = \psi_b$ is of no consequence. This is because the two halves of g are each intended to be single-valued functions on their own and independent of each other.) The values and signs of the first- and second-order partial derivatives of g with respect to ψ and y are given in Table 1. The iso-attractiveness contours of g are linear and those associated with the maximization of g subject to (1) are labeled g in Figure 1. (Increased attractiveness shifts the iso-attractiveness curves down and to the right in $\Psi_b^+ \times Y$, and down and to the left in $\Psi_b^- \times Y$.) Using Lagrange's theorem on constrained maximization at interior points of $\Psi_b^+ \times Y$ and $\Psi_b^- \times Y$, it is easily seen that for b in B,

$$\psi_b^+ = b + \frac{\alpha}{2\beta},$$

$$y_b^+ = \frac{\alpha^2}{4\beta^2},$$

and

$$\psi_b^- = -\frac{1}{b} - \frac{\alpha}{2\beta},$$

$$y_b^- = \frac{\alpha^2}{4\beta^2}.$$

Geometrically, these values of ψ_b^+, y_b^+, ψ_b^- and y_b^- are the co-ordinates of the unique points of tangency in Figure 1 between iso-attractiveness

[7] See Katzner [7].

contours and the potential surprise density function. The comparative static conclusions that

$$\frac{\partial \psi_b^+}{\partial b} > 0, \qquad \frac{\partial y_b^+}{\partial b} = 0.$$
$$\frac{\partial \psi_b^-}{\partial b} > 0, \qquad \frac{\partial y_b^-}{\partial b} = 0, \tag{3}$$

follow immediately. As already suggested, the left- and right-hand derivatives in (3) describe, respectively, the changes in the maximizing utility and potential surprise magnitudes as variation in b induces movement from one potential surprise density function to another. (Although the assertion, for example, that $\partial\psi_b^+/\partial b > 0$ at b′ in B, says something about how ψ_b^+ varies with b in a small neighborhood about b′, without the assumption that the artifice ξ is differentiable, no parallel statement with respect to x, where $b = \xi(x)$, is possible.) Observe also that the symmetry of the two halves of the attractiveness function together with the symmetry, for each b in B, of the potential surprise density functions over the sets where $b \le \psi \le b + 1$ and $-\frac{1}{b} - 1 \le \psi \le -\frac{1}{b}$, leads to (i) symmetric values for ψ_b^+ and ψ_b^-, and to (ii) the equality $y_b^+ = y_b^-$. However, there is little reason for such symmetries to hold in general.

For Example 2, which is based on the family of potential surprise density functions (2), add the attractiveness function

$$g(\psi,y,b) = \begin{cases} \psi(1 - y), & \text{on } \Psi_b^+ \times Y, \\ \psi(y - 2), & \text{on } \Psi_b^- \times Y. \end{cases}$$

The relevant partial derivatives of g appear in Table 2 and the iso-attractiveness contours corresponding to its constrained maximization are labeled g in Figure 2. Again, from the theorem of Lagrange, at b in B

$$\psi_b^+ = \frac{b + 1}{2},$$

$$y_b^+ = \frac{1 - b}{2},$$

and

$$\psi_b^- = -\frac{1}{2b} - 1,$$

$$y_b^- = 1 - \frac{1}{2b},$$

and these values are indicated as the co-ordinates of appropriate tangencies in Figure 2. Clearly[8]

$$\frac{\partial\psi_b^+}{\partial b} > 0, \qquad \frac{\partial y_b^+}{\partial b} < 0,$$
$$\frac{\partial\psi_b^-}{\partial b} > 0, \qquad \frac{\partial y_b^-}{\partial b} > 0. \tag{4}$$

Note that when b = 1, the attractiveness function over $\Psi_b^+ \times Y$ is maximized subject to the potential surprise density function at the "corner" point (1,0), and when b = ½, the constrained maximum of the attractiveness function over $\Psi_b^- \times Y$ occurs at the corner (-2,0). However, even in these cases, there is still a tangency between an iso-attractiveness contour and the potential surprise density function at the maximizing point. Notice also that the iso-attractiveness contours in $\Psi_b^+ \times Y$ are asymptotic to the line y = 1, while those in $\Psi_b^- \times Y$ intersect y = 1. The latter contours, if extended, would be asymptotic to the line y = 2. Moreover, without the symmetry of the attractiveness function of Example 1 (the potential surprise density function remains symmetric), the symmetry of the values ψ_b^+ and ψ_b^- and the equality between y_b^+ and y_b^- fail.

Returning to the general situation, suppose that unique constrained maxima of the attractiveness function exist, as they do in the previous examples, for all b in B. Then for each x in X or, equivalently, for each b in B, the decision-maker focuses his attention on two pairs (ψ_b^-,y_b^-) and (ψ_b^+,y_b^+). Suppose further that the decision-maker has a continuously differentiable decision function

$$Q(\psi_b^-,y_b^-,\psi_b^+,y_b^+),$$

defined over the collection of all possible vectors $(\psi_b^-,y_b^-,\psi_b^+,y_b^+)$, and such that

$$\frac{\partial Q}{\partial\psi_b^-} > 0, \qquad \frac{\partial Q}{\partial\psi_b^+} > 0,$$
$$\frac{\partial Q}{\partial y_b^-} > 0, \qquad \frac{\partial Q}{\partial y_b^+} < 0, \tag{5}$$

everywhere. Note Q may be expressed as a function of b alone.

---

[8] In this case, the comparative static partial derivatives are actually total derivatives.

Furthermore, substitution of the 1-1 correspondence $b = \xi(x)$ into this latter expression of Q, reduces Q to a function of x. Assume that the decision-maker makes his decision by choosing b (or x) to maximize Q over its domain.

If Q is taken as

$$Q(\psi_b^-, y_b^-, \psi_b^+, y_b^+) = \psi_b^- + y_b^- + \psi_b^+ - y_b^+, \tag{6}$$

then, in Example 1, Q as a function of b is

$$Q(b) = b - \frac{1}{b},$$

for all b in B. This result is obtained by substituting the constrained maximization solution values previously derived into (6). Since $dQ(b)/db > 0$ on the interior of B, the decision-maker chooses that x in X corresponding to $b = 1$. Similarly, the same Q turns up in Example 2, giving the decision associated with $b = 1$ as in Example 1. It should be remembered here that to keep the Shackle-Vickers representation of the decision process, and hence the results of the present section (and those of the next), independent of the arbitrary selections of both the ordinal utility function that produces the values of ψ, and the artifice ξ that determines the values of b, it has been assumed, in part, that alterations in either of these functions are exactly offset by corresponding and appropriate changes in f, g and Q.

III

Before analyzing the comparative statics of the maximization of the attractiveness function subject to the potential surprise density function in the general Shackle-Vickers model, consider first the questions of the existence and uniqueness of such constrained maxima. For situations in which the potential surprise density function and both halves of the attractiveness function are continuous, in which the density function is identical to the line $y = 1$ except for a single interval in Ψ, and in which the directions of increasing attractiveness are as described in Example 1 (the same directions also apply to Example 2), the existence of constrained maxima poses no difficulty. Under these conditions (which are fulfilled in both Examples 1 and 2) the subset of $\Psi_b^+ \times Y$ consisting of the points on or above the density function, as well as that of $\Psi_b^- \times Y$ defined similarly, are compact. Hence, since half of the attractiveness function is continuous over each of these sets, appropriate constrained maxima always exist. The question of whether these maxima are unique turns on the shape of the iso-attractiveness contours in relation to the shape of the potential surprise density function. If, as in the case of Example 1, the iso-attractiveness contours are linear and the potential surprise density function is appropriately strictly convex, or if, as in Example 2, the iso-attractiveness contours are strictly concave and the potential surprise density function is appropriately linear, then both constrained maxima are unique. Obviously, other combinations of shapes can also produce uniqueness.

With other forms of the potential surprise density function, such as the elongated S-shape introduced by Shackle (e.g., [8], p. 155) and reproduced in Figure 3, and with other kinds of attractiveness functions, the questions of existence and uniqueness of constrained maxima become more complex, and affirmative answers to them more problematical. In Figure 3, for example, a unique constrained maximum exists over $\Psi_b^+ \times Y$ because the curvature of the iso-attractiveness contours relative to the density function is sharp enough to permit it; but with the potential surprise density function crossing each iso-attractiveness contour at a single point, and with all of these curves asymptotic to the line $y = 1$, no unique constrained maximum exists over $\Psi_b^- \times Y$. (Here, too, directions of increasing attractiveness are down and to the right on $\Psi_b^+ \times Y$ and down and to the left on $\Psi_b^- \times Y$.) Still other iso-attractiveness contours and potential surprise density functions can result in corner solutions (recall Example 2). When constrained maxima exist that are not unique, the Shackle-Vickers model needs to be enriched if it is to determine, and hence explain, the decision of the decision-maker. Of course, if constrained maxima do not even exist, then the Shackle-Vickers model is incapable of explaining any decisions at all.

As indicated earlier, the comparative static analysis of the constrained maximization of the attractiveness function is concerned with determining, when possible, the signs of the derivatives of ψ_b^-, y_b^-, ψ_b^+ and y_b^+ with respect to b. For this purpose, the derivatives of appropriate functions and the relevant unique maxima are hereafter assumed to exist. In addition, for reasons of simplicity, only attractiveness functions g that are independent of b are considered.

It has already been observed in two special cases that from (5), when the derivatives of ψ_b^-, y_b^-, ψ_b^+ and y_b^+ are signed as in (3) from Example 1 or as in (4) from Example 2, the derivative, obtained using (6),

$$\frac{dQ(b)}{db} = \frac{\partial Q(\psi_b^-, y_b^-, \psi_b^+, y_b^+)}{\partial \psi_b^-} \frac{\partial \psi_b^-}{\partial b} + \frac{\partial Q(\psi_b^-, y_b^-, \psi_b^+, y_b^+)}{\partial y_b^-} \frac{\partial y_b^-}{\partial b}$$

$$+ \frac{\partial Q(\psi_b^-, y_b^-, \psi_b^+, y_b^+)}{\partial \psi_b^+} \frac{\partial \psi_b^+}{\partial b} + \frac{\partial Q(\psi_b^-, y_b^-, \psi_b^+, y_b^+)}{\partial y_b^+} \frac{\partial y_b^+}{\partial b} > 0,$$

for all interior b in B. This means that if b′ and b″ are in B, then b′ > b″ if and only if Q(b′) > Q(b″). Now a change from, say, b″ to b′ generally involves a movement of both halves of the potential surprise density function. Of course, the direction and extent of the movement of each half, to the right or left, depends on the posited form of the family of potential surprise density functions and on the manner in which b enters into the specification of f. In the cases of Examples 1 and 2, to pass from b″ to b′, where b′ > b″, implies a rightward shift of both halves of the potential surprise density function, that is,

$$f(\psi, b') < f(\psi, b''), \qquad b'' < \psi < b' + 1, \tag{7}$$

$$f(\psi, b') > f(\psi, b''), \qquad -\frac{1}{b''} - 1 < \psi < -\frac{1}{b'} . \tag{8}$$

In such a circumstance, the potential surprise density function given b′ is said to dominate that given b″. Generalizing on the basis of the discussion to this point, a broader definition of dominance (rightward shift) of potential surprise density functions can be stated as follows: f(ψ,b′) dominates f(ψ,b″) whenever (7) holds for all ψ in $\Psi_{b'}^+$, such that $f_\psi(\psi, b') > 0$, and (8) holds for all ψ in $\Psi_{b'}^-$, such that $f_\psi(\psi, b') < 0$. The following proposition is a simple consequence of previous argument. It applies to all functional forms of f and g that satisfy its hypotheses.

<u>Theorem 1</u>: Let Q be defined as in (6) and let f and g be such as to produce either inequalities (3) or (4) for all b′ and b″ in the interior of B. Assume f(ψ,b′) dominates f(ψ,b″) if and only if b′ > b″. Then f(ψ,b′) dominates f(ψ,b″) if and only if Q(b′) > Q(b″).

The notion of dominance described above is similar, at least in spirit, to those for stochastic environments given by Hadar and Russell [2]. Furthermore, Theorem 1 parallels their results relating stochastic dominance to the more preferred alternatives.

Theorem 1 also suggests another notion of dominance with respect to the objects of choice. For all b′ and b″ in B, refer to b′ as dominating b″ provided that Q(b′) > Q(b″). The same notion could be

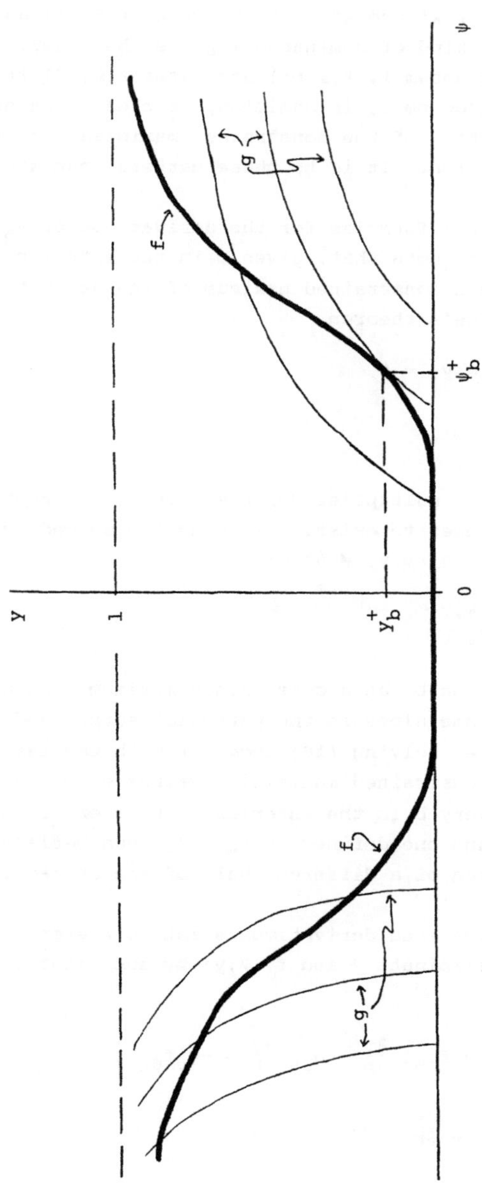

Figure 3

expressed in terms of x′ and x″ in X, where b′ = ξ(x′) and b″ = ξ(x″). In general, neither kind of dominance implies the other. But under the hypotheses of Theorem 1, f(ψ,b′) dominates f(ψ,b″) if and only if b′ dominates b″. Theorem 1, in addition, is clearly an outgrowth of the comparative statics of the constrained maximization of the attractiveness function. It is to these matters that attention now turns.

To derive general formulas for the derivatives of ψ_b^-, y_b^-, ψ_b^+ and y_b^+ with respect to b, note that, given b in the interior of B, the conditions defining a constrained maximum of the attractiveness function are, by Lagrange's theorem,

$$\begin{aligned} &-\lambda f_\psi(\psi,b) + g_\psi(\psi,y) = 0, \\ &\lambda + g_y(\psi,y) = 0, \\ &f(\psi,b) = y, \end{aligned} \tag{9}$$

where λ is a Lagrange multiplier dependent on b, and appropriate derivatives are assumed to exist. Dividing the second equation of (9) into the first (when $g_y(\psi,y) \neq 0$) gives

$$f_\psi(\psi,b) = -\frac{g_\psi(\psi,y)}{g_y(\psi,y)}, \tag{10}$$

which says that, given b, at a constrained maximum, iso-attractiveness contours have the same slope as the potential surprise density function. When possible, solving (10) together with the last equation of (9) expresses the constrained maximizing values of ψ and y as functions of b. For every b in the interior of B, there is one system (9) defined on $\Psi_b^+ \times Y$ and one defined on $\Psi_b^- \times Y$, each reflecting the constrained maximization of a different half of the attractiveness function.

Assuming the required derivatives exist, differentiate (9) with respect to b, and eliminate λ and $f_\psi(\psi,y)$ by substitution from (9) and (10). This gives

$$\frac{g_\psi}{g_y}\lambda_b + (g_{\psi\psi} + g_y f_{\psi\psi})\frac{\partial\psi}{\partial b} + g_{\psi y}\frac{\partial y}{\partial b} = -g_y f_{\psi b},$$

$$\lambda_b + g_{y\psi}\frac{\partial\psi}{\partial b} + g_{yy}\frac{\partial y}{\partial b} = 0,$$

$$-\frac{g_\psi}{g_y}\frac{\partial\psi}{\partial b} - \frac{\partial y}{\partial b} = -f_b,$$

where functional arguments have been dropped to simplify notation.

From Cramer's rule (with $g_{\psi y} = g_{y\psi}$) and (10),

$$\frac{\partial\psi}{\partial b} = - \frac{f_b g_{\psi y} + g_y f_{\psi b} + f_\psi f_b g_{yy}}{\left(\frac{1}{g_y}\right)^2 [(g_y)^2 (g_{\psi\psi} + g_y f_{\psi\psi}) - 2g_\psi g_y g_{\psi y} + (g_\psi)^2 g_{yy}]}, \tag{11}$$

$$\frac{\partial y}{\partial b} = \frac{f_\psi f_b g_{\psi y} + f_b g_{\psi\psi} + g_y f_b f_{\psi\psi} + g_\psi f_{\psi b}}{\left(\frac{1}{g_y}\right)^2 [(g_y)^2 (g_{\psi\psi} + g_y f_{\psi\psi}) - 2g_\psi g_y g_{\psi y} + (g_\psi)^2 g_{yy}]}. \tag{12}$$

As suggested above, equations (11) and (12) have different expressions on $\Psi_b^+ \times Y$ and $\Psi_b^- \times Y$ for each b in the interior of B. Both are well-defined as long as their denominators do not vanish.

The derivatives of ψ and y with respect to b, as determined in (11) and (12) are not possible to sign in general. Even if, around the maxima, (i) the potential surprise density function were convex with $f_{\psi\psi} \geq 0$, (ii) the attractiveness function were strictly quasi-concave with $g_y < 0$, and (iii) the bordered Hessian determinant

$$(g_y)^2 g_{\psi\psi} - 2g_\psi g_y g_{\psi y} + (g_\psi)^2 g_{yy} < 0,$$

thus implying that the denominators in (11) and (12) were negative, the signs in the numerator could still go either way.[9] The same would be true if the convexity of the density function were strict with $f_{\psi\psi} > 0$. However, there are two situations of immediate interest, one a slight generalization of Example 1 and the other a slight generalization of Example 2, in which (11) and (12) can be signed. The situation generalizing Example 1 yields the comparative static inequalities (3), while that generalizing Example 2 produces inequalities (4).

First suppose that $f_{\psi\psi} = f_{\psi b} = g_{\psi\psi} = g_{yy} = 0$ as in Table 2 (for Example 2) in neighborhoods of the appropriate maxima, for some b in the interior of B. Then in light of (10), equations (11) and (12) reduce to

$$\frac{\partial\psi}{\partial b} = -\frac{1}{2} f_\psi f_b,$$

$$\frac{\partial y}{\partial b} = \frac{1}{2} f_b.$$

---

[9] A similar assertion holds with a nonpositive bordered Hessian determinant as long as the convexity of the density function is strengthen so that $f_{\psi\psi} < 0$.

Applying the sign conditions for f_ψ and f_b in Table 2 yields Theorem 2:

<u>Theorem 2</u>: Let b be in the interior of B, and $f_{\psi\psi} = f_{\psi b} = g_{\psi\psi} = g_{yy} = 0$ in neighborhoods of the maxima (ψ_b^+, y_b^+) in $\Psi_b^+ \times Y$ and (ψ_b^-, y_b^-) in $\Psi_b^- \times Y$. If $f_\psi > 0$ and $f_b < 0$ in the neighborhood of (ψ_b^+, y_b^+), then

$$\frac{\partial \psi_b^+}{\partial b} > 0 \quad \text{and} \quad \frac{\partial y_b^+}{\partial b} < 0.$$

Also, if $f_\psi < 0$ and $f_b > 0$ in the neighborhood of (ψ_b^-, y_b^-), then

$$\frac{\partial \psi_b^-}{\partial b} > 0 \quad \text{and} \quad \frac{\partial y_b^-}{\partial b} > 0.$$

Next, let $g_{\psi\psi} = g_{\psi y} = g_{yy} = 0$ as in Table 1 (for Example 1) in neighborhoods of the appropriate maxima, for b in the interior of B. Then using (10)-(12),

$$\frac{\partial \psi}{\partial b} = -(g_y)^2 \frac{f_{\psi b}}{f_{\psi\psi}},$$

$$\frac{\partial y}{\partial b} = (g_y)^2 \frac{f_b f_{\psi\psi} - f_\psi f_{\psi b}}{f_{\psi\psi}}.$$

Example 1 has the further property that $f_b f_{\psi\psi} = f_\psi f_{\psi b}$ at most points in $\Psi \times B$, thus rendering

$$\frac{\partial y}{\partial b} = 0.$$

To obtain the second result, now add the sign conditions for $f_{\psi b}$ and $f_{\psi\psi}$ in Table 1:

<u>Theorem 3</u>: Let b be in the interior of B, and $g_{\psi\psi} = g_{\psi y} = g_{yy} = 0$ and $f_b f_{\psi\psi} = f_\psi f_{\psi b}$ in neighborhoods of the maxima (ψ_b^+, y_b^+) in $\Psi_b^+ \times Y$ and (ψ_b^-, y_b^-) in $\Psi_b^- \times Y$. If $f_{\psi b} < 0$ and $f_{\psi\psi} > 0$ in both neighborhoods, then

$$\frac{\partial \psi_b^+}{\partial b} > 0, \qquad \frac{\partial \psi_b^-}{\partial b} > 0,$$

and

$$\frac{\partial y_b^+}{\partial b} = \frac{\partial y_b^-}{\partial b} = 0.$$

Additional sufficient conditions that permit the signing of (11) and (12), although likely to be more complex, are certainly possible.

And the development of such conditions can only enrich the comparative static analysis of the Shackle-Vickers model and thereby add to our understanding of it.

References

[1] Deaton, A., and J. Muellbauer, Economics and Consumer Behavior. Cambridge: Cambridge University Press, 1980.

[2] Hadar, J., and W.R. Russell, "Rules for Ordering Uncertain Prospects," American Economic Review 59 (1969): 25-34.

[3] Hadar, J., and W.R. Russell, "Stochastic Dominance and Diversification," Journal of Economic Theory 3 (1971): 288-305.

[4] Hadar, J., and W.R. Russell, "Diversification of Interdependent Prospects," Journal of Economic Theory 7 (1974): 231-240.

[5] Katzner, D.W., "Potential Surprise, Potential Confirmation and Probability," Journal of Post Keynesian Economics 9 (Fall, 1986): 58-78.

[6] ________, "More on the Distinction between Potential Confirmation and Probability," Journal of Post Keynesian Economics 10 (Fall, 1987): 65-83.

[7] ________, "The Shackle-Vickers Approach to Decision-Making in Ignorance," mimeograph.

[8] Shackle, G.L.S., Decision Order and Time in Human Affairs, 2nd ed. Cambridge: Cambridge University Press, 1969.

[9] Vickers, D., Financial Markets in the Capitalist Process. Philadelphia: University of Pennsylvania Press, 1978, Pt. 3.

[10] ________, Money Capital in the Theory of the Firm. Cambridge: Cambridge University Press, 1987, Ch. 12.

STOCHASTIC DOMINANCE AND TRANSFORMATIONS OF RANDOM VARIABLES

Jack Meyer
Department of Economics
Michigan State University
East Lansing, MI 48824

1. Introduction

During the past twenty years, the term stochastic dominance (SD) has been used by economists to describe a particular set of rules for ranking random variables. These rules apply to pairs of random variables, and indicate when one is to be ranked higher than the other by specifying a condition which the difference between their cumulative distribution functions (CDF) must satisfy. Various SD ranking procedures have been employed in both empirical and theoretical analysis. First degree stochastic dominance, second degree stochastic dominance, and Rothschild and Stiglitz' definition of increasing risk are prominent examples.

A variety of empirical studies have used these SD rules to determine which elements in a choice set are undominated (efficient) in both the pairwise and convex stochastic dominance senses. In addition, theoretical studies involving randomness have often determined the effect of replacing a random parameter by one which dominates it under a particular SD definition. In each of these applications, the SD definitions can be used directly without modification. This is possible since comparing the random variables in a choice set can be carried out by comparing their CDFs; also, replacing one random variable by another in a decision model is accomplished by replacing one CDF with another in the expected utility calculation. Thus, the various SD ranking criteria can be used without modification in these applications.

For another set of applications or questions it is advantageous to adapt the stochastic dominance ranking procedure to include the ranking of transformations of random variables. This is the case whenever the emphasis in the analysis is on pairs of random variables which are related to one another by means of a transformation, or on sets of random variables where each are related to a common random variable by means of a transformation. These types of relationships arise when instruments such as insurance or put or call options are modeled. Insurance or option contracts can be used by an agent to transform the current random variable. In evaluating the usefulness of such transformations, one is concerned with comparing a new random variable with the original when they are not unrelated, but instead, the one is obtained from the other by means of a transformation. The stochastic dominance question becomes: which transformations are such that the welfare of a particular set of agents is increased when they are applied to a given random variable? Determining the effect of a particular legal instrument, such as an insurance contract, asking whether or not it alters a given random variable so that the resulting random variable dominates the original one for some particular group of agents, or asking which of several such insurance policy alternatives is best for a particular group of agents, are questions of interest. They can be dealt with directly by examining SD rankings of transformations. For these and other applications of SD ranking rules, the focus is on transformations of random variables. Extending the domain of the stochastic dominance discussion to include ranking and categorizing these transformations is precisely the point of this paper.

Transformations of random variables have been discussed and used to some extent in the stochastic dominance literature, especially in the risk analysis portion. Hadar and Russell (1971, 1974) have dealt with special cases of the transformation question, emphasizing its use in dealing with portfolios of random variables. Sandmo (1971) and others have used a particular linear, risk altering, transformation in discussing the comparative statics of risk. Recently, Cheng, Magill, and Shafer (1987) have used the transformation approach to address the comparative statics of first degree stochastic dominant shifts in a random variable within a general decision model context. The general transformation question and approach, however, has not been systematically explored or explicitly presented in the detail which occurs here.

The next section defines what is meant by a transformation of a random variable and gives the notation and assumptions used throughout the remainder of the paper. Following this the transformation question is examined within the context of first and second degree stochastic dominance. Certain examples of transformations available through insurance contracts and put and call option contracts are discussed. Finally, the work is extended to a form of stochastic dominance which allows the mean of the random variable to be decreased, and yet the random variable to be improved.

2. The General Transformation Question

The general problem of concern is the ranking of a pair of random variables y and z, where y and z are each obtained from random variable x by means of a transformation; that is, $y = m(x)$ and $z = n(x)$. The results presented will focus on the relationship between the transformations m(x) and n(x), which leads to specific forms of stochastic dominance. The special case, where $n(x) = x$, represents the situation where one is asking if a transformation m(x) leads to an improvement over the current random variable. This is the question posed most frequently in the literature, and is dealt with here as a special case.

This problem is of interest for a variety of reasons, but mainly because many of the risk altering instruments available in the market place come in the form of transformations, and are most directly modeled as such. Insurance contracts, and put or call option contracts are major examples. These instruments can be used by an agent to create a new random variable which is a modification of, and replaces, the current one. The agent often has available several such transformations and must choose among them. It would be advantageous to be able to call upon general results concerning transformations of random variables when discussing, designing, or ranking such instruments.

Throughout the analysis it is assumed that x is a continuously distributed random variable with support in the interval [a,b]. Its density function is denoted f(x) and its CDF by F(x). The transformations are assumed to be defined at all points in [a,b], and to be nondecreasing, continuous, and piecewise differentiable. Thus, the problem of interest is: given x, a continuously distributed random variable with support in [a,b], for which nondecreasing, continuous, and piecewise differentiable functions m(x) and n(x) does $y = m(x)$ dominate $z = n(x)$ according to a specified stochastic dominance rule. $G(\cdot)$ and $g(\cdot)$ will be used to denote the CDF and density of y, and likewise, $H(\cdot)$ and $h(\cdot)$ for random variable z.

The utility functions will be denoted $u(\cdot)$, and are assumed to possess continuous and piecewise differentiable first derivatives. As the literature has shown, stochastic dominance is defined by a certain relationship between the CDFs describing the random variables, but can be equivalently specified or interpreted as unanimous preference for the one random variable over the other by all expected utility maximizing agents within a specified group. This latter meaning of the term stochastic dominance will be emphasized here.

Before presenting answers to this question, comments concerning the restrictions placed on the transformations, and on x, are in order. First, the nondecreasing assumption concerning m(x) and n(x) combined with monotonic preferences in the expected utility model ensure that the transformations will not reverse the preference order over outcome levels for the original random variable. That is, the ranking of the various realizations of x are not altered by the transformations considered. This seems to be a feature of transformations representing most insurance contracts (possibly for moral hazard reasons), and is very important in allowing one to give the relationship between the CDFs describing random variables x, y and z in a simple way. The continuity and piecewise differentiability restriction can be replaced with a slightly weaker condition at the expense of complicating the notation and proofs.

The continuous nature of random variable x is also advantageous and not overly restrictive. If random variable x were allowed to be discretely distributed, then only particular discrete random variables could be derived from x by means of transformations. This is because the transformation process can only shift or accumulate probability, and cannot redistribute "lumps" which already exist. It is to eliminate the handling of this complication that x is assumed to be continuously distributed.

3. First Degree Stochastic Dominance

First degree stochastic dominance (FSD) is defined by stating a requirement concerning cumulative distribution functions. Random variable y dominates random variable z in the first degree, if the CDF for y lies below that for z at all points; that is $G(\cdot) \le H(\cdot)$. It is well known that this condition is necessary and sufficient for $Eu(y) \ge Eu(z)$ for all nondecreasing utility functions. In fact, this particular equivalence is the major factor in giving meaning to first degree stochastic dominance in economic research. The question addressed in this section is when do transformations m(x) and n(x) lead to random variables y = m(x) and z = n(x), where y dominates z in the first degree? That is, when does $G(\cdot)$ lie below $H(\cdot)$, or when is Eu(m(x)) greater than or equal to Eu(n(x)) for all utility functions which are nondecreasing? While the result presented is quite obvious, and the most important part of it has been established elsewhere, the framework developed and the techniques used allow us to move smoothly into the more interesting second degree stochastic dominance case.

Theorem 1: Given random variable x with density f(x) and support in the interval [a,b], random variable y = m(x) dominates z = n(x) in the first degree if and only if $(m(x) - n(x))\, f(x) \geq 0$ for all x in $[a,b]$.

<u>Proof</u>: A Taylor's series expansion of $u(m(x))$ about $u(n(x))$ implies that $Eu(m(x)) - Eu(n(x)) = Eu'(p(x))\,(m(x) - n(x))$ for some $p(x)$ between $m(x)$ and $n(x)$. The right hand side of this equality is nonnegative under the conditions of the theorem, hence the left hand side is, and sufficiency is established. To show necessity assume that $(m(x) - n(x))\cdot f(x) < 0$ for some x^* in $[a,b]$. This implies that $m(x) < n(x)$, and $f(x) > 0$ at that point. One can now construct a utility function which is nondecreasing and such that $Eu(m(x)) < Eu(n(x))$. To do so, let $x_o = \sup\{x: m(x) \geq n(x) \text{ and } x < x^*\}$ and $x_1 = \inf\{x: m(x) \geq n(x) \text{ and } x > x^*\}$. The nondegenerate interval $[x_o,x_1]$ contains x^* and is such that $m(x) < n(x)$ at all points. Define $u(\cdot)$ to be constant for all values less than $m(x_o)$, strictly increasing on the interval $[m(x_o), m(x_1)]$, and constant for all values greater than $m(x_1)$. $Eu(m(x)) < Eu(n(x))$ for this utility function. Q.E.D.

Hadar and Russell (1974) present a special case of this result where $n(x)$ is assumed to be the identity function; for this case they show sufficiency of the condition $m(x) \geq x$. Hadar and Russell (1971, 1974) also explicitly consider the case where $m(x)$ is linear, and determine the conditions on the parameters in the linear transformation sufficient to ensure that the resulting random variable dominates the current one in the FSD sense. Their use of these results is primarily in discussion of stochastic dominance in the portfolio problem with two risky assets. Sandmo (1971) has also dealt with the special case where $n(x) = x$, but requires that $m(x) = x + \theta$ where θ is a constant greater than zero. He uses that particular transformation to determine the comparative static effect of increasing a random output price for a competitive firm. Recent work by Cheng, Magill and Shafer (1987) also use this same transformation approach, assuming that $n(x) = x$ and that $m(x) \geq x$, in order to develop results concerning the comparative static effect of a first degree stochastic dominant change in a random variable within a general decision model context. These applications indicate that the transformation approach is useful in discussing comparative statics of random variable changes and other issues.

Before turning to other forms of stochastic dominance, two points need emphasis. First, the relationship required concerning $m(x)$ and $n(x)$ does depend on $f(x)$; that is, the condition imposed on the transformations does depend on how the original random variable is distributed. For FSD this dependence is particularly simple in that the restriction depends only on whether $f(x)$ is zero or not. Results concerning other forms of stochastic dominance will also display this dependence on $f(x)$, but will not be of so simple a nature. Second, since the condition concerning $m(x)$ and $n(x)$ depends on $f(x)$, one can ask the additional question of which transformations lead to first degree stochastic dominance for all initial random variables x? Obviously, the answer here is that $m(x)$ must be greater than or equal to $n(x)$ for all x in [a,b], a restriction not much different than that posed in Theorem 1. For other forms of stochastic dominance the relationship between the answer to these two questions will not be nearly so close, nor will the second question be of much interest. Next the case of second degree stochastic dominance is discussed.

4. Second Degree Stochastic Dominance

As in the case of FSD, second degree stochastic dominance (SSD) is defined by a condition on the difference between two CDFs. Random variable y is said to dominate z in the second degree if

$$\int_a^x [H(s) - G(s)]ds \geq 0 \quad \text{for all } x \text{ in } [a,b].$$

This condition is equivalent to $Eu(y) \geq Eu(z)$ for all nondecreasing and concave utility functions. The following theorem uses this definition to develop a ranking rule which applies to transformations of random variables.

<u>Theorem 2</u>: Given random variable x with density $f(x)$ and support in the interval [a,b], random variable $y = m(x)$ dominates $z = n(x)$ in the second degree if and only if

$$\int_a^x [(m(s) - n(s)]\cdot f(s)ds \geq 0 \quad \text{for all } x \text{ in } [a,b].$$

<u>Proof</u>: Define $Eu(\theta) = Eu[n(x) + \theta(m(x) - n(x))]$. Thus, $Eu(0) = Eu(n(x))$, and $Eu(1) = Eu(m(x))$. Signing $dEu(\theta)/d\theta$ for all θ in [0,1] is sufficient for signing $Eu(1) - Eu(0)$ or $Eu(m(x)) - Eu(n(x))$. Now $dEu(\theta)/d\theta = E[u'(n(x) + \theta(m(x) - n(x))]\cdot[m(x) - n(x)]$. Integrating this by parts one obtains

$$[u'(n(b)+\theta(m(b)-n(b))]\cdot\int_a^b [m(s)-n(s)]\cdot f(s)ds -$$

$$\int_a^b u''(n(x)+\theta(m(x)-n(x))\cdot(n'(x)+\theta(m'(x)-n'(x))\cdot\int_a^x (m(s)-n(s))f(s)dsdx.$$

The conditions stated are sufficient to sign this expression for all in [0,1], hence sufficiency is established. To show necessity a proof by contradiction using a constructed utility function will be employed as in the FSD case. First note that $Eu(\theta)$ is concave in θ. Thus, $dEu(\theta)/d\theta > 0$ at $\theta = 0$ is necessary for $Eu(m(x)) > Eu(n(x))$. I.e., $Eu'(m(x))\cdot(n(x)-m(x)) > 0$ is required. Assume the condition in the theorem is violated at some point x_1. Then there exists a nondegenerate interval $[x_o,x_1]$ such that $m(x) - n(x) < 0$ on this interval, $\int_a^{x_o} (m(s)-n(s))\cdot f(s)ds \leq 0$ and $\int_a^{x_1} (m(s)-(n(s))\cdot f(s)ds < 0$. Define $u(x)$ by $u'(x) = 1$ for $x < x_o$, $u'(x) = (x_1 - x)/(x_1 - x_o)$ for x in $[x_o,x_1]$ and $u'(x) = 0$ for $x > x_1$. Then $dEu(\theta)/d\theta < 0$ at $\theta = 0$, and $Eu(m(x)) < Eu(n(x))$ for this utility function. Q.E.D.

Fewer special cases of this result have been discussed in the literature than for the FSD condition. It appears that the only case examined is where $n(x) = x$, and $m(x)$ is assumed to be linear. Hadar and Russell (1971, 1974) deal with this case in the portfolio context, and find the parameter values for a linear transformation $m(x)$ which lead to SSD over the original random variable. The risk analysis literature examines this same case with the additional requirement that the transformation not alter the mean value of the random variable. Such a linear transformation was used by Sandmo in discussing the comparative statics of a special type of an increase in the riskiness of a random variable. This transformation takes the specific form $m(x) = x + \theta\cdot(x - \mu)$ for $\theta \geq 0$ where μ is the mean of random variable x. Other than these two cases, SSD transformations do not appear to have been discussed in a general way.

Notice that the condition imposed on the transformations by SSD depends on the distribution of the random variable. The relationship between this condition and the density $f(x)$ is not so simple as in the FSD case. Furthermore, if one wishes to examine conditions on $m(x)$ and $n(x)$ which imply SSD for all random variables x, one must impose the same condition as in the FSD case, namely $m(x) \geq n(x)$ for all x in $[a,b]$. Sufficiency of this condition is obvious. To show necessity one need only note that if $m(x) < n(x)$ for some interval then one can use a random variable x, whose support is in that interval, to construct a counterexample. It is not very useful to have FSD and SSD conditions which are the same, and hence, the question of which transformations lead to SSD for all random variables is not as interesting as the one posed in Theorem 2 where a specific random variable is assumed.

This SSD condition listed in Theorem 2 can also be translated into a similar condition relating to Rothschild and Stiglitz' (1971) definition of an increase in risk. All that needs to be done is to impose the mean preserving requirement. Work by Meyer and Ormiston (1987) does this, and uses the transformation approach to discuss the comparative static effect of an increase in risk for a general decision model. That form of stochastic dominance will not be discussed here.

These FSD and SSD results have obvious application in ranking transformations which arise in either the insurance or options market applications. This is demonstrated by discussing three examples; two are different forms of insurance policies, and the third is a call option. Transformations are used to model these risk altering instruments.

First consider the situation of owning an asset such as a house or an automobile whose value is random. This may be due to events such as natural catastrophes like wind damage or flood, or losses caused by other agents through theft or collision. Let x denote this random value and assume that its support is the interval [a,b]. The value b is the value of the asset if no loss occurs. One type of insurance policy that can be purchased to alter this random variable x, is the deductible policy in which the insurance company promises to reimburse all losses in excess of some stated amount d (the deductible) in return for a payment of size δ (the premium). Such an insurance policy is represented by transformation

$$n(x) = \begin{cases} b - d_n - \delta_n & \text{for } x < b - d_n \\ x - \delta_n & \text{for } x \geq b - d_n \end{cases}$$

This transformation is continuous and piecewise differentiable. A similar transformation with deductible d_m and premium δ_m defines transformation m(x).

Two interesting questions concerning these insurance policies can be addressed using Theorems 1 and 2. One can ask when is policy m(x) better than n(x) for either the FSD or SSD groups of agents, or which if any deductible policy dominates the alternative of not purchasing insurance at all? Forming the difference m(x) - n(x) allows the first question to be answered. It is assumed that m(x) and n(x) are labeled so that $d_m < d_n$. For these parameter values

$$m(x) - n(x) = \begin{cases} d_n - d_m + \delta_n - \delta_m & a \leq x \leq b - d_n \\ b - d_m - \delta_m - x + \delta_n & b - d_n < x < b - d_m \\ \delta_n - \delta_m & b - d_m \leq x \leq b \end{cases}$$

The first thing to notice is that m(x) dominates n(x) in the first degree if the premium charged under m(x) is smaller than that under n(x). Of course, experience in choosing among policies with varying sizes for the deductible indicates that it is unlikely for the premium charged to be smaller for policies with lower deductibles. Furthermore, it is typical for the reduction in the premium to be a fraction of the increase in the deductible. Thus it is further assumed that $\delta_m > \delta_n$, and that $d_n - d_m > \delta_m - \delta_n$.

Under this restriction the difference m(x) - n(x) is first positive and constant, then declines with slope minus 1, and finally is constant and negative. Such functions satisfy the SSD condition if the $\int_a^b [m(x) - n(x)]\cdot f(x)dx \geq 0$; that is, if the mean value of m(x) is at least as large as the mean value of n(x). Since the difference between the mean value of x and the mean value of the transformation is the expected gain to the provider of the insurance policy, one can conclude that among all deductible policies <u>with the same expected gain to the provider</u>, the one with the lowest deductible ($d_m = 0$) is preferred by all risk averse agents. Hence, if all agents are risk averse, insurance policies with different levels for the deductible cannot be sold unless the provider has different expected gains from the various policies. This assumes the same f(x) for all agents.

In addressing the question of whether any risk averse agent would prefer such a deductible policy over no insurance at all, one must examine the difference m(x) - x. This difference is given by

$$m(x) - x = \begin{cases} b - d_m - \delta_m - x & \text{when } x < b - d_m \\ -\delta_m & \text{when } x \geq b - d_m \end{cases}$$

As long as $d_m + \delta_m$ is not larger than (b - a), FSD does not apply. Making such an assumption, the function m(x) - x is first positive and declining and then negative and declining, and finally negative and constant. Thus, the SSD condition is satisfied only if the expected value of m(x) is greater than or equal to the expected value of x. Since providers of insurance are unlikely to supply insurance under this condition where expected gain is nonpositive, not all risk averse agents will purchase an insurance policy with such deductible features, only those with sufficient risk aversion.

The next type of insurance contract to be considered involves coinsurance. For this type of insurance the provider insures an asset whose value is random by promising to reimburse a fixed percentage, θ, of the difference (b - x) between the asset's maximum value and its actual value, while charging a premium δ. Transformation m(x) =

$x + \theta_m \cdot (b - x) - \delta_m$ represents such a contract, and n(x) is similarly defined using parameters θ_n and δ_n. Their difference, $m(x) - n(x) = (\theta_m - \theta_n)(b - x) - (\delta_m - \delta_n)$. Dominance in the first degree is displayed if one contract both reimburses a higher percentage of the loss and charges a lower premium. Rule this out by assuming that $\theta_m > \theta_n$ and $\delta_m > \delta_n$. To eliminate FSD completely one must further assume that the difference in premiums cannot exceed the maximum difference in the size of the reimbursement, that is, $\delta_m - \delta_n < (b - a)(\theta_m - \theta_n)$. For these parameter restrictions, the above difference is a linear function which is first positive and then negative. Thus, SSD of m(x) over n(x) occurs if the two transformations are such that the expected value of m(x) is at least as large as that of n(x). This immediately leads to conclusions concerning the optimal value of θ, and whether or not all risk averse agents would choose to purchase such a policy, similar to those found concerning deductibles in the previous example. Among all contracts with coinsurance provisions and yielding the same expected gain to the provider, all risk averse agents prefer the reimbursement percentage to be set at 100%. Not all risk averse agents would choose such a policy if the provider has an expected gain strictly greater than zero, only those with sufficiently large risk aversion measures would do so. Although it will not be presented here, it is straightforward to similarly model insurance contracts which have both coinsurance and deductible provisions, or to compare policies with deductible features with those having coinsurance attributes.

Turning now to another type of instrument which is available to agents to alter the random value of an asset they possess, consider put and call option contracts to modify the value of common stock. These contracts provide the buyer of the option with the right to either buy (call) or sell (put) shares of common stock at a fixed price referred to as the striking price. On the other hand, the seller of such an option contract incurs the obligation to either sell or buy the common stock at the agreed upon striking price if the contract purchaser decides to exercise the option. To model one such option transaction using the transformation notation, let x represent the random value of one hundred shares of a given common stock. An investor who owns the common stock can sell a call contract (100 shares) with striking price x_m for a price of $\$p_m$. This investment of selling a call option while owning the common stock can be represented by the following transformation. The original random value x becomes m(x) when the stock is held and the call option is sold.

$$m(x) = \begin{cases} x + p_m & \text{when } x < x_m \\ x_m + p_m & \text{when } x \geq x_m \end{cases}$$

That is, this sale of the call option while holding the common stock alters the value of the total investment by adding the option price to the stock value in the event that the option is not exercised, and fixes the investment's value at the option price plus the striking price if the option is exercised. Similar notation applies to selling a call option with a different striking price x_n ($x_n > x_m$) and selling price p_n. To compare the investment alternatives of selling call options with different striking prices, one forms the difference $m(x) - n(x)$.

$$m(x) - n(x) = \begin{cases} p_m - p_n & a \leq x < x_m \\ (x_m + p_m) - (x + p_n) & x_m \leq x \leq x_n \\ (x_m + p_m) - (x_n + p_n) & x_n < x \leq b \end{cases}$$

The FSD condition implies that the call option represented by $m(x)$ dominates that represented by $n(x)$ only if its selling price is higher and the sum of its selling and striking price is also higher. If this case is ruled out, but $p_m > p_n$, then the above difference is first positive and constant, then declining at rate minus one, and finally negative and constant. This is exactly the same as in the deductible insurance example above, and analysis of its implications is straightforward. All investors who are risk averse prefer the lowest striking price possible if the call options are priced so that their expected values are the same. Not all risk averse investors would choose to sell such call options if their expected values exceeded their selling prices. Since the theory concerning the buyer of the call option, who is the provider of such an investment alternative, is less well understood than in the insurance case, it is more difficult to predict whether these call options would sell at a price which is greater than or less than their expected value.

While this example deals with the selling of a call option, the purchase of a put option contract can also be modeled using a similar transformation. One can also model the simultaneous purchase or sale of put or call contracts with differing striking prices, although the transformations involved become cumbersome.

The examples just discussed show that the SSD ranking of transformations can be used as long as the preferred transformation has at least as high an expected value as the other one. For both the insurance and the put and call option examples just discussed, this allows comparison of different contracts yielding the same expected value to the provider, but does not allow comparison with the no contract case if the provider requires a positive expected gain in order to supply the contract. For the insurance examples the provider can be expected to require a positive expected value, while for the options example it is not clear whether the buyer of the call option requires a positive expected return or not. Thus, for at least the question of who would purchase insurance, it is clear that a form of stochastic dominance, which allows the provider of the transformation to gain in an expected value sense, and yet the acquirer of the transformation to prefer it to the no insurance alternative, would be a desirable addition. The next section deals briefly with one such form of stochastic dominance.

5. Stochastic Dominance With Respect to a Function

The final form of stochastic dominance to be discussed is a generalization of the SSD concept which allows the reference agent to be arbitrary rather than the risk neutral agent. The set of all risk averse agents can be equivalently described as the set of all agents more risk averse than the risk neutral agent. Thus, one can generalize the SSD ranking procedure by examining the set of all agents more risk averse than some agent with utility function $k(x)$. Of course, the case where $k(x) = x$ is the SSD assumption. Meyer (1977) referred to this as second degree stochastic dominance with respect to a function, and the notation SSD(k) has been used.

Theorem 3: Given random variable x with density $f(x)$ and support in the interval $[a,b]$, random variable $y = m(x)$ dominates $z = n(x)$ in the SSD(k) sense if and only if

$$\int_a^x [k(m(s)) - k(n(s))]\cdot f(s)ds \geq 0 \quad \text{for all } x \text{ in } [a,b].$$

Proof: As in the earlier work concerning this form of stochastic dominance, the proof is simply a change of variables exercise applied to the SSD result. Pratt (1964) has shown that all agents more risk averse than $k(x)$ have utility functions $u(x)$ which can be written as $u(x) = v(k(x))$, where $v(\cdot)$ is a concave and increasing function. Thus, $Eu(m(x)) - Eu(n(x))$ is equal to $Ev(k(m(x))) - Ev(k(n(x)))$ for such $v(\cdot)$, and Theorem 2 applies directly to the transformations $k(m(x))$ and $k(n(x))$. Q.E.D.

As mentioned in the previous section, the main purpose of introducing this result is to allow one to choose a reference agent with utility function k(x) so that the provider of transformation m(x) can have an expected gain (Em(x) < Ex), and yet broad classes of agents can still choose m(x) over the current random variable. k(x) functions displaying sufficient risk aversion do this. Hence, even if insurance companies will provide insurance only if the expected value to them is positive, all agents more risk averse than a certain level would still choose to obtain such insurance.

This concludes this paper. Much can still be done concerning transformations and stochastic dominance, especially applying these results, but also extending them, using such concepts as Fishburn's (1974) convex stochastic dominance, and to other forms of stochastic dominance. Hopefully the results presented provide the necessary first steps for such work.

References

Cheng, H., M. Magill, and W. Shafer, "Some Results on Comparative Statics under Uncertainty," *International Economic Review* 28 (1987): 493-507.

Fishburn, P., "Convex Stochastic Dominance with Continuous Distribution Functions," *Journal of Economic Theory* 7 (1974): 143-158.

Hadar, J., and W. Russell, "Rules for Ordering Uncertain Prospects," *American Economic Review* 59 (1969): 25-34.

Hadar, J., and W. Russell, "Stochastic Dominance and Diversification," *Journal of Economic Theory* 3 (1971): 288-305.

Hadar, J., and W. Russell, "Stochastic Dominance in Choice Under Uncertainty," in *Essays in Economic Behavior Under Uncertainty*, eds. M. Balch, D. McFadden and S. Wu, 133-150. North Holland, 1974.

Hanoch, G., and H. Levy, "The Efficiency Analysis of Choices Involving Risk," *Review of Economic Studies* 36 (1969): 335-346.

Meyer, J., "Second Degree Stochastic Dominance with Respect to a Function," *International Economic Review* 18 (1977): 477-487.

Meyer, J., and M. Ormiston, "Deterministic Transformations of Random Variables and the Comparative Statics of Risk," *Journal of Risk and Uncertainty* (forthcoming 1989).

Pratt, J., "Risk Aversion in the Small and the Large," *Econometrica* 32 (1964): 122-136.

Rothschild, M., and J. Stiglitz, "Increasing Risk I: A Definition," *Journal of Economic Theory* 3 (1971): 66-84.

Sandmo, A., "The Competitive Firm Under Price Uncertainty," *American Economic Review* 61 (1971): 65-73.

REPRESENTATIVE SETS FOR STOCHASTIC DOMINANCE RULES

W.R. Russell and T.K. Seo
Southern Methodist University
Dallas, TX 75275

1. Introduction

Advising someone as to his best course of conduct is always treacherous and trying to steer his economic course can be perilous to personal relationships. If we knew his utility function, economists might say, we could confidently and with courage make optimal selections for anyone. But economic counselors would likely know, at most, only some salient characteristics of the advisee. Depending on what and how much we know about a client's utility function we could more or less sharply delineate the options which are inferior for him. This idea is at the root of all studies under the topic of "stochastic dominance rules." Given incomplete information about a person's utility function the best that we can do is to classify him accordingly to one or more sets of utility functions. He may be one of any number of people whose utility functions are members of some given set. We know no more or less about his utility function than any other in the set. Any choice between two uncertain prospects appropriate to him would likewise be appropriate to anyone else whose utility function is in the same set because this set defines the limits of information about the utility functions we consider. It is equivalent then to ask: "If we know Tom's utility function can be characterized as thus and so which choice should he make?" or, "If everyone we consider has utility functions which can be characterized as thus and so, which choice should they unanimously make?" The latter question is in the spirit of stochastic dominance research. Primarily, stochastic dominance rules dictate procedures for discovering unanimous orderings of uncertain prospects appropriate for utility functions within specified sets.

In principle, the underlying decision criterion for stochastic dominance need not be maximization of expected utility, but in execution to date, there has been limited progress in the search for a better criterion. The number of stochastic dominance rules, however, has increased over the years. The most prominent rules known in the literature are the First Degree Stochastic Dominance (FSD) rule, the Second Degree Stochastic Dominance (SSD) rule, the Mean-Preserving Spread (MPS), and the Third Degree Stochastic Dominance (TSD) rule.

Each of the rules for unanimous choice apply to a well-defined set of utility functions, (e.g., risk-averters, risk-preferrers, etc.), and within each set of functions are, of course, a tremendous number of different functional forms. Our task in this paper is to reduce some of the complexity of working with dominance rules by presenting and illustrating the usefulness of working with specific proper subsets of "representative" utility functions rather than with all admissible ones in the original set. We shall see that applications of a stochastic dominance rule for a representative subset will in fact yield unanimous orderings for all members of the original utility set.

To proceed, we assume that agents are assumed to possess von Neumann-Morgenstern utility functions and rank any given set of uncertain prospects by expected utilities. Let F, G, ... denote probability distribution functions, (or, distributions) of random prospects. We assume that all the distributions in this paper are right-continuous, with finite first moments, μ_F, μ_G, etc. All integrations in this paper are performed with respect to probability measures, so they are Lebesgue-Stieltjes integrals. Then integrants can be replaced by other functions which are identical except at the set of measure zero. Any convex or concave function defined on an interval has, at most, two points of discontinuity. And utility functions considered in this paper are measurable with respect to <u>all</u> probability measures, and are integrable with respect to all probability measures on a closed interval. For this reason, we can assume without loss of generality in our proofs involving integrals that the given utility functions are continuous.

2. Representative Sets for Risk Averters and Risk Preferrers

The second degree stochastic dominance theorem asserts that for any given pair of random prospects X and Y, X SSD Y if and only if all risk averters prefer X over Y. In this section, we identify a proper subset of risk averse agents, to be called a <u>representative</u> set, with the property that all agents in this smaller group prefer X over Y if and only if X SSD Y. The existence of such a representative set is somewhat surprising inasmuch as we ordinarily expect that the smaller the group of agents, the less restrictive would be the corresponding decision rule, and conversely. More remarkable are some of the properties of the representative sets. It turns out that all agents in this group have utility functions of an extremely simple form (consisting of two linear pieces), and this fact has been utilized in a study of portfolios ([4]). Secondly, any given concave utility function can be arbitrarily closely approximated by a linear combination of such utility functions. And thirdly, all agents in this group are completely ordered by risk premiums of Arrow and Pratt.

2.1. Risk Averters

Let U_2^- be the set of all nondecreasing concave functions on $(-\infty,\infty)$, which are integrable with respect to all probability measures with finite means.[1] It has been established in the literature ([3], [5]) that F is unanimously preferred or indifferent to G by all risk averters with utility functions in U_2^-, if and only if

$$\int_{-\infty}^{c}(G(x)-F(x))dx \geq 0, \qquad \text{for all } c \in (-\infty,\infty). \tag{1}$$

Let $u_c^-(x) = \text{Min}\{(x-c), 0\}$. Certainly, u_c^- is an element of U_2^-, so if (1) holds, F is preferred or indifferent to G by all agents with utility functions of type u_c^-, $c \in (-\infty,\infty)$. We want to verify the converse; that is, if F is preferred or indifferent to G by all agents with utility functions in R_2^-, where

$$R_2^- = \{u_c^- \mid c \in (-\infty,\infty)\},$$

then (1) is satisfied. To see this, assume that

$$\int_{-\infty}^{\infty}u_c^-(x)dF(x) \geq \int_{-\infty}^{\infty}u_c^-(x)dG(x), \qquad \text{for all } c \in (-\infty,\infty). \tag{2}$$

Now $\int_{-\infty}^{\infty}u_c^-(x)dF(x) = \int_{-\infty}^{c}(x-c)dF(x) = (x-c)F(x)\Big|_{-\infty}^{c} + \int_{-\infty}^{c}F(x)dx = \int_{-\infty}^{c}F(x)dx,$ the last equality being obtained by the fact that F has a finite mean so that $\lim_{x\to-\infty} xF(x) = 0$. Similarly, we have $\int_{-\infty}^{\infty}u_c^-(x)dG(x) = \int_{-\infty}^{c}G(x)dx$. We then immediately see that (2) is equivalent to (1). This establishes the desired result:

<u>Theorem 1</u>: The following three statements are equivalent.

(i) $\int_{-\infty}^{\infty}u(x)dF(x) \geq \int_{-\infty}^{\infty}u(x)dG(x)$, for all $u \in U_2^-$.

[1] In [11], it has been shown that $u \in U_2^-$ if and only if $|u(x)/x|$ is uniformly bounded for sufficiently small x.

(ii) $\int_{-\infty}^{\infty} u_c^-(x)dF(x) \geq \int_{-\infty}^{\infty} u_c^-(x)dG(x)$, for all $u_c^- \in R_2^-$.

(iii) $\int_{-\infty}^{c} (G(x)-F(x))dx \geq 0$, for all $c \in (-\infty,\infty)$.

This theorem implies that unanimous choice of F over G by those agents with utility functions in R_2^- yields the same choice by all risk averters. In this sense, R_2^- is regarded as a collection of "representatives" for the set of all risk averters U_2^-. Utility functions of the u_c^--type have been discussed by Markovitz ([6]) who also pointed out that agents with such utility functions behave as if they minimize expected loss, where loss is defined by $-(x-c)$.

2.2. Risk Preferrers

Now let us consider U_2^+, the set of all nondecreasing convex functions on $(-\infty,\infty)$ which are integrable with respect to all probability measures with finite means. Let

$$R_2^+ = \{u_c^+ \mid c \in (-\infty,\infty)\},$$

where $u_c^+(x) = \text{Max}\{(x-c), 0\}$. The following theorem shows that R_2^+ is a set of representatives for risk preferrers.

<u>Theorem 2</u>: The following three statements are equivalent.

(i′) $\int_{-\infty}^{\infty} u(x)dF(x) \geq \int_{-\infty}^{\infty} u(x)dG(x)$, for all $u \in U_2^+$.

(ii′) $\int_{-\infty}^{\infty} u_c^+(x)dF(x) \geq \int_{-\infty}^{\infty} u_c^+(x)dG(x)$, for all $u_c^+ \in R_2^+$.

(iii′) $\int_{c}^{\infty} (G(x)-F(x))dx \geq 0$, for all $c \in (-\infty,\infty)$.

<u>Proof</u>: Define $u^*(x) = -u(-x)$ and $F^*(x) = 1-F(-x)$. It is apparent that u is F-integrable if and only if u^* is F^*-integrable, and that the correspondence ϕ: $U_2^+ \to U_2^-$, $\phi(u) = u^*$, is one-to-one and onto. Since,

$$\int_{-\infty}^{\infty} u(x)dF(x) = - \int_{-\infty}^{\infty} u^*(x)dF^*(x),$$

and similarly for G and G^*, we see that (i′) is equivalent to

$$\int_{-\infty}^{\infty} u^*(x)dF^*(x) \leq \int_{-\infty}^{\infty} u^*(x)dG^*(x), \quad \text{for all } u^* \in U_2^-. \tag{3}$$

By Theorem 1, (3) is equivalent to

$$\int_{-\infty}^{\infty} u_c^-(x)dF^*(x) \le \int_{-\infty}^{\infty} u_c^-(x)dG^*(x), \qquad \text{for all } u_c^- \in R_2^-. \tag{4}$$

Now the L.H.S. of (4) $= \int_{-\infty}^{\infty} u_c^+(-t)dF(t) = \int_{-\infty}^{\infty} -u_{-c}^+(t)dF(t)$, and similarly, the R.H.S. of (4) $= \int_{-\infty}^{\infty} -u_{-c}^+(t)dG(t)$, hence, (4) is equivalent to

$$\int_{-\infty}^{\infty} u_{-c}^+(x)dF(x) \ge \int_{-\infty}^{\infty} u_{-c}^+(x)dG(x), \qquad \text{for all } c \in (-\infty,\infty),$$

which is equivalent to (ii').

Also, by Theorem 1, (3) is equivalent to

$$\int_{-\infty}^{c} (G^*(x)-F^*(x))dx \ge 0, \qquad \text{for all } c \in (-\infty,\infty).$$

After replacing F^* and G^* by F and G, respectively, and changing variable,

$$\int_{c}^{\infty} (G(x)-F(x))dx \ge 0, \tag{4'}$$

for all $c \in (-\infty,\infty)$. Q.E.D.

We may now raise a question about the relationship between risk averters and risk preferrers. If F is unanimously preferred over G by risk averters, under what conditions will risk preferrers unanimously prefer G over F? Suppose that $F \underset{\tilde{a}}{\ge} G$, i.e., F is preferred or indifferent to G by all risk averters with utility functions in U_2^-. Now the difference of the means can be expressed as:

$$\int_{-\infty}^{\infty} xd(F(x)-G(x)) = x(F(x)-G(x))\Big|_{-\infty}^{c} + \int_{-\infty}^{\infty}(G(x)-F(x))dx.$$

Since F has a finite mean, $\lim_{x\to-\infty} xF(x) = 0 = \lim_{x\to\infty} x(1-F(x))$; and similarly for G, so that $x(F(x)-G(x))\Big|_{-\infty}^{\infty} = 0$. But, by (iii) of Theorem 1, $\int_{-\infty}^{\infty}(G(x)-F(x))dx \ge 0$, hence, $\mu_F - \mu_G = \int_{-\infty}^{\infty} xd(F(x)-G(x)) \ge 0$.

Now if we further suppose that $G \underset{\tilde{p}}{\ge} F$, i.e., G is preferred or indifferent to F by all risk preferrers with utility functions in U_2^+, then we have, by applying Theorem 2, $\mu_G \ge \mu_F$. Hence, $\mu_F = \mu_G$. Conversely, if $\mu_F = \mu_G$, then it is immediate to see the relationship between (iii) of Theorem 1 and (iii') of Theorem 2. Specifically, we have:[2]

Theorem 3:

(i) $F \underset{\tilde{a}}{\geq} G \rightarrow (\mu_F = \mu_G \leftrightarrow G \underset{\tilde{p}}{\geq} F)$.

(ii) $F \underset{\tilde{p}}{\geq} G \rightarrow (\mu_F = \mu_G \leftrightarrow F \underset{\tilde{a}}{\geq} G)$.

(iii) $\mu_F = \mu_G \rightarrow (F \underset{\tilde{a}}{\geq} G \leftrightarrow G \underset{\tilde{p}}{\geq} F)$.

2.3. Mean Preserving Spread

Let U_2 be the set of all concave functions as defined by Rothschild and Stiglitz on [0,1]. In particular, U_2 includes all decreasing concave functions. In their study of increasing risk, Rothschild and Stiglitz ([10]) has established that F is preferred or indifferent to G by all agents with utility functions in U_2, if and only if, $\mu_F = \mu_G$ and the SSD condition (1) hold. Since R_2^- has been shown to be a representative set for U_2^-, the group of agents U_2 can be represented by

$$R_2 = R_2^- \cup \{-I\}$$

where $-I(x) \equiv -x$, for all x.[3] Formally stated,

Theorem 6: The following three statements are equivalent.

(i) $\int_0^1 u(x)dF(x) \geq \int_0^1 u(x)dG(x)$, for all $u \in U_2$.

(ii) $\mu_F = \mu_G$ and $\int_0^c (G(x)-F(x))dx \geq 0$, for all $c \in [0,1]$.

(iii) $\int_0^1 v(x)dF(x) \geq \int_0^1 v(x)dG(x)$, for all $v \in R_2$.

---

[2]Theorem 3 is already known in the literature. See, for example, Mosler [8].

[3]Precisely stated R_2^- should be modified as

$$\left\{ u_c^- \big|_{\text{rst on } [0,1]} \;\middle|\; u_c^- \in R_2^- \right\}.$$

3. Two Applications of the Representative Sets

3.1. Proof of the SSD Theorem

The stochastic dominance theorems are known to be valid but it may or may not be recognized that several published proofs ([3], [5], etc.) are either incorrect, or incomplete even under some unnecessarily restrictive assumptions. We take this as an opportunity to demonstrate the use of our representative set to provide a valid proof of the SSD rule not based on proof by contradiction. A correct proof of the FSD rule can be established easily without the concept of representative sets so it is of lesser interest here and we will omit it.

Proofs of the SSD rule (i.e., the equivalence between (i) and (iii) in Theorem 1) have leaned on the method of proof by contradiction or reductio ad absurdum. The fact is that such arguments are delicate and unless utmost care is taken it is easy to fall into error, and importantly, even when the proof is correct it often sheds little understanding on the connection between the two statements one is trying to establish. It is prudent therefore to avoid this mode of argumentation where possible. In this section, we are going to avoid proof by contradiction by utilizing representative sets in our proposed proof of the SSD rule. To do this we must make use of the following two lemmas whose proofs are provided in the Appendix:

Lemma 1: Let u be a continuous convex function on [0,1]. Then there is a sequence of functions $\{\hat{u}_n\}$

$$\hat{u}_n(x) = \alpha_{0n}x + \sum_{i=1}^{n-1} \alpha_{in}(x-c_{in})^+ + \beta_n, \qquad 0 \le x \le 1,$$

$$\alpha_{in} \ge 0,\ (i \ne 0),\quad c_{in} \ge 0,\quad \alpha_{in},\ c_{in},\ \beta_n \text{ are real constants,}$$

$$(x-c_{in})^+ \equiv \text{Max}\{(x-c_{in}),\ 0\} \equiv u^+_{c_{in}}(x),$$

such that $\{\hat{u}_n\}$ converges uniformly to u. If u is nondecreasing on [0,1], then $\alpha_{0n} \ge 0$. If u is decreasing for some subinterval of [0,1], then $\alpha_{0n} \le 0$ and $c_{0n} = 0$ for sufficiently large n.

Lemma 2: Let u be a continuous convex function defined on the real line $(-\infty,\infty)$, and let u be integrable with respect to every probability measure with finite first moments.[4] Then, there exist a function h and a sequence $\{g_n\}$ of functions such that

(i) $|g_n(x)| < |h(x)|$ for all x,

(ii) h is integrable with respect to every probability measure with finite first moments on $(-\infty,\infty)$,

(iii) $\{g_n\}$ converges pointwise to u, and

(iv) g_n can be expressed as u_n in Lemma 1.

If u is not integrable, then the condition (ii) as is modified as

(ii') $h = u + \xi$, for some integrable function ξ.

And all other conditions remain the same.

To commence our proof of Theorems 1 and 2 we observe that it has already been properly shown that (ii) and (iii) of Theorem 1 are equivalent, and similarly, by using the correspondence ϕ defined in the argumentation of Theorem 2, (ii') and (iii') of Theorem 2 are equivalent. Hence, it remains to be proven that (ii)→(i) and (ii')→(i'). But again by the correspondence ϕ, it suffices to show only one of these implications. Since we formulated the lemmas in terms of convex functions, we shall prove (ii')→(i'), which will complete our proofs of Theorems 1 and 2.

Assume (ii') and take any $u \in U_2^+$. By Lemmas 1 and 2, there is a sequence $\{g_n\}$ of functions converging pointwise to u, and

$$\int_{-\infty}^{\infty} g_n(x)dF(x) = \sum_{i=1}^{n-1} \alpha_{in} \int_{-\infty}^{\infty} u_{c_{in}}^+(x)dF(x) + \beta_n$$

$$\geq \sum_{i=1}^{n-1} \alpha_{in}^+ \int_{-\infty}^{\infty} u_{c_{in}}^+(x)dG(x) + \beta_n = \int_{-\infty}^{\infty} g_n(x)dG(x),$$

the inequality being obtained by (ii') of Theorem 2 and the fact that α_{in} are nonnegative. Now, Lemma 2, (i), and (ii) permit us to apply the Lebesgue Dominated Convergence Theorem, and

$$\int_{-\infty}^{\infty} u(x)dF(x) = \lim_{n\to\infty} \int_{-\infty}^{\infty} g_n(x)dF(x) \geq \lim_{n\to\infty} \int_{-\infty}^{\infty} g_n(x)dG(x) = \int_{-\infty}^{\infty} u(x)dG(x).$$

Q.E.D.

3.2. Extension of Mean Preserving Spread to $(-\infty,\infty)$

As we have seen, Rothschild and Stiglitz restricted the domain of the concave utility functions to [0,1]. We shall show that the results

---

[4] A necessary and sufficient condition that a convex function defined on $[0,\infty)$ or $(-\infty,\infty)$ has a finite expected value for every random variable with finite moment is provided in [11]. Since we do

for the mean preserving spread rule continue to hold when the domain is extended to the whole real line. Our proof is another application of representative sets.

Let U_2 be the set of all concave functions defined on $(-\infty,\infty)$, which are integrable with respect to all probability measures with finite means.[5] We want to show that Theorem 6 remains valid after replacing [0,1] by $(-\infty,\infty)$. By Theorem 1 or section 3.1 above, it is clear that (ii) and (iii) of the "modified" Theorem 6 are equivalent. Hence, we are left only to prove that (iii)→(i).

Assume that (iii) holds, and take any $u \in U_2$. If u is nondecreasing, then $u \in U_2^-$, hence (iii) implies (i) for this u, by section 3.1. Therefore, we assume that u is decreasing at some portion of $(-\infty,\infty)$. Now $u^*(x) = -u(-x)$ is convex which is decreasing somewhere on the real line. Then there is a real number a such that u^* is monotonically nonincreasing on $(-\infty,a)$ and is monotonically nondecreasing on (a,∞). For sufficiently large n_o, $a \in (-n,n)$ for all $n \ge n_o$. Now by Lemmas 1 and 2, there is a sequence $\{g_n\}$ of functions converging pointwise to u^* and for all $n \ge n_o$,

$$g_n(x) = \alpha_{0n}x + \sum_{i-1}^{n-1} \alpha_{in}u^+_{c_{in}}(x) + \beta_n,$$

with $\alpha_{0n} \le 0$, $\alpha_{in} \ge 0$, $i = 1,\ldots,(n-1)$. Noting $-u^+_{c_{in}}(-x) = u^-_{-c_{in}}(x)$, we have

$$-g_n(-x) = \alpha_{0n}x + \sum_{i-1}^{n-1} \alpha_{in}u^-_{-c_{in}}(x) - \beta_n,$$

so that,

$$\int_{-\infty}^{\infty} -g_n(-x)dF(x) = \alpha_{0n} \int_{-\infty}^{\infty} xdF(x) + \sum_{i-1}^{n-1} \alpha_{in} \int_{-\infty}^{\infty} u^-_{-c_{in}}(x)dF(x) - \beta_n$$

$$\ge \alpha_{0n} \int_{-\infty}^{\infty} xdG(x) + \sum_{i-1}^{n-1} \alpha_{in} \int_{-\infty}^{\infty} u^-_{-c_{in}}(x)dG(x) - \beta_n$$

$$= \int_{-\infty}^{\infty} -g_n(-x)dG(x),$$

where the inequality was obtained by (iii) of Theorem 6 and the fact that $\mu_F = \mu_G$, and $\alpha_{in} \ge 0$, for $i = 1,\ldots,(n-1)$. Since $\{g_n\}$ converges

not explicitly use it in this paper, we will not divulge the exact nature of this condition.

[5]Such a function for utility has been characterized in [11].

to u^* in a manner described in Lemma 2, so does $\{-g_n(-x)\}$ converge to $-u^*(-x) = u(x)$ for each x, in such a way that the Lebesgue Dominated Convergence Theorem can be applied. Therefore,

$$\int_{-\infty}^{\infty} u(x)dF(x) = \lim_{n\to\infty} \int_{-\infty}^{\infty} -g_n(-x)dF(x) \geq \lim_{n\to\infty} \int_{-\infty}^{\infty} -g_n(-x)dG(x)$$

$$= \int_{-\infty}^{\infty} u(x)dG(x),$$

which is (i) of Theorem 6. Q.E.D.

4. Generalized Mean Preserving Spread

Meyer ([7]) has generalized the Rothschild and Stiglitz ([10]) concept of increasing risk based on the mean preserving spread notion (which we discussed above) by using a definition closely related to the Mean Utility Preserving Spread of Diamond and Stiglitz ([1]). Following Meyer, consider the set U of strictly increasing twice differentiable functions on [0,1],[6] and let u_o be any element in U. Then define $U(u_o)$ to be the set of all utility functions with absolute risk aversion measures greater than or equal to the absolute risk aversion measure of u_o. Formally,

$$U(u_o) = \{u \mid -u''(x)/u'(x) \geq -u_o''(x)/u_o'(x), \quad \text{for all } x \in [0,1]\}.$$

It has been shown by Meyer that F is preferred or indifferent to G by all agents with utility functions in $U(u_o)$, if and only if

$$\int_0^c (G(x)-F(x))du_o(x) \geq 0, \quad \text{for all } c \in [0,1]. \tag{11}$$

We propose to find a set of representatives for $U(u_o)$ by using Meyer's integral condition (11). Letting $z = u_o(x)$, $F^*(z) = F(u_o^{-1}(z))$, and $G^*(z) = G(u_o^{-1}(z))$, (11) can be written as

$$\int_{u_o(0)}^{u_o(c)} (G^*(z)-F^*(z))dz \geq 0, \quad \text{for all } u_o(c) \in [u_o(0), u_o(1)].$$

By Theorem 1, this is equivalent to

---

[6]We can accommodate the range, $(-\infty,\infty)$, but for simplicity, we restrict to the closed unit interval as Meyer did.

$$\int_{u_o(0)}^{u_o(1)} u_c^-(z)(G^*(z)-F^*(z))dz \geq 0, \quad \text{for all } c \in [0,1],$$

or, with a change of variable,

$$\int_0^1 u_c^-(u_o(x))(G(x)-F(x))dx \geq 0, \quad \text{for all } c \in [0,1].$$

Hence, if we let

$$R_2^-(u_o) = \{u_c^- \circ u_o | \ c \in [0,1]\}.$$

where $(u_c^- \circ u_o)(x) = u_c^-(u_o(x))$, for all $x \in [0,1]$, we see that $R_2^-(u_o)$ is a set of representatives for $U(u_o)$. That is,

Theorem 7: The following three statements are equivalent.

(i) $\int_0^1 u(x)dF(x) \geq \int_0^1 u(x)dG(x)$, for all $u \in U(u_o)$.

(ii) $\int_0^c (G(x)-F(x))du_o(x) \geq 0$, for all $c \in [0,1]$.

(iii) $\int_0^1 (v(x)dF(x) \geq \int_0^1 (v(x)dG(x)$, for all $v \in R_2^-(u_o)$.

5. A Representative Set for First Degree Stochastic Dominance

Up to this point, the specification of the set of utilities depended importantly on the sign of the second derivative of the functions. As is well-known, the first degree dominance rule is applicable when this sign is unknown. We will find a representative set for this class of functions.

Let U_1 be the set of all nondecreasing functions on $(-\infty,\infty)$ which are integrable with respect to all probability measures with finite means.[7] It has been shown in the literature ([3], [9]) that F is preferred or indifferent to G by all nonsatiating agents with utility functions U_1, if and only if,

$$G(x)-F(x) \geq 0, \quad \text{for all } x \in (-\infty,\infty). \tag{5}$$

In the following we are going to show that the sets of representatives for risk averters and preferrers, R_2^- and R_2^+, give rise to a

[7] In [11], it has been shown that $u \in U_1$ if and only if $|u(x)/x|$ is uniformly bounded for sufficiently large $|x|$.

representative set for U_1. Consider

$$R_1 = \{u^-_{c_1} \circ u^+_{c_2} \mid c_1 \in [0,\infty),\ c_2 \in (-\infty,\infty)\},$$

where "o" indicates the mapping composition. Being a composition of nondecreasing functions, R_1 is clearly a subset of U_1. It is of considerable interest that every element in the representative sets of risk averters and risk preferrers, we described above, can be recovered as a limit of utility functions which are scale transformations of elements in R_1.

It is our intention to show that the set R_1 defined above is a representative set for U_1. For this, it is sufficient to show that (5) is equivalent to

$$\int_{-\infty}^{\infty}(u^-_{c_1} \circ u^+_{c_2})(x)d(F(x)-G(x)) \geq 0, \tag{6}$$

for all $c_1 \in [0,\infty)$ and $c_2 \in (-\infty,\infty)$. Noting that

$$\begin{aligned} (u^-_{c_1} \circ u^+_{c_2})(x) &= -c_1, && x < c_2, \\ &= x - c_1 - c_2, && c_2 \leq x < (c_2 + c_1), \\ &= 0, && (c_2 + c_1) \leq x, \end{aligned}$$

we have, after some manipulation, the L.H.S. of (6) = $\int_{c_2}^{c_1+c_2} (G(x)-F(x))dx$, so that (6) is equivalent to

$$\int_{c_2}^{c_1+c_2} (G(x)-F(x))dx \geq 0, \tag{7}$$

for all $c_1 \in [0,\infty)$ and $c_2 \in (-\infty,\infty)$. Certainly (5) implies (7). To see the converse, assume that (5) is not true. Then, by the right-continuity of F and G, there are x_o and a positive a, such that $(G(x)-F(x)) < 0$, for all $x \in (x_o-a,\ x_o+a)$. Hence, if we put $c_2 = x_o$ and $c_1 = a$, we immediately see that the inequality in (7) is reversed. Thus, (7) implies (5). Summarizing the arguments above, we have established the desired theorem:

<u>Theorem 4</u>: The following two statements are equivalent.

(i) $\int_{-\infty}^{\infty} u(x)dF(x) \geq \int_{-\infty}^{\infty} u(x)dG(x)$, for all $u \in U_1$.

(ii) $\int_{-\infty}^{\infty} u(x)dF(x) \geq \int_{-\infty}^{\infty} u(x)dG(x)$, for all $u \in R_1$.

6. A Representative Set for Third Degree Stochastic Dominance

When considering a class of risk averters we may be willing to separate out a subset by specifying only those with a positive third derivative. Whitmore ([12]) solves the problem of providing an optimal rule for just this group of risk averters.

Let U_3 be the set of all nondecreasing functions on [0,1], which have monotonically nonincreasing convex first derivatives.[8] Then, Whitmore ([12]) has shown that F is preferred to G by all agents with utility functions in U_3, if and only if,

$$\int_0^x \int_0^y (G(z)-F(z))dzdy \geq 0, \quad \text{for all } x \in [0,1], \tag{8}$$

and

$$\int_0^1 (G(x)-F(x))dx \geq 0. \tag{9}$$

Using these Whitmore's integral conditions, we shall find a representative set for U_3 which is inspired by the representative set obtained earlier for the group of risk averters. Noting that $-u'$ belongs to U_2 for every $u \in U_3$, we define,

$$f_c(t) = -2\int_0^t u_c^-(x)dx = 2ct - t^2 - c^2, \quad 0 \leq t \leq c,$$

$$= 0, \quad c < t,$$

for each $c \in [0,1]$, and

$$R_3 = \{f, f_c | \ c \in [0,1]\},$$

where $f(t) \equiv t$, for all $t \in [0,1]$. It can now be seen that R_3 is a representative set for U_3. Firstly, note that every element in R_3 belongs to U_3. Next, since $f(t) \equiv t$ belongs to R_3, (9) is satisfied, if F is unanimously preferred to G by all the agents with utility functions in R_3. Finally assume that

---

[8] Although we could extend to unbounded domains, we shall limit the analysis to the closed bounded interval, as Whitmore did.

$$\int_0^1 f_c(x)dF(x) \geq \int_0^1 f_c(x)dG(x), \tag{10}$$

for all $f_c \in R_3$. Then it is easy to see that

$$\int_0^1 f_c(x)dF(x) = \int_0^c (2cx - x^2 - c^2)dF(x) = -2 \int_0^c \int_0^x F(t)dtdx.$$

Similarly, we may obtain,

$$\int_0^1 f_c(x)dG(x) = -2 \int_0^c \int_0^x G(t)dtdx,$$

so that, (10) holds if and only if,

$$\int_0^c \int_0^x (G(t)-F(t))dtdx \geq 0, \quad \text{for all } c \in [0,1],$$

which, clearly, is (8). Hence, we have established the following:

Theorem 5: The following statements are equivalent.

(i) $\int_0^1 u(x)dF(x) \geq \int_0^1 u(x)dG(x), \quad \text{for all } u \in U_3.$

(ii) $\int_0^1 u(x)dF(x) \geq \int_0^1 u(x)dG(x), \quad \text{for all } u \in R_3.$

7. Conclusion

The explosion of works on stochastic dominance over recent years is traceable to the important works by Quirk and Saposnik ([9]), and Fishburn ([2]). Similar results, independently discovered, appeared subsequently in papers by Hadar and Russell ([3]), Hanoch and Levy ([5]), Rothschild and Stiglitz ([10]). Whitmore ([12]), Meyer ([7]), and Mosler ([8]) added important extensions and generalizations. Presently, the volume of work based on this concept and available in the literature is truly amazing. While the concept has direct applicability to problems requiring unanimous choice, its usefulness ranges far beyond this application. The concept has introduced a convenient structure for analyzing optimal decisions when information on preferences is limited in various ways; it has clarified our thinking about portfolios; it has permitted us to separate mentally the notion of riskiness from the more crude one of variability; and it serves as a touchstone for research in nonexpected utility maximization criteria.

With the advances also come the requirement and burden of greater technical expertise as the cost for further progress. Our paper addresses this trend. We seek to provide a way to simplify proof procedures for future investigations. By using only representative sets instead of dealing with the full set of admissible utility functions the analysis cannot be made more difficult, but we certainly expect that in most instances it should be made much more manageable. Indeed, we suggest that even the stage of conceptualizing one's idea becomes easier as the representative set serves to indicate the nature of the function you can limit your thinking to and still capture unanimity of the admissible set.

We cannot, of course, anticipate where the greatest and most advantageous use of the approach we suggest here can be found but we have provided two simple applications to illustrate how the representative sets may be used. We trust other applications will be found. As in the case of any development of techniques we can only evaluate the contribution after passage of time.

Appendix

Before we commence the proof of the two lemmas used in the body of this paper a few remarks may be in order. While the lemmas may appear obvious to some, the proofs are not readily available so we are impressed to provide them for completeness. The proof of Lemma 1 is rather lengthy and detailed but the detailing here provides some compensation in the reduction of the argumentation for Lemma 2. The proof of Lemma 1 is based on the observation: Any given convex function u, which is continuous can be uniformly approximated within any closed bounded subinterval by a polygonal function whose curve is inscribed in the graph of u. And such a polygonal function can be expressed as u_n in the statement of Lemma 1.

Proof of Lemma 1: Since u is continuous on [0,1], u is uniformly continuous. Take any $\epsilon > 0$. Then there is a sufficiently large n, depending upon ϵ, such that

$$|u(x) - u(y)| < \epsilon, \quad \text{for all } |x - y| \le \frac{1}{n}, \quad x,y \in [0,1].$$

Consider the partition $p_n = [c_0, c_1, \ldots, c_n]$ of [0,1] such that $c_i = \frac{i}{n}$, $i = 0,1,\ldots,n$.

Case 1. u is nondecreasing on [0,1].

Define

$$c_{-1} = 0,$$

$$\beta_i = u(c_i) - u(c_{i-1}),$$

$$\alpha_i = \frac{1}{c_{i+1} - c_1} [\beta_{i+1} - \beta_i]$$

$$i = 0,1,\ldots,(n-1).$$

By convexity of u and noting the fact that $c_i - c_{i-1} = \frac{1}{n}$ for all $i \geq 1$, we have $\beta_i \geq \beta_{i-1}$ for all i, so that

$$\alpha_i \geq 0, \quad i = 0,1,\ldots,(n-1) \tag{A.1}$$

Also for each i,

$$\sum_{j=0}^{i} \alpha_j(c_{i+1} - c_j) = \sum_{j=0}^{i} \frac{c_{i+1} - c_j}{c_{j+1} - c_1} [\beta_{j+1} - \beta_j]$$

$$= \sum_{j=0}^{i} (i+1-j)(\beta_{j+1} - \beta_j) = -(i+1)\beta_0 + \beta_1 + \beta_2 + \ldots + \beta_{i+1}$$

$$= \beta_1 + \ldots + \beta_{i+1} = u(c_{i+1}) - u(c_0),$$

so that,

$$u(c_{i+1}) = u(c_0) + \sum_{j=0}^{i} \alpha_j(c_{i+1} - c_j)$$

$$i = 0,1,\ldots,n-1 \tag{A.2}$$

If we put $\hat{u}_n(x) = u(c_0) + \sum_{j=0}^{n-1} \alpha_j(x - c_j)^+$, $0 \leq x \leq 1$, then by (A.1), it only remains to show that $|\hat{u}_n(x) - u(x)| < \epsilon$, for all $x \in [0,1]$. For this, choose any k, $0 \leq k \leq n-1$, and any $x \in [c_k, c_{k+1}]$. Then $\hat{u}_n(c_k) \leq \hat{u}_n(x) \leq u_n(c_{k+1})$, because $\hat{u}_n$ is nondecreasing. Now,

$$\hat{u}_n(c_k) = u(c_0) + \sum_{j=0}^{k-1} \alpha_j(c_k - c_j) = u(c_k),$$

by (A.2), and similarly $\hat{u}_n(c_{k+1}) = u(c_{k+1})$. Hence

$$u(c_k) \leq \hat{u}_n(x) \leq u(c_{k+1}), \quad \text{for all } x \in [c_k, c_{k+1}],$$

$$k = 0,1,\ldots,n-1.$$

Since $|u(c_{k+1}) - u(c_k)| < \epsilon$, and $u(c_k) \leq u(x) \leq u(c_{k+1})$ for all $x \in [c_k, c_{k+1}]$, we immediately see that

$$|\hat{u}_n(x) - u(x)| < \epsilon, \quad \text{for all } x \in [0,1].$$

By the very construction of $\hat{u}_n$, $\{\hat{u}_n\}$ converges uniformly to u.

<u>Case 2</u>. u is decreasing on [0,a] for some $0 \le a \le 1$.

We assume that n is so large that u is decreasing on the first subinterval $[c_0,c_1]$. Consider the (nonpositively sloped) straight line

$$y = f(x) = n(u(c_1) - u(c_0))x + u(c_0),$$

which passes through the points $(c_0, u(c_0))$ and $(c_1, u(c_1))$. Then $f(c_1) \le f(x) \le f(c_0) = f(0) = u(c_0)$, for all $x \in [c_0,c_1]$, and $f(c_1) = u(c_1)$, so that $u(c_1) \le f(x) \le u(c_0)$ for all $x \in [c_0,c_1]$, i.e.,

$$|u(x) - f(x)| < \epsilon, \quad x \in [c_0,c_1]. \tag{A.3}$$

Define u_1 as $u_1(x) = u(x) - f(x)$, $x \in [0,1]$. It can be readily seen that u_1 is convex on [0,1] and $u_1(c_1) = 0$. Moreover, u_1 is nondecreasing on $[c_1,1]$, as can be seen below: let $x_1 > x_2 \ge c_1 > c_0$. Then

$$\frac{u_1(x_1) - u_1(x_2)}{x_1 - x_2} = \frac{u(x_1) - u(x_2)}{x_1 - x_2} - \frac{u(c_1) - u(c_0)}{c_1 - c_0},$$

and by the convexity of u, the right hand side is nonnegative. This implies $u_1(x_1) \ge u_1(x_2)$ for $x_1 \ge x_2 \ge c_1$. Briefly summarizing:

$$u_1(c_1) = 0,$$

u_1 is nondecreasing convex on $[c_1,1]$.

We then repeat all the arguments in <u>Case 1</u> to u_1 on $[c_1,1]$ and we may obtain

$$u_{1n}(x) = \sum_{j=1}^{n-1} \alpha_{1j}(x - c_j)^+,$$

satisfying

$$\alpha_{1j} \ge 0, \quad \text{and}$$

$$|u_1(x) - u_{1n}(x)| < \epsilon, \quad x \in [c_1,1] \tag{A.4}$$

Finally, by letting $\alpha_{10} = n(u(c_1) - u(c_0))$ (≤ 0), so that $f(x) = \alpha_{10}x + u(c_0)$, we define

$$\hat{u}_{1n}(x) = u(c_0) + \sum_{j=1}^{n-1} \alpha_{1j}(x - c_j)^+ + \alpha_{10}x.$$

By (A.3) and (A.4), we now see that $|u(x) - \hat{u}_{1n}(x)| < \epsilon$, $x \in [0,1]$, and $\alpha_{10} \le 0$, $c_0 = 0$, $\alpha_{1j} \ge 0$, $j = 1,\ldots,n$. The convergency of $\{\hat{u}_{1n}\}$ to u is clearly uniform. Q.E.D.

Taking advantage of the constructive proof of Lemma 1, we can prove Lemma 2 in short steps.

Proof of Lemma 2: By Lemma 1, there exists a function $\hat{u}_n$ such that $|\hat{u}_n(x) - u(x)| < \epsilon$. From this, it is readily seen that there exists a function g_m of type $\hat{u}_k$ in Lemma 1, such that

$$|g_m(x) - u(x)| < 2^{-m}, \quad \text{for all } x \in [-m,m],$$

$$m = 1,2,\ldots.$$

Thus, g_m converges pointwise to u. Consider the elementary function $\xi = \sum_{m=1}^{\infty} 2^{-m} I_{A_m}$, $A_m = (-m, 1-m) \cup [m-1, m)$, $m = 1,2,\ldots$, where I_{A_m} is the indicator of A_m. Clearly, ξ is measurable. Since u is assumed to be integrable, so is $h = u + \xi$. Finally, by the construction of g_m, it is apparent that $g_m - h$ is uniformly bounded for all x. Q.E.D.

References

[1] Diamond, P.A., and J.E. Stiglitz, "Increases in Risk and in Risk Aversion," Journal of Economic Theory 8 (1974): 337-360.

[2] Fishburn, P.C., Decision and Value Theory. New York: Wiley, 1964.

[3] Hadar, J., and W.R. Russell, "Rules for Ordering Uncertain Prospects," American Economic Review 59 (1969): 25-34.

[4] Hadar, J., and T.K. Seo, "Asset Proportions in Optimal Portfolios," Review of Economic Studies 55 (1988): 459-468.

[5] Hanoch, G., and H. Levy, "The Efficiency Analysis of Choices Involving Risk," Review of Economic Studies 29 (1969): 140-146.

[6] Markowitz, H.M., Portfolio Selection. New York: Wiley, 1959.

[7] Meyer, J., "Increasing Risk," Journal of Economic Theory 11 (1975): 119-132.

[8] Mosler, K.C., Entscheidungsregeln bei Risiko: Multivariate Stochastische Dominanz. Berlin: Springer-Verlag, 1982.

[9] Quirk, J.P., and R. Saposnik, "Admissibility and Measurable Utility Functions," Review of Economic Studies 29 (1962): 140-146.

[10] Rothschild, M., and J.E. Stiglitz, "Increasing Risk I: A Definition," Journal of Economic Theory 3: 225-243.

[11] Russell, W.R., and T.K. Seo, "Admissible Sets of Utility Functions in Expected Utility Maximization," Econometrica 46 (1978): 181-184.

[12] Whitmore, G.A., "Third-Degree Stochastic Dominance," American Economic Review 60 (1970): 457-459.

STOCHASTIC DOMINANCE FOR THE CLASS OF COMPLETELY MONOTONIC UTILITY FUNCTIONS

G.A. Whitmore
McGill University
Montreal, Canada

1. Introduction

According to the expected utility axioms, a decision maker with utility function u(x) for wealth x assigns the following subjective value to an uncertain prospect with cumulative distribution function F(x).

$$E(u;F) = \int_0^\infty u(x)dF(x) \tag{1}$$

It is assumed here that wealth level x is positive and that prospect F has moments of all orders.

A stochastic dominance rule identifies efficient or undominated prospects among a given choice set, for any decision maker whose utility function is a member of a specified class U. The stochastic dominance rules which have been developed to date include rules for decision makers who prefer more wealth to less, who are risk averse, who exhibit decreasing absolute risk aversion, who can borrow or lend wealth at a riskless rate, and others. See, for example, Blackwell and Girshick (1954), Quirk and Saposnik (1962), Fishburn (1964), Hadar and Russell (1969), Hanoch and Levy (1969), Rothschild and Stiglitz (1970), Whitmore (1970), Vickson (1975, 1977), Levy and Kroll (1978). Fishburn and Vickson (1978) and Levy and Kroll (1978) give an overview of these rules. The utility classes corresponding to the stochastic dominance rules of the first-, second- and third-degrees, for example, are

$$\text{First-degree:} \quad U_1 = \{u \mid u^{(1)} \geq 0\}, \tag{2a}$$

$$\text{Second-degree:} \quad U_2 = \{u \mid u \in U_1,\ u^{(2)} \leq 0\}, \tag{2b}$$

$$\text{Third-degree:} \quad U_3 = \{u \mid u \in U_2,\ u^{(3)} \geq 0\}, \tag{2c}$$

where u is assumed to be a differentiable function of requisite degree and $u^{(n)}$ denotes the nth derivative of u.

2. Theory

The three utility classes in (2) have appealing economic rationales. U_1 includes all utility functions for which more wealth is preferred to less wealth. U_2 includes all utility functions in U_1 which also reflect risk-averse attitudes. U_3 includes, as a proper subset, all utility functions in U_2 which also exhibit nonincreasing absolute risk aversion.

The pattern of alternating signs of the successive derivatives that define the classes in (2) has been noted by many investigators. Jean (1980), in particular, has derived the stochastic dominance rules for utility classes in which n successive derivatives of u alternate in sign, for any chosen n. These nth-degree stochastic dominance rules involve comparison of the successive integrals of the cumulative distribution functions for prospects.

It is natural to consider the analytical extension of Jean's sequence of utility classes, namely, the following utility class comprised of functions with derivatives of all orders that alternate in sign.

$$U_\infty = \{u \mid (-1)^{n-1}u^{(n)} \geq 0,\ n = 1,2,\ldots\} \tag{3}$$

No compelling economic rationale for this extension is apparent although it can be shown that all functions in the class exhibit nonincreasing absolute risk aversion. Moreover, U_∞ is included in U_3 and can be shown to contain many of the families of utility functions which are used routinely by investigators, such as the linear, exponential, logarithmic and power families. Furthermore, one might argue that a perfectly rationale economic decision maker will have preferences which undergo the smooth and systematic change with wealth level which is implied by the conditions defining U_∞. The alternating signs of the derivatives imply that each derivative decays monotonically with increasing wealth. Thus, the class might be called quite reasonably the class of <u>completely monotonic</u> utility functions. Despite the lack of a strong economic rationale for the extension, this paper examines what can be gained conceptually and mathematically by considering it. The results suggest that the examination is worthwhile.

Brumelle and Vickson (1975) show that the classes of utility functions that have been of interest to investigators, including the classes in (2), constitute convex cones in their respective function spaces, i.e., the classes have the following property.

$$\text{For any } u_1, u_2 \in U \text{ and } c_1, c_2 \geq 0,\ c_1u_1 + c_2u_2 \in U. \tag{4}$$

It can be shown that the completely monotonic class U_∞ is also a convex cone of utility functions.

It follows from the property in (4) that any utility function u in a conical class U can be written as a positive linear combination of the extremal functions of the class U. For example, the set of extremal functions of the class U_1 is the set of step functions

$$h_a(x) = \begin{cases} 1 & x \geq a \\ 0 & x < a \end{cases} \quad \text{for all values a.} \tag{5}$$

Although the extremal functions in (5) are not in the class U_1 as defined in (2a), they are contained in the closure of U_1. Once the extremal functions of any given utility class are identified, the corresponding stochastic dominance rule is, in principal, readily derived. Specifically, the expected utility of one prospect will be at least as large as the expected utility of another prospect for all $u \in U$ if and only if this relation holds for all the extremal functions of U. With respect to (5), for example, the expected utility of a prospect F for extremal function $h_a(x)$ is given by

$$E(h_a;F) = \int_0^\infty h_a(x)dF(x) = 1 - F(a).$$

Clearly, the expected utility for one prospect F_1 will be as great as that of another prospect F_2 for all extremal functions of U_1 only if

$$1 - F_1(a) \geq 1 - F_2(a) \quad \text{for all a} \tag{6a}$$

or equivalently, only if

$$F_2(a) \geq F_1(a) \quad \text{for all a.} \tag{6b}$$

The condition in (6b) is none other than the stochastic dominance rule for utility class U_1.

The extremal functions of the utility class U_∞ are provided by Bernstein's theorem (Phelps, 1966, p. 11). In this context, Bernstein's theorem provides that the first derivative of every $u \in U_\infty$ is representable in the following integral form

$$u^{(1)}(y) = \int_0^\infty \exp(-ay)dB(a) \qquad y \in (0,\infty) \tag{7}$$

where B(a) is a Borel measure on $[0,\infty]$ which is unique to $u^{(1)}$. Integrating (7) over the interval [0,x] and reversing the order of integration of y and a gives

$$u(x) = \int_0^\infty \int_0^x \exp(-ay)\,dy\,dB(a) + u(0)$$

$$= \int_0^\infty \{[1 - \exp(-ax)]/a\}\,dB(a) + u(0). \quad (8)$$

This representation of $u(x)$ is valid provided $u(0)$ is finite. The function $[1 - \exp(-ax)]/a$ is taken to be x when $a = 0$ and 0 when $a = \infty$. Thus, every $u \in U_\infty$ can be uniquely represented, up to a constant, as a positive linear combination of functions of the form

$$h_a(x) = [1 - \exp(-ax)]/a \quad \text{for all } a \in [0,\infty]. \quad (9)$$

The $h_a(x)$ in (9) are therefore the extremal functions of the completely monotonic utility class U_∞.

The family of extremal functions in (9) is the family of exponential utility functions, including the linear and zero functions as limiting cases. Convex linear combinations of exponential functions have been considered as general purpose utility functions by other researchers. See, for example, Hildreth (1974) and Keeney and Raiffa (1976, p. 170).

Table 1 gives the generic Bernstein representation of several common families of utility functions that are in the completely monotonic class. The representations are readily derived using the Laplace-Stieltjes transform because $u^{(1)}(y)$ in (7) is the transform of $B(a)$.

The expected value of the extremal function in (9), with respect to the prospect F, is given by

$$E(h_a;F) = [1 - M_F(a)]/a \quad \text{for } a > 0 \quad (10)$$

where M_F denotes the Laplace-Stieltjes transform of F. For $a = 0$, $E(h_a;F) = \mu_F$, the mean of F. It follows from (10) that the stochastic dominance rule for the completely monotonic utility class is given by

> The expected utility of one prospect F_1 is at least as great as that of another prospect F_2 for all $u \in U_\infty$ if and only if
>
> $$M_2(a) \geq M_1(a) \quad \text{for all } a > 0$$
>
> where M_i denotes the Laplace-Stieltjes transform of F_i, $i = 1,2$. (11)

The certainty equivalent value of a prospect with Laplace-Stieltjes transform $M(a)$ for the exponential utility function

$u(x) = -\exp(-ax)$ is

$$C(a) = -[\ln M(a)]/a \quad \text{for } a > 0. \tag{12}$$

C(a) will be referred to subsequently as the <u>certainty equivalent function</u> of the prospect. Note that C(a) is expressed in the same wealth units as the prospect. Also, note that C(a) is the certainty equivalent value of the prospect to a decision maker having a constant risk aversion coefficient equal to a.

TABLE 1

BERNSTEIN REPRESENTATIONS FOR SEVERAL COMMON FAMILIES OF UTILITY FUNCTIONS

Family	u(x)	dB(a)/da
Exponential	$-\exp[-\alpha(\beta + x)$ $0 < \alpha$	$\alpha\exp(-\beta a)\delta(a - \alpha)$
Power-1	$(\beta + x)^{\alpha}$ $0 < \alpha < 1,\ 0 \leq \beta$	$\alpha a^{-\alpha}\exp(-\beta a)/\Gamma(1 - \alpha)$
Logarithmic	$\ln(\beta + x)$ $0 < \beta$	$\exp(-\beta a)$
Power-2	$-(\beta + x)^{-\alpha}$ $0 < \alpha,\ 0 < \beta$	$\alpha a^{\alpha}\exp(-\beta a)/\Gamma(1 + \alpha)$

Where: $\delta(\ )$ denotes the Dirac delta function
$\Gamma(\ )$ denotes the gamma function

An equivalent statement of the stochastic dominance rule in (11) in terms of the certainty equivalent function is

> The expected utility of one prospect F_1 is at least as great as that of another prospect F_2 for all $u \in U_\infty$ if and only if
>
> $C_1(a) \geq C_2(a) \quad$ for all $a > 0$
>
> where C_i denotes the certainty equivalent function of F_i, $i = 1,2$. (13)

The stochastic dominance rule for the completely monotonic utility class, whether expressed in form (11) or (13), will be referred to subsequently as the CMSD rule. It can be shown that the CMSD rule is mathematically implied by Jean's conditions for nth-degree stochastic dominance when n is made to approach infinity. The limit of the inequality in (13) as a approaches 0 is $\mu_1 \geq \mu_2$ where μ_i denotes the mean of F_i, i = 1,2. The limit of (13) as a approaches ∞ is $m_1 \geq m_2$ where m_i represents the smallest possible outcome of F_i, i = 1,2. More precisely, for any prospect F, $m = \inf[x| F(x) > 0]$.

3. Applications and Discussion

If a prospect, defined by random variable X, has the discrete distribution (x_i,p_i), i = 1,2,..., then its certainty equivalent function is

$$C(a) = -(1/a)\ln\{E[\exp(-aX)]\} = -(1/a)\ln[\sum_i p_i\exp(-ax_i)] \tag{14}$$

A useful graphical procedure for checking on CMSD relations which may exist among a finite collection of prospects is to plot their certainty equivalent functions on the same graph. If $C_1(a)$ lies entirely above $C_2(a)$ for all a > 0 then prospect F_1 is preferred to prospect F_2 by all decision makers with completely monotonic utility functions, i.e., F_1 dominates F_2 by CMSD.

Figure 1 illustrates the graphical procedure for discrete distributions. Figure 1a gives the discrete probability distributions of three prospects, F_1, F_2, and F_3, in the form of a decision table having three acts (which correspond to the prospects) and four outcome states with the probabilities noted. Figure 1b shows the plot of C(a) against log(a) for each of these prospects. A logarithmic scale for a is used to amplify the detail at small values of a and yet retain the full dynamic range of the graph. Note that $C_2(a)$ lies entirely above $C_1(a)$, indicating that F_2 dominates F_1 by CMSD. Also note that $C_2(a)$ and $C_3(a)$ cross once at a = 0.018 [log (a) = -1.7]. Thus, neither F_2 nor F_3 dominates the other by CMSD. Since the curve for F_3 lies above that for F_2 when a > 0.018, it is clear that more risk averse decision makers would prefer F_3 to F_2. Since the curve for F_2 lies above that for F_3 when a < 0.018, decision makers who are less risk averse would prefer F_2 to F_3. As stated earlier, the quantity C(a) approaches the mean value of the prospect when a approaches 0. Hence, the ranking of prospects at a = 0 is that which would be assigned to the prospects by a risk neutral decision maker. A graph of certainty equivalent functions summarizes, in a simple visual way, the relative attractiveness of competing prospects to decision makers with varying degrees of risk aversion.

(a) Decision table showing the payoff distributions for three prospects F_1, F_2, and F_3

	Outcome States			
	S_1	S_2	S_3	S_4
Probability	0.25	0.25	0.25	0.25
Prospect				
F_1	70	50	30	10
F_2	20	30	30	90
F_3	30	30	40	50

(b) Plot of the certainty equivalent functions for prospects F_1, F_2, and F_3

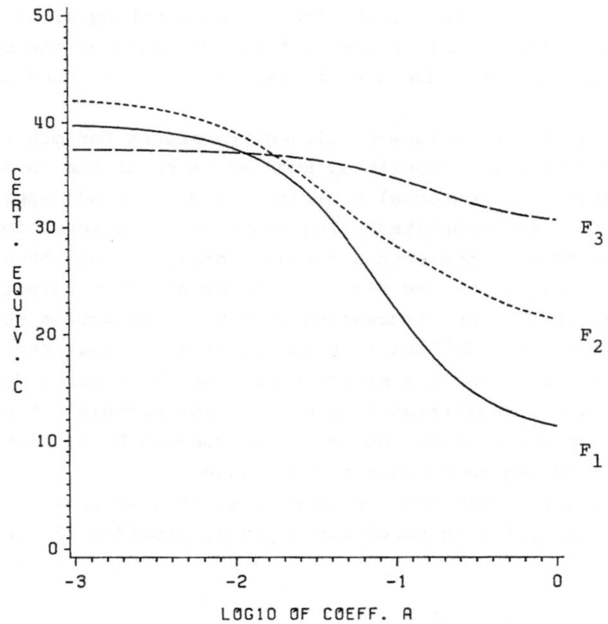

Figure 1b

Figure 1. A graphical assessment of completely monotonic stochastic dominance for three discrete prospects

As a further illustration of the CMSD rule, consider two normally distributed prospects, F_1 and F_2, with means and variances represented by μ_1, μ_2 and σ_1^2, σ_2^2, respectively. A strict interpretation of the theory presented here does not admit normally distributed prospects. Provided, however, that the probability in the negative region of the distributions is negligible in each case, CMSD may be applied to normally distributed prospects with no effects of practical consequence. In this case, the inequality in (13) takes the form

$$\mu_1 - a\sigma_1^2/2 \geq \mu_2 - a\sigma_2^2/2 \quad \text{for all } a > 0. \tag{15}$$

This set of inequalities can hold only if both

$$\mu_1 \geq \mu_2 \quad \text{and} \quad \sigma_2^2 \geq \sigma_1^2.$$

This pair of conditions defines the mean-variance criterion. When the graphical procedure is applied to normally distributed prospects, the plot of C(a) against a is a line with an intercept equal to the mean and a negative slope equal to one-half the variance of the distribution. Such a graph provides a pictorial check on the conditions in (15).

Knowledge of the Laplace-Stieltjes transforms for other common cumulative distribution functions, such as those of the inverse Gaussian, gamma, and lognormal families, allows a ready application of the CMSD rule to prospects having these distributional forms.

CMSD dominance represents a stronger ordering rule than any nth-order rule, n = 1,2,..., and also a stronger ordering rule than the rule for the class of non-increasing absolute risk averse utility functions. This fact follows from the observation that the completely monotonic utility class is a strict subset of the classes defining these other rules. Referring to Figure 1, for example, it can be shown that prospect F_2 does not dominate prospect F_1 by first-, second- or third-degree stochastic dominance.

The certainty equivalent function C(a) of a prospect X can be expanded in the following power series in a, provided the series converges.

$$C(a) = \mu + \sum_{r=2}^{\infty} \kappa_r (-a)^{r-1}/r! \tag{16}$$

Here $\kappa_r = E\{(X-\mu)^r\}$ is the rth cumulant or central moment of X. Thus, the set of inequalities defining the CMSD rule in (13) is, in fact, a set of inequalities governing the central moments of the dominating and dominated prospects. For example, it can be seen from (16) that if two prospects have the same mean then the dominating prospect must have the smaller variance κ_2.

It has long been desired to be able to construct efficient portfolios of prospects based on stochastic dominance principles. The analytical tractability of the Laplace-Stieltjes transform offers some promise of a method for constructing CMSD efficient portfolios of prospects. If for example X_i, $i = 1,\ldots,n$, are the random variables associated with n prospects having a joint Laplace-Stieltjes transform $M(a_1,\ldots,a_n)$ defined as follows

$$M(a_1,\ldots,a_n) = E\{\exp(-\sum_{i=1}^{n} a_i X_i)\} \tag{17}$$

then the following convex linear combination, denoted by Y, is the random variable associated with a portfolio of the prospects having the weight vector $\lambda = (\lambda_1,\ldots,\lambda_n)$ where $\lambda_i \geq 0$ for all i and $\Sigma\lambda_i = 1$.

$$Y = \lambda_1 X_1 + \ldots + \lambda_n X_n$$

The Laplace-Stieltjes transform of Y is

$$M(a\lambda_1,\ldots,a\lambda_n) = E\{\exp(-a \sum_{i=1}^{n} \lambda_i X_i)\} = E\{\exp(-aY)\} \tag{18}$$

and the certainty equivalent of Y is

$$C(a\lambda_1,\ldots,a\lambda_n) = -(1/a)\ln\{M(a\lambda_1,\ldots,a\lambda_n)\}. \tag{19}$$

To generate portfolios which are in the CMSD efficient set, one can find the weight vectors $\lambda(a)$ which maximize (19) for each value of $a > 0$. Of course, portfolios consisting of the one or several prospects having the highest expected value are in the CMSD efficient set and correspond to $a = 0$. The set of portfolios $L_0 = \{\lambda(a), a \geq 0\}$ produced by this procedure is a subset of the CMSD efficient set, corresponding as it does to the set of most preferred portfolios of decision makers having constant risk aversion. Although set L_0 sometimes constitutes the entire CMSD efficient set, denoted here by L, it is generally somewhat smaller than L. The exact structure of L, and its relationship to L_0, is the subject of ongoing study.

To illustrate the set L_0, refer again to the three prospects in the decision problem of Figure 1a. Figure 2 shows the composition of portfolios constructed from prospects F_1, F_2 and F_3 that make up the set L_0. As in Figure 1b, this graph employs log(a) on the horizontal scale. When $a = 0$, the portfolio consists of F_2 only. Between $a = 0$ and $a = 0.065$ [$\log(a) = -1.2$], the portfolios contain a mixture of prospects F_2 and F_3. Above a = 0.065, the portfolios contain a mix- of all three prospects. As a approaches ∞, the limiting portfolio is $\lambda = (1/3, 0, 2/3)$.

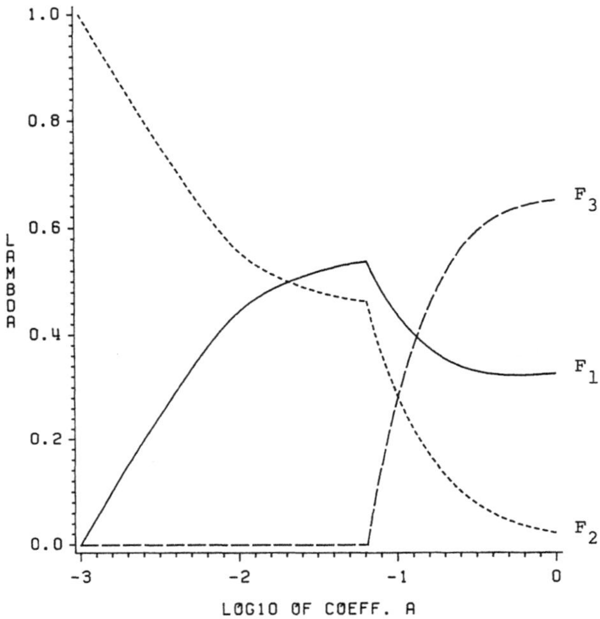

Figure 2. The composition of CMSD efficient portfolios in the set $L_0 = \{\lambda(a), a \geq 0\}$ for decision makers exhibiting constant absolute risk aversion in the decision problem of Figure 1a. L_0 is a subset of the entire CMSD efficient set L.

A <u>levered</u> portfolio is one consisting of a risky prospect represented by random variable X and a riskless prospect represented by the fixed outcome A, i.e., $Y = \lambda X + (1-\lambda)A$. It is found in this case that

$$C_Y(a\lambda, a(1-\lambda)) = \lambda C_X(a\lambda) + (1-\lambda)A \qquad (20)$$

where C_Y and C_X denote the certainty equivalent functions of Y and X, respectively. Thus, the certainty equivalent of the levered portfolio is a corresponding weighted average of the riskless prospect A and the certainty equivalent of the risky prospect X, where the latter is evaluated for risk aversion coefficient $a\lambda$ rather than a. Following the approach of Levy and Kroll (1978), suppose a levered portfolio involving a prospect X_1 and riskless prospect A is found to dominate a prospect X_2 by CMSD, i.e., $Y_* = \lambda_* X_1 + (1-\lambda_*)A$ dominates X_2 by CMSD for some λ_*. Then it can be shown that any levered portfolio of X_2, say $Y_2 = \lambda_2 X_2 + (1-\lambda_2)A$ with $\lambda_2 > 0$, will be dominated by CMSD by a suitably chosen levered portfolio of X_1, namely, $Y_1 = \lambda_1 X_1 + (1-\lambda_1)A$ where $\lambda_1 = \lambda_2 \lambda_*$. In this case, one might say that prospect X_1 dominates prospect X_2 by CMSD with riskless leverage, or CMSDR for short, adopting a mneumonic of the Levy and Kroll type. For the three prospects in Figure 1a, for example, a levered portfolio of prospect F_2 and the riskless prospect A = 36 dominates prospect F_3. Specifically, letting X_2 and X_3 denote the random variables corresponding to F_2 and F_3, respectively, the levered portfolio $(1/3)X_2 + (2/3)(36)$ dominates X_3 by CMSD. Thus, if a riskless prospect A = 36 were available for portfolio building in the decision problem then prospect F_2 would dominate prospect F_3 with this riskless leverage, i.e., F_2 would dominate F_3 by CMSDR.

References

Blackwell, D., and M.A. Girshick, Theory of Games and Statistical Decisions. New York: Wiley, 1954.

Brumelle, S.L., and R.G. Vickson, "A Unified Approach to Stochastic Dominance." In Stochastic Optimization Models in Finance, eds. W.T. Ziemba and R.G. Vickson. New York: Academic Press, 1975.

Fishburn, P.C., Decision and Value Theory. New York: Wiley, 1964.

Fishburn, P.C., and R.G. Vickson, "Theoretical Foundations of Stochastic Dominance." In Stochastic Dominance, eds. G.A. Whitmore and M.C. Findlay. Lexington, Massachusetts: Heath, 1978.

Hadar, J., and W.R. Russell, "Rules for Ordering Uncertain Prospects," American Economic Review 59 (1969): 25-34.

Hanoch, G., and H. Levy, "The Efficiency Analysis of Choices Involving Risk," Review of Economic Studies 36 (1969): 335-346.

Hildreth, C., "Expected Utility of Uncertain Ventures," Journal of the American Statistical Association 69 (1974): 9-17.

Jean, W.H., "The Geometric Mean and Stochastic Dominance," Journal of Finance 35 (1980): 151-158.

Keeney, R.L., and H. Raiffa, Decisions with Multiple Objectives: Preferences and Value Tradeoffs. New York: Wiley, 1976.

Levy, H., and Y. Kroll, "Ordering Uncertain Options with Borrowing and Lending," Journal of Finance 33 (1978): 553-573.

Phelps, R.R., Lectures on Choquet's Theorem. Princeton, New Jersey: D. Van Nostrand, 1966.

Quirk, J.P., and R. Saposnik, "Admissibility and Measurable Utility Functions," Review of Economic Studies 29 (1962): 140-146.

Rothschild, M., and J.E. Stiglitz, "Increasing Risk I: A Definition," Journal of Economic Theory 2 (1970): 225-243.

Vickson, R.G., "Stochastic Dominance Tests for Decreasing Absolute Risk Aversion I: Discrete Random Variables," Management Science, Application Series, 21 (1975): 1438-1446.

________, "Stochastic Dominance Tests for Decreasing Absolute Risk Aversion II: General Random Variables," Management Science, Application and Theory Series 23 (1977): 478-489.

Whitmore, G.A., "Third-Degree Stochastic Dominance," American Economic Review 60 (1970): 457-459.

PART II
Estimation and Testing

THE STOCHASTIC DOMINANCE ESTIMATION OF DEFAULT PROBABILITY

Mary S. Broske and Haim Levy
Oklahoma State University, and
The Hebrew University, Jerusalem and
The University of Florida, Gainesville

The purpose of this paper is two-fold: (1) to present a stochastic dominance technique which can be used to quantify differences in cumulative probability distributions of data, and (2) to demonstrate this technique by quantifying the probability of default as assessed by the bond market. We suggest, then, that the contribution of this paper lies in its introduction of a new methodology which we then use to answer a question in economics and finance.

Section 1 provides an overview of the literature. In Section 2, we present our model and the algorithm for implementing our technique. In Section 3 we present our data and empirical results. Regarding the empirical results, we should say at the outset that the main contribution of this paper consists of the new methodology suggested and not in the empirical results. While we obtain meaningful empirical results, there is a room for more empirical tests which may improve the data, cover different subperiods, etc. Section 4 presents our summary and conclusions, and discusses both our empirical results and our evaluation of the usefulness of and the implications of our stochastic dominance technique.

1. Literature Review

The Stochastic Dominance criteria when applied to two distributions insure that if F dominates G by the given degree of stochastic dominance (first, second or third degree), then all investors with a utility function which is a member of the associated set of utility functions (first degree, $u' \geq 0$, second degree, $u' \geq 0$, $u'' \leq 0$, third degree, $u' \geq 0$, $u'' \leq 0$, $u''' \geq 0$) will gain greater or equal expected utility from investing in F.

The stochastic dominance criteria are based on the von Neumann-Morgenstern axioms. If these axioms hold, and as a result F is preferred to G, then it follows that the expected utility of F is greater than or equal to the expected utility of G with a strict inequality holding for at least one utility function of the associated set. Thus, we can state the relationship between expected utility and stochastic dominance as follows:

$$E_F u(x) \geq E_G u(x) \Longleftrightarrow F \text{ dominates } G$$

The various stochastic dominance rules are stated as follows:

F dominates G by First Degree Stochastic Dominance (FSD) if $F(x) \leq G(x)$ for all x, and by Second Degree Stochastic Dominance (SSD) if $\int_{-\infty}^{x} [G(t) - F(t)]dt \geq 0$ for all x. Note that in all cases to have a strict dominance we need a strict inequality for at least one value. For brevity's sake, we will not emphasize this requirement in the rest of the paper. The SSD can be written also in terms of the distributions' quantiles as follows: F dominates G by SSD if and only if,

$$\int_{0}^{p} (Q_F(t) - Q_G(t))dt \geq 0$$

for all p where p is probability.[1] For more details on the stochastic dominance rules see Josef Hadar and William Russell (1969), Giora Hanoch and Haim Levy (1969), Michael Rothschild and Joseph Stiglitz (1970), Haim Levy and Yoram Kroll (1978), and G.A. Whitmore (1970).

As we demonstrate the usefulness of the stochastic dominance technique by applying it to an unanswered question, i.e., what is the magnitude of default probability, it is necessary to review prior attempts to answer this question. First, we recognize that bond ratings are assigned in an attempt to assist potential investors in ranking bonds in order of the likelihood that the bond will default prior to maturity. Thus, a rating of Aaa (Moody) or AAA (Standard and Poor) is assigned to bonds perceived by the rating agency as having a negligible probability of default. The second category is Aa or AA (Moody and S and P, respectively), followed by A (for both) and Baa or BBB (Moody and S and P, respectively). Bonds rated below this last

---

[1]Similarly, FSD can be rewritten in terms of the quantiles as $Q_F(P) \geq Q_G(P)$ for all values P, when the F distribution quantile is defined as $Pr(X \leq Q_F(P)) = P$, and $Q_G(P)$ is defined similarly. The third degree stochastic dominance is given as follows: F dominates G if and only if

$$\int_{-\infty}^{x} \int_{-\infty}^{v} [G(t) - F(t)]dt\, dv \geq 0$$

for all x and in addition $E_F(x) \geq E_G(x)$. If, however, F and G intersect only once SSD and TSD coincide, namely yield the same dominance relationship. We concentrate in this paper on risk of default derived from SSD but a similar algorithm can be developed for TSD.

category are considered speculative. Only issues of the Federal Government are assumed to have no risk of default, as the Congress has the authority to issue money to settle its debt.

There seem to be certain criteria in common use by all bond analysts in setting the rating (Cohen, Zinbarg and Zeikel, 1977, p. 388). Perhaps one-half of all bonds are rated identically by different agencies and where there are differences, they are usually not greater than one category (Cohen, Zinbarg, and Zeikel, 1977, p. 385). The prediction of bond ratings on the basis of publicly available information has been investigated. Robert Kaplan and Gabriel Urwitz (1979) provide a thorough survey of statistical models of bond ratings. Kaplan and Urwitz's work as well as studies they survey indicate that reasonably accurate predictions of bond ratings can be obtained by the use of publicly available data.

The prediction of bankruptcy from publicly available information has also been documented, and is primarily associated with Edward I. Altman (1968, 1971 and 1977). Multiple discriminant analysis was utilized to develop a bankruptcy classification model which uses financial statement data and market data.

The relationship of bond rating to the probability of default has also been analyzed empirically. The classic study of the relationship of bond rating to the frequency of default is that of W. Braddock Hickman (1958). He concluded that for the period 1900-1943, the probability of default (as indicated by the occurrence of default) was inversely related to the quality of the bond as reflected in the bond rating. Hickman (1960) reported the number of defaults by bond rating broken down by decade for the twenties and thirties and for the two decades together. Gordon Pye (1974) concluded that Hickman's data indicate that almost all the spread between Aaa and Baa bonds in the twenties and thirties would have to be a default premium rather than a risk premium. He defined the default premium as the difference between the yield (the coupon rate, or promised return) and the expected return (the yield to maturity), (Pye, 1974, p. 49). Pye found virtually no incidence of default in the fifties and sixties for bonds rated Baa or better and concluded that for the post-war period, the probability of default is so small as to be insignificant.

In conclusion, given the usefulness of publicly available information in predicting bond ratings and the inverse relationship between bond ratings and the incidence of default, we assume that we are justified in using market data and publicly available information (the assigned bond rating) in our study of the derived relative probabilities of default as assessed by the market.

2. The Model

A. Introduction

As mentioned in the introduction, the purpose of this study is to present a stochastic dominance technique which can quantify differences in cumulative probability distributions. We use this technique to quantify the probability of default as assessed by the market. In order to find this estimate, we adopt the following framework. Investors who are assumed to be risk-averters consider investing either in Government bonds or in corporate bonds, say corporate bonds rated Aaa. We denote the cumulative distribution of the rates of return on the investment in Government bonds by $F_G(x)$ and the cumulative distribution of the rates of return on the investment in Aaa bonds by $F_{Aaa}(x)$. The investor considers putting 1 dollar either in $F_G(x)$ or in $F_{Aaa}(x)$. For any finite holding period (e.g., one month, one year, etc.), the risk involved in each investment includes two main components: (a) the risk of changes in the rate of interest, and (b) the risk of default. As we are interested in measuring only default risk, we attempt to neutralize type (a) risk. In order to do this, we compare the distributions of rates of return of the two types of bonds while holding maturity (or, alternatively, duration) and all other relevant factors except default risk constant.

Given two cumulative distributions, $F_G(x)$ and $F_{Aaa}(x)$, we expect that if type (a) risk is held constant, the investor will pay a higher price for $F_G(x)$ as it is default-free. Thus having a lower price for option $F_{Aaa}(x)$ implies that the holding period rates of return on this option will be higher than the comparable holding period rates of return on the Government bond.

Taking into account the default risk, <u>on an ex ante basis</u> we expect that neither $F_G(x)$ nor $F_{Aaa}(x)$ will dominate the other by Second Degree Stochastic Dominance (SSD). However, by using <u>ex-post</u> rates of return, we analyze only bonds of firms which did not default and thus we expect on an <u>ex-post</u> basis to observe that $F_{Aaa}(x)$ dominated $F_G(x)$ by SSD and may be even FSD. In other words, when investing in corporate bonds we can distinguish between two states (θ):

θ_1 -- no default, a case where the investor obtains an observation drawn out of $F_{Aaa}(x)$ as observed in the past.

θ_2 -- default, a case where the investor gets either zero return or gets some compensation depending on how severe is the default.

As we are using ex-post data, we examine only firms which did not default during the period covered in the study. The expost-data, since they include only firms which did not default, consider only θ_1, and θ_2 is not represented explicitly in the data. We take the expost-data (state θ_1) and incorporate state θ_2 in the following manner. We expect that with ex-post data, $F_{Aaa}(x)$ will dominate $F_G(x)$. Then we derive from distribution $F_{Aaa}(x)$ a new distribution $F_{Aaa'}(x)$ which assigns some probability to state θ_2. We change this probability until neither $F_G(x)$ nor $F_{Aaa'}(x)$ dominates the other by SSD. This probability which results in neither dominating the other is the risk of default of the Aaa bond as assessed by the market. Assuming that the market is efficient and is in equilibrium, and that investors are risk averters, neither $F_G(x)$ nor $F_{Aaa'}(x)$ dominates the other by SSD.

Before moving to the derivation of and illustration of the use of the suggested technique, three comments are called for:

(1) We do not claim that the ex-post distributions are necessarily stable and represent ex-ante distributions. Moreover, we can claim that in periods of inflation the ex-ante distributions will be shifted. However, ex-post data are used to estimate the extra premium required by bondholders in the past for possible default in the future. From this we can make conclusions about the probability of default which prevailed in the past, or as assessed by the market in the past. If there is additional information regarding the future, the future probability of default may change.

(2) Even in the past, the probability of default as assessed by the market may vary from year to year. Indeed, we will distinguish in this study between years of economic prosperity or stability in the economy and years of recession or contraction in the economy. We expect to find the derived probability of default to be larger in recession years. However, for practical reasons (and because of statistical limitations) we will not measure the default risk as attributed to every year. Rather, we distinguish between two periods, prosperity (or stability) and recession, as mentioned above.

(3) The methodology suggested in this paper, can be applied to individual bonds, to a portfolio of bonds or to a mix of individual bond with any other risky assets. If, for example, one assumes that only one bond is held in the portfolio then F_G and F_A represent one government bond and one individual corporate bond distributions respectively. However, in the empirical section we analyze portfolio of bonds of different categories since we are interested in the analysis the probability of default of the various categories of bonds rather than of individual bonds. The same technique can be applied to individual bonds if one would like to estimate the probability of default of a particular firm. The analysis presented in this paper (regarding

one individual bond or a portfolio of bonds) can be extended easily to incorporate other risky assets (e.g., the market portfolio X_m) under the following two scenarios:

(a) If the return on X_m and the return on bonds are statistically independent (the empirical evidence shows that the correlation of the returns on bonds and stocks is not significantly different from zero), all the results of this paper are valid without any change (see Levy and Kroll (1978)).

(b) In the more general case when the returns on the market portfolio and on bonds are dependent, one can use the same methodology of this paper except we find the probability of default by analyzing the <u>conditional</u> probability distributions of $Y|X_m$ and $X'|X_m$ where Y and X' are returns on two categories (or individual bonds) and X_m is the return on the market portfolio. To be more specific, Levy and Levy (1984) proved that if the conditional distribution, say, of $Y|X_m$ dominates the conditional distribution $X'|X_m$ then any combination of the type $\alpha Y + (1-\alpha)X_m$ dominates any combination of the type $\alpha X' + (1-\alpha)X_m$. While this framework is the most general one since it allows assigning a probability of default to each individual bond held in a large portfolio, its empirical test is not simple, since it requires an estimation of conditional probability distributions. Note that while the empirical test in this specific case is quite involved, the methodology developed in this paper, in principle, applies also to this case.

Finally, as we shall see when we employ the marginal distributions and not the conditional distributions, we obtain that the lower the bond's rating the higher the probability of default as assigned by the market. This evidence provides at least a partial support to case (a) above. Namely, returns on bonds and on stocks are approximately independent hence one can ignore the market portfolio in the bonds default analysis. The justification for ignoring X_m is that a dominance of Y' over X (or vice versa) implies a dominance also in a portfolio context, of $\alpha Y' + (1-\alpha)X_m$ over $\alpha X + (1-\alpha)X_m$.

B. The Definition of Default

In a one-period setting with no taxes, the holder of a bond which was issued at par and which matures at the end of that period is promised a return of $(1 + C)$, where C is the coupon rate. Risk for the bondholder is the probability of realizing a return less than the promised return as a result of the firm defaulting on the bond agreement. Default occurs when the firm has generated earnings before interest and taxes (EBIT) less than the principal and interest legally owed to the bondholder at maturity. There exists a distribution of possible levels of EBIT, only one of which will be the outcome at the end of the period. Thus, there are two equivalent statements of the default risk inherent in the ownership of a bond:

$$\text{Default risk} = \Pr[0 \le (1 + r) < (1 + C)] \tag{1}$$

where r is the realized rate of return on the bond, and alternatively:

$$\text{Default risk} = \Pr[\text{EBIT} < (1 + C)B] \tag{2}$$

where B is the face value of the bond.

C. Measuring the Probability of Default

In deriving the probability of default, we shall consider two cases:

<u>Case 1</u>: Default results in zero return.
<u>Case 2</u>: Default results in a return greater than zero but less than the promised return of (1 + C).

The return to the bondholder in Case 1, (1 + r), is as follows:

$$(1 + r) = \begin{cases} 0 & \text{if default} \\ (1 + C) & \text{if no default} \end{cases}$$

The return to the bondholder in Case 2, is X where $0 \le X \le (1 + C)$ in case of default, and (1 + C) in case of no default. The value of X is a function of the magnitude of the firm's EBIT.

We define δ as the probability of default which when incorporated in the risky distribution would eliminate the dominance of one distribution over the other. For this derivation, we shall use Aaa bonds as representing the risky investment (distribution F), and government bonds (GOVT) as the default risk-free investment (distribution G).

Since we study only bonds which did not default, we expect that F will dominate G and will be preferred by all risk averters (and maybe even by all investors). Namely, we expect to find with <u>ex-post</u> data that:

$$\int_0^x (G(t) - F(t))dt \ge 0 \quad \text{for all values of x}$$

If such an event indeed occurs, it seems that all risk-averters would be better off investing in F rather than G. This conclusion is obviously wrong since corporate bonds are exposed to default risk and Government bonds are not. Thus, we change F by incorporating the market estimate of default until:

$$\int_0^x (G(t) - F_\delta(t))dt \quad \text{is negative for at least one value of } x,$$

namely until the dominance exactly disappears where F_δ is derived from F by incorporating probability of default. That value of δ which causes the dominance to disappear is the market estimate of the risk of default.

We present below a method to find this critical value δ. The algorithm is based on the assumption that default results in a zero return to the bondholder (Case 1). We know that in practice, if default occurs, the bondholder will get less than the promised return. However, there is no reason to think that the level of the payoff under default should be a function of the bond rating. We make a simplifying assumption that if two firms having different bond ratings default, then the investor gets the same level of payoff from each. As it is only the probability of default, not the level of the payoff that varies with bond ratings, we have introduced no bias into our corporate bond comparisons.

We turn now to explain the method of the derivation of $F_\delta(x)$, hence of the probability of default δ.

Let us denote as before by F(x) the distribution of the <u>ex-post</u> returns on corporate bonds and by G(x) the distribution of the ex-post return on Government bonds. When the probability of default is incorporated into F(x) we obtain a new distribution $F_\delta(x)$ given by:

$$F_\delta(x) = \begin{cases} \delta & \text{if } x = 0 \\ \delta + (1-\delta)F(x) & \text{if } x > 0 \end{cases}$$

Obviously, where $F(x) = 1$, $F_\delta(x) = 1$. Note that $F_\delta(x)$ is state dependent and can be written as $F_\delta(x,\theta)$. For brevity sake we simply write in the rest of the paper $F_\delta(x)$.

Thus, $F_\delta(x)$ is shifted upward relative to F(x). Moreover, the higher δ, the higher will be the upward shift in F(x). Essentially, we shift F(x) by changing δ, until neither F(x) nor G(x) dominates the other.

Figure 1a illustrates the hypothetical distributions F(x) and G(x). In this specific case, G(x) does not dominate F(x) by SSD since up to point x_0 we have:

$$\int_{-\infty}^{x_0} [F(t) - G(t)]dt < 0$$

On the other hand, F(x) dominates G(x) if and only if:

$$\int_{-\infty}^{x_1} [G(t) - F(t)]dt \geq 0$$

(See Figure 1a.) Note that, in this specific case, if the integral is positive up to the value x_1, it can be readily seen from Figure 1a that the integral is positive up to any other value x which implies that F(x) dominates G(x). Employing ex-post returns reveals that in most cases, indeed F(x) dominates G(x) by SSD, as demonstrated in Figure 1a.

Figure 1b, demonstrates the shift in F(x) induced by incorporating the probability of default. The new distributions are $F_{\delta_1}(x)$ and $F_{\delta_2}(x)$ for two values δ_1 and δ_2, respectively, when $\delta_1 > \delta_2$. It is clear that for any $\delta > 0$, $F_\delta(x)$ does not dominate G(x) since the left tail of $F_\delta(x)$ is always above the left tail of distribution G(x) (not shown in Figure 1b but shown in Figure 1a). Hence for small values x (say close to zero) we have

$$\int_{-\infty}^{x} [G(t) - F_\delta(t)]dt < 0$$

which implies that $F_\delta(x)$ does not dominate G(x) by SSD. However, we may find that G(x) dominates $F_\delta(x)$. Thus, we are looking for the maximum value of δ denoted by δ^* such that also G(x) does not dominate $F_\delta(x)$. Suppose that for δ_1 we find that G(x) does not dominate $F_{\delta_1}(x)$. So, we gradually increase δ (say to δ_2) until we find that G(x) exactly dominates $F_\delta(x)$. Namely, we have

$$\int_{-\infty}^{x} [F_{\delta_2}(t) - G(t)]dt \geq 0$$

for all values x, and for δ-ϵ ($\epsilon > 0$) we have at least one value x_0 such that

$$\int_{-\infty}^{x_0} [F_{\delta_2-\epsilon}(x) - G(t)]dt < 0.$$

Hence, in this example δ_2 is the maximum value, δ^* where the no-dominance condition of G(x) over F (x) exactly disappears.[2] Such a

---

[2]Note that one can reach the critical value δ by a different approach, start with $\delta = 1$ to obtain the obvious condition

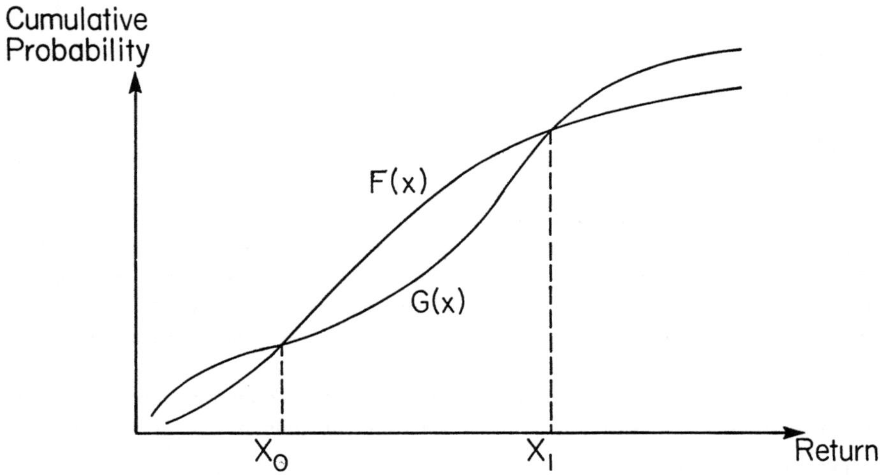

Figure 1a

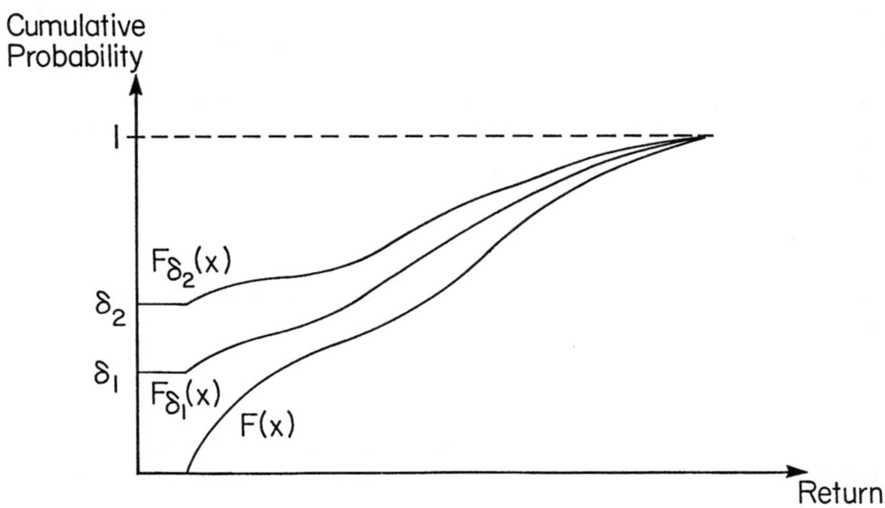

Figure 1b

value always exists, since one may go to the extreme where $\delta = 1$, a case where by definition G(x) dominates $F_{\delta=1}(x)$. Nevertheless in most cases there is no need to go to the extreme value $\delta = 1$, since the no-dominance condition disappears for relatively low values of δ.

Before we turn to the algorithm, note that δ^* is the maximum probability of default as assigned by the market. This is the maximum value such that neither $F_\delta(x)$ nor G(x) dominates the other. For any value greater than δ^*, G(x) dominates $F_\delta(x)$ by SSD.

The basic principle of finding δ^* is demonstrated by Figure 1a or 1b. Working with sample data, however, is much more complicated since the two cumulative distributions under consideration may intersect many times and the integral condition for dominance should be calculated for each intersection point and for various values of δ. Thus, we need an algorithm for solving for the critical value of δ^*.

We employ the quantile approach for SSD which asserts that G(x) dominates $F_\delta(x)$ if and only if for each value P we have

$$\int_0^P [Q_G(t) - Q_{F_\delta}(t)]dt \geq 0$$

(see Levy and Kroll (1978b)), when Q(P) stands for the distribution quantiles and P is a probability, hence,

$$0 \leq P \leq 1.$$

Dealing with <u>ex-post</u> data we have n observations of returns to each

---

$$\int_{-\infty}^{x} [F_{\delta=1}(t) - G(t)]dt > 0$$

for all values x hence G(x) dominates $F_{\delta=1}$. Decrease δ gradually, hence F (x) is shifted <u>downward</u> until the dominance exactly disappears. Suppose that this occurs for $\delta = \delta^{**}$. Thus,

$$\int_{-\infty}^{x} [F_{\delta^{**}}(t) - G(t)] \geq 0$$

for all values x but for $\delta^{**} - \epsilon$ ($\epsilon > 0$) we have

$$\int_{-\infty}^{x_0} [F_{\delta^{**}-\epsilon}(t) - G(t)]dt < 0$$

for at least one value x_0. Then δ^{**} is the maximum probability of default as assessed by the market. Since it does not matter if one starts with $\delta = 0$ and increases it until dominance appears at the first time, or if one starts with $\delta = 1$ and decreases it until dominance disappears at the first time, it is obvious that $\delta^* = \delta^{**}$ and the two approaches yield the same result.

Dealing with <u>ex-post</u> data we have n observations of returns to each distribution. Hence the cumulative distribution function are step functions with a step height of $\frac{1}{n}$. Levy and Kroll (1979) proved that in such a case there is no need to check the integral inequality at all points P and it is sufficient to check the integral condition only at points when either $F_\delta(x)$ or $G(x)$ increase, namely only at the beginning of each step of $F_\delta(x)$ and $G(x)$.

Suppose that we have n observations of $G(y)$ which we denote by y_i $(i = 1,2,\ldots,n)$ and n observations of $F_\delta(z)$ which we denote by $z_1, z_2,\ldots,z_n$. We add to distribution $F_\delta(z)$ an observation of $z = 0$ with a probability δ. We assign a probability of $\frac{1}{n}$ for each observation of G. We also assigned a probability of $\frac{1}{n}$ for each observation taken from F, but the cumulative probability function of F_δ (which consists of n+1 observations) is given by,

$$F_\delta(z) = \begin{cases} \delta & z = 0 \\ \delta + (1-\delta)F(z) & > 0 \end{cases}$$

Hence, while the height of each step of F and G is $\frac{1}{n}$, the height of the steps of F_δ are not equal to $\frac{1}{n}$ any more, as we shall see below:

We employ the following procedure in solving for δ^*:

(1) Order (rank) the observations of the given variable for z and then for y from the smallest value to the largest.

(2) Define the cumulative distributions $F_\delta(z)$ and $G(y)$. We know that z contains some implied level of delta. Since we have discrete distributions, the cumulative probability (the step function) at any point can be represented as an interval as follows (employ the definition of $F_\delta(z)$ given above)

0	$0 < p \le \delta$
z_1	$\delta < p \le [(1-\delta)\left(\frac{1}{n}\right) + \delta]$
z_2	$[(1-\delta)\left(\frac{1}{n}\right) + \delta] < p \le [(1-\delta)\left(\frac{2}{n}\right) + \delta]$
z_3	$[(1-\delta)\left(\frac{2}{n}\right) + \delta] < p \le [(1-\delta)\left(\frac{3}{n}\right) + \delta]$
.	
.	
.	
z_n	$[(1-\delta)\left(\frac{n-1}{n}\right) + \delta] < p \le 1$

where n is the number of observations. For G(y) we get the following simple step functions:

$$y = \{y_1\colon 0 < p \le \tfrac{1}{n},\ y_2\colon \tfrac{1}{n} < p \le \tfrac{2}{n},\ \ldots,\ y_n\colon \tfrac{n-1}{n}\ n < p \le 1\}$$

(3) Calculate $(y - z)h$ for each change in probability where h is the height of the relevant step given below. Call these areas, 1 . . . . 2n. Formulas for each area $(y - z)h$ is given by:

Area	$(y - z)h$
1.	$(y_1 - 0)\delta$
2.	$(y_1 - z_1)\left(\frac{1}{n} - \delta\right)$
3.	$(y_2 - z_1)\left[\left(\frac{1}{n}(1 - \delta) + \delta\right) - \frac{1}{n}\right]$
4.	$(y_2 - z_2)\left[\frac{2}{n} - \left(\frac{1}{n}(1 - \delta) + \delta\right)\right]$
.	
.	
.	
2n - 1.	$(y_n - z_{n-1})\left[\frac{n-1}{n}(1 - \delta) + \delta\right] - \frac{n-1}{n}$
2n.	$(y_n - z_n)\left[\frac{n}{n} - \left(\frac{n-1}{n}(1 - \delta) + \delta\right)\right]$

(4) Begin with a large value for δ (so that $G(y)$ dominates $F_\delta(x)$ by SSD) and reduce it until the cumulative difference is no longer greater than zero (i.e. until exact SSD results and for any further reduction in δ, $G(y)$ ceases to dominate $F_\delta(z)$.

In order to have dominance of $G(y)$ over $F_\delta(z)$, we need that the cumulative area $1,2,\ldots,2n$ will be non-negative up to the end of each area, $i = 1,2,\ldots,2n$. This requirement can be written in a more compact way, (which is easy to run on the computer) as follows: Define the following variables:

$$\alpha_i = (y_{i+1} - z_i)[\delta\left(1 - \tfrac{i}{n}\right)], \quad i = 0,1,\ldots,n-1 \quad \text{and} \quad \alpha_n = 0 \tag{1}$$

$$\beta_i = (y_i - z_i)\left[\frac{1}{n} + \delta\left(\frac{i-1}{n} - 1\right)\right], \quad i = 1,\ldots,n \quad \text{and} \quad \beta_0 = 0 \tag{2}$$

$$_i = \alpha_i + \beta_i, \quad i = 0,1,\ldots,n \tag{3}$$

The following two rules must hold for the δ which results in precise SSD:

$$\text{Rule 1:} \quad \sum_{i=0}^{I} \psi_i \ge 0 \quad \text{for all } I \tag{4}$$

$$\text{Rule 2:} \quad \sum_{i=1}^{I} \psi_i - \beta_i \ge 0 \quad \text{for all } I \tag{5}$$

We decrease δ gradually until the first negative sign appears either in (4) or in (5), which implies that the dominance of G(y) over $F_\delta(z)$ no longer holds.

Figure 2 demonstrates the technique suggested in this paper when we have four observations for F and G. Since we add the value z = 0 with probability δ to F, F_δ contains five observations. We check whether G(y) dominates $F_\delta(z)$. Thus, whenever G(y) lies below $F_\delta(z)$ we assign a plus sign to the area between the two cumulative distributions and a minus sign is assigned whenever G(y) is above $F_\delta(z)$. We require that the cumulative total area between the two distributions will be non-negative at any point. However, Levy and Kroll (1979) proved that it is sufficient to check the area only for points with a change in the step function. Hence in order to have a dominance of G(y) over $F_\delta(z)$ we require that the following will hold simultaneously,

$$\alpha_1 > 0, \quad \alpha_1 + \beta_1 > 0, \quad \alpha_1 + \beta_1 + \alpha_2 > 0, \quad \text{etc.} \quad \text{(see Figure 2).}$$

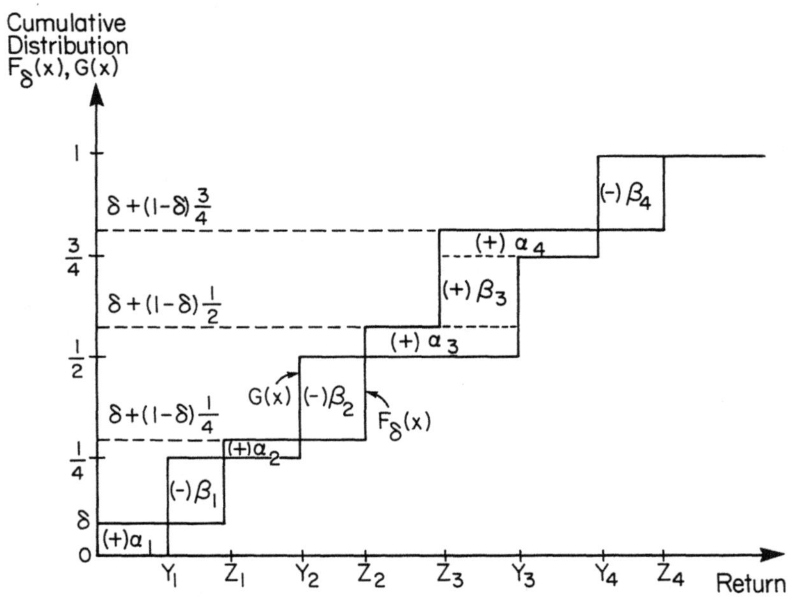

Figure 2

This can be rewritten in a compact way as,

$$\sum_{i=0}^{I} \Psi_i \geq 0 \quad \text{for all I, and}$$

$$\sum_{i=0}^{I} \Psi_i - \beta_i \geq 0 \quad \text{for all I when } \Psi_i, \beta_i \text{ and I are as defined before.}$$

3. Data and Empirical Results

In order to calculate the relative probabilities of default, it is desirable to control for the many other dimensions along which bonds may differ, such as coupon rate, callability, maturity (or duration),[3] sinking fund provisions (if any), tax features, and status in the event of bankruptcy. Ideally, one would analyze data on bonds matched for all relevant characteristics except bond rating in order to obtain accurate measures of relative probabilities of default as indicated by bond ratings.

This study is based on two sets of data taken from two different sources. In both cases an effort has been done to neutralize all factors apart from the default risk (see below), though we realize that working with actual data a perfect matching of the bonds for all other variables is impossible.

This study covered the years 1971 through 1980, and employed two different data sets--one set consisted of bonds maturing in 10 (or less) years for which various issues of the Federal Reserve Bulletin were the source, and the other set consisted of bonds maturing in 20 years, for which Moody's Bond Record served as the source.

The Federal Reserve Bulletin data set consisted of 120 monthly observations of yields to maturity[4] reported for Aaa and Baa corporate bonds (data were not published for Aa or for A bonds) and for

---

[3]By controlling for maturity (or duration), we are holding constant market segmentation. Thus, the existence of market segmentation would not affect the validity of our results.

[4]As a matter of fact, one can take rates of return on bonds for any assumed holding period and apply the technique advanced in this paper. The yield-to-maturity seems to be appropriate for a large segment of the bond market, e.g., institutional investors, pension funds, etc. More importantly, there is a mathematical bias present when delta is calculated based on holding period returns. The bias results from the fact that decreasing price levels may result in a negative holding period return, or even a series of negative holding period returns. In such an event, the distribution of holding period returns will shift to the left and the resulting delta values will be decreased (thus biased).

government bonds neither due nor callable in less than 10 years. Each observation of yield to maturity, as reported in the Federal Reserve Bulletin, is an average of daily yields to maturity for that rating category. These daily figures, on which the average is calculated by the Federal Reserve Bulletin, are provided by Moody's Investors Service. The 120 observations of the monthly average of daily yields to maturity for a given bond rating category are treated as a frequency distribution of yields to maturity, where the likelihood (probability) of the occurrence of a given yield to maturity is 1/120. Thus, we are treating months as possible states of the world where the probabilities of occurrence are equal.

The data from Moody's Bond Record (the second data set) included 465 bonds and were hand-collected. They consisted of a stratified sample, where the strata were the four investment grade categories (Aaa, Aa, A and Baa). There were not enough Government bonds to include them. For a given bond rating category, the number of bonds was the smaller of 10 or the population. When the population was larger than 10, bonds were included, in alphabetical order, until 10 had been identified as meeting the following criteria for matching purposes: (1) 20 years to maturity, (2) investment grade rating assignment, (3) presence of a sinking fund and of a call feature, (4) non-subordination, (5) domestic issue, (6) no missing data for any period in the 10 years covered by the study, and (7) no rating change. The matching requirements made it necessary to use 12/31 and 6/30 as the dates of data collection for each year in the study, rather than month-end dates, as we would have preferred. In order to keep maturity constant at 20 years, a new set of bonds was chosen at each observation collection date. For a given collection date, for a given rating category, a non-weighted average of the yields to maturity was calculated. These averages of yields to maturity for a given category, say Aaa, (there would be 20 averages) together served as the frequency distribution of yields to maturity for that rating category.

As we recognize the importance of the level of economic activity on the magnitude of the relative probabilities of default, we separated the 10 year period into periods of economic expansion and periods of economic contraction as defined by the National Bureau of Economic Research, Inc. Expansionary periods were identified as 1971 through 1973 and 1976 through 1979. Periods of economic contraction were identified as 1974 through 1975 and also 1980. There were, as a result, 84 months of economic expansion and 36 months of economic contraction. As described above for the full data sets, frequency distributions were constructed for these sub-periods of expansion and of contraction.

Tables 1 and 2 present the relative probabilities of default which result from applying the algorithm respectively to the Federal Reserve Bulletin data and to the Moody's Bond Record data sets described above. The Fortran program written to apply the algorithm reiteratively tests until it has found the last value of delta for which both rules of the algorithm hold. A reduction in the value of delta by 0.001 would result in the cumulative difference in the cumulative probability distributions being strictly less than zero. The values of delta in the tables are to be read as percents, that is, 0.013 is read as 1.3 percent.

TABLE 1
RELATIVE PROBABILITIES OF DEFAULT OF CORPORATE BONDS AND GOVERNMENT BONDS WHEN THE INVESTMENT HORIZON IS TEN YEARS
(Based on 1971-1980 Federal Reserve Data)

	Aaa vs. Govt.	Baa vs. Govt.	Baa vs. Aaa
Total Period	0.013	0.023	0.011
Economic Expansion	0.012	0.021	0.010
Economic Contraction	0.014	0.027	0.013

TABLE 2
RELATIVE PROBABILITIES OF DEFAULT OF CORPORATE BONDS WHEN THE INVESTMENT HORIZON IS TWENTY YEARS
(Based on 1971-1980 Moody Data)

	Aa vs. Aaa	A vs. Aaa	Baa vs. Aaa	A vs. Aa	Baa vs. Aa	Baa vs. A
Total Period	0.003	0.006	0.012	0.003	0.010	0.007
Economic Expansion	0.003	0.005	0.011	0.003	0.009	0.006
Economic Contraction	0.004	0.007	0.014	0.003	0.012	0.009

Three aspects of the relative probabilities of default as emerge from this study are of interest: (1) the relationship of delta to the level of economic activity, including both the relative magnitude of deltas and the relative sensitivities of deltas to a change in the level of economic activity, (2) the relative probabilities of default of high grade corporate bonds (say Aaa) over the government bonds in comparison to the relative probabilities of default of low grade corporate bonds (say Baa) over the same government bonds, and (3) the relationship between the default probability and the different investment horizons, for the default risk structure relevant for a given individual is a function of his/her investment horizon. The default risk structure for a given investment horizon, of course, is based on the market's assessment of the relative probabilities of default for different bond rating categories.

The default risk structure is a function of the level of economic activity. As the likelihood of default (the probability of default) is related to the state of the economy, we expect to observe that the magnitudes of the relative probabilities of default will be greater in periods of economic contraction than in periods of economic expansion. An examination of Tables 1 and 2 leads to the conclusion that the relative probabilities of default for every pairwise comparison except one (A vs. Aa is unchanged in Table 2) are larger in periods of economic contraction than they are in periods of economic expansion.

Tables 1 and 2 also reveal that the lower the agency rating the higher δ. Thus, our method and the agency rating provide consistent indication of the risk attached to each bond category.

Before moving to an analysis of the impact of the length of the investment horizon on the magnitudes of the relative probabilities of default, it is necessary to assign a more precise interpretation to the values of delta as presented in Tables 1 and 2. There are two distinctive features of the data used to calculate Table 1 deltas which need elaboration and which affect the comparison of these results with those of Table 2. First, as was noted earlier, Table 1 data are for government bonds which are neither due nor callable in less than ten years and for corporate bonds with ten years to maturity whereas the data for Table 2 are for callable bonds with twenty years to maturity. Thus, the ten-year horizon deltas and the twenty-year horizon deltas differ in the degree which maturity has been held constant. As a result, the Table 1 deltas are biased when compared with Table 2 deltas, but there is no reason to assume bias <u>within</u> the Table 1 results when corporate bonds are compared with one another. As corporate bonds in general possess a call feature, no bias is expected to exist either in Table 1 Baa versus Aaa deltas or in any pairwise comparisons in Table 2. Rather, a call feature is assumed for all corporate bonds with no difference between bond rating categories as to its presence or lack of presence. There is a difference in callability as noted when government bonds and corporate bonds are compared, as in Table 1. The difference in the degree to which maturity is held constant in the 10-year versus the 20-year data and the difference in callability of government bonds and corporate bonds impinge on the strict interpretation of the calculated relative probabilities of default for the 10-year investment horizon when compared with the 20-year investment horizon.

As the corporate bond data for deltas presented in Table 1 and Table 2 are characterized by maturity matching of 10 and of 20 years respectively, and by no bias expected in the treatment of callability, it is valid to analyze deltas calculated for the pairwise comparison of Baa corporate bonds versus Aaa corporate bonds. Such a comparison is presented in Table 3. It should be noted that the relative probability of default consistently increases with the length of the investment horizon. It is interesting to note that the differences in the relative probabilities of default (reflected in column 3) are consistently of the same magnitude, and do not vary with the definition of the period (total, economic expansion, or economic contraction). It also should be noted that the difference in the magnitude of delta when periods of economic expansion are compared with periods of economic contraction is invariant with respect to the length of the investment horizon. Thus, we conclude that the increase in deltas when the 20-year investment horizon is compared with the 10-year investment horizon is strictly a function of the difference in the horizon and is not affected by the state of economic activity. In other words, the level of economic activity has no more effect on the default risk faced by an investor with a 20-year investment horizon than it does on an investor with a 10-year investment horizon.

Finally, a comment on possible sampling errors is called for. Since we employ ex-post data it is possible that we find dominance-- in the sample but such dominance does not exist in the population. Kroll and Levy (1980) showed that for large sample sizes, this type of error is very small, and in our case, the sample satisfies the requirement of being large enough. Moreover, if indeed we have sampling errors (say neither distribution dominates the other in the population, but such dominance is revealed in the sample), we would expect delta to be zero for one-half of the pairwise comparisons, and about one-half of the times to be positive. Namely, the sample may reveal that the distribution of corporate bonds starts left of that of the Government bond, a case where delta is, by definition, equal to zero.

TABLE 3

THE IMPACT OF THE INVESTMENT HORIZON ON THE MAGNITUDE OF THE RELATIVE PROBABILITY OF DEFAULT OF Baa CORPORATE BONDS OVER Aaa CORPORATE BONDS

	20 Year Horizon Baa vs. Aaa (1)	10 Year Horizon Baa vs. Aaa (2)	Difference in Delta (1) - (2)
Total Period	0.012	0.011	0.001
Economic Expansion (a)	0.011	0.010	0.001
Economic Contraction (b)	0.014	0.013	0.001
Difference in Delta (b) - (a)	0.003	0.003	0.000

Looking only at the "total period" category (see Tables 1, 2 and 3) we find that delta is positive in 10 out of 10 cases. If there is no dominance in the population, we expect that $Pr(\delta > 0) = Pr(\delta = 0) = 1/2$, (i.e., equal probability that each distribution starts from the left), and the probability of getting 10 out of 10 positive deltas under a null hypothesis is very small $[(1/2)^{10}]$, which strongly indicates that our results are not due to sampling errors.

4. Concluding Remarks

In this paper we suggest a stochastic dominance method for quantifying the differences in cumulative probability distributions. We use our technique to quantify bond default risk. We look at the cumulative distribution of yield to maturity on different bonds and find that one class (say Aaa) dominates Government bonds by first or second degree stochastic dominance. Since this cannot hold in equilibrium, we conclude that the Aaa bonds are exposed to the risk of default while the Government bonds are not. We change the distribution of Aaa in a systematic manner until the dominance disappears. From this new distribution we estimate the probability of default as assigned by the market.

Our results were consistently in the right direction, and were correctly related to the level of economic activity. The probabilities of default estimated were larger in periods of economic contraction than in periods of economic expansion and varied directly with the investment horizon.

Finally, our method has many potential applications. We have demonstrated it in addressing one economic question, but its usefulness as a tool of analysis is quite promising in many other situations. In general, it can be used whenever one wishes to quantify the remaining dimension along which two distributions differ, and we anticipate applying this tool to related questions in future research.

References

Altman, Edward I., "Financial Ratios, Discriminant Analysis and the Prediction of Corporate Bankruptcy," Journal of Finance (September 1968): 589-609.

________, "Railroad Bankruptcy Propensity," Journal of Finance (May 1971): 333-345.

Altman, Edward I., Robert G. Haldeman, and P. Narayan, "ZETA Analysis," Journal of Banking and Finance (June 1977): 29-54.

Bierwag, G.O., and George Kaufman, "Coping with the Risk of Interest Rate Fluctuations: A Note," Journal of Business (July 1977): 364-370.

Board of Governors of the Federal Reserve System, Federal Reserve Bulletin, Washington, D.C.

Broske, Mary S., "The Measurement of Bond Default Risk," Research in Finance (1984).

Cohen, Jerome B., Edward D. Zinbarg, and Arthur Zeikel, Investment Analysis and Portfolio Management, 3rd Edition. Homewood, Ill.: Richard D. Irwin, Inc., 1977.

Hadar, Josef, and William R. Russell, "Rules for Ordering Uncertain Prospects," American Economic Review (March 1969): 25-34.

Hanoch, Giora, and Haim Levy, "The Efficiency Analysis of Choices involving Risk," Review of Economic Studies (June 1969): 335-346.

Hickman, W. Braddock, Corporate Bond Quality and Investor Experience. Princeton, NJ: Princeton University Press, 1958.

________, Statistical Measures of Corporate Bond Financing Since 1900. Princeton, NJ: Princeton University Press, 1960.

Hopewell, Michael, and George Kaufman, "Bond Price Volatility and Term to Maturity: A Generalized Respecification," American Economic Review (September 1973): 749-753.

Jensen, Michael C., "The Performance of Mutual Funds in the Period 1945-64," Journal of Finance (May 1968): 389-416.

Kapian, Robert S., and Gabriel Urwitz, "Statistical Models of Bond Ratings: A Methodological Inquiry," Journal of Business (April 1979): 231-261.

Kaufman, George, "Duration, Planning Period and Tests of the Capital Asset Pricing Model," Journal of Financial Research (Spring 1980): 1-9.

Kroll, Yoram, "State Contingent Stochastic Dominance," unpublished manuscript, 1981.

Kroll, Yoram, and Haim Levy, "Sampling Errors and Portfolio Efficient Analysis," Journal of Financial and Quantitative Analysis (September 1980): 655-688.

Levhari, David, and Haim Levy, "The Capital Asset Pricing Model and the Investment Horizon," *Review of Economics and Statistics* (February 1978): 92-104.

Levy, Haim, "The CAPM and the Investment Horizon," *Journal of Portfolio Management* (Winter 1981): 32-40.

Levy, Haim, and Yoram Kroll, "Efficiency Analysis with Borrowing and Lending: Criteria and Their Effectiveness," *Review of Economics and Statistics* (February 1979): 125-130.

Levy, Haim, and Yoram Kroll, "Investment Decision Rules, Diversification, and the Investor's Initial Wealth," *Econometrica* (September 1978a): 1231-1237.

Levy, Haim, and Yoram Kroll, "Ordering Uncertain Options with Borrowing and Lending," *Journal of Finance* (1978b): 553-573.

Levy, Haim, and Azriel Levy, "Ordering Uncertain Options under Inflation," (September 1984): 1223-1229.

Moody's Investors Service, *Moody's Bond Record* (July 1981).

National Bureau of Economic Research, Inc., *NBER Reporter* (Spring 1981).

Pinches, George E., and Kent A. Mingo, "A Multivariate Analysis of Industrial Bond Ratings," *Journal of Finance* (March 1973): 1-18.

Pye, Gordon, "Gauging the Default Premium," *Financial Analysts Journal* (January-February 1974): 49-52.

Rothschild, Michael, and Joseph E. Stiglitz, "Increasing Risk: I. A Definition," *Journal of Economic Theory* (1970): 225-243.

Sharpe, William F., "Mutual Fund Performance," *Journal of Business* (January 1966): 119-138.

Treynor, Jack L., "How to Rate Management of Investment Funds," *Harvard Business Review* (January-February 1965): 63-75.

von Neumann, John, and Oskar Morgenstern, *Theory of Games and Economic Behavior*, 3rd Edition. Princeton, NJ: Princeton University Press, 1953.

Weinstein, Mark I., "The Systematic Risk of Corporate Bonds," *Journal of Financial and Quantitative Analysis* (September 1981): 257-280.

Whitmore, G.A., "Third Degree Stochastic Dominance," *American Economic Review* (1970): 457-459.

TESTING FOR STOCHASTIC DOMINANCE

Daniel McFadden[1]
Department of Economics
Massachusetts Institute of Technology
Cambridge, MA 02139, USA

1. Introduction

It is often useful in economic analysis to formulate and test necessary conditions for optimizing behavior; this obviates the need for complete, and perhaps tenuous, maintained hypotheses on the objective function of the decision-maker. For example, the weak axiom of revealed preference can be tested without assuming a parametric family of preferences. For consumers who choose among uncertain alternatives by maximizing von Neumann-Morgenstern utility, it is also useful to identify necessary conditions and to develop methods that allow them to be tested econometrically. One such necessary condition is that an optimal prospect cannot be inferior to another feasible prospect for all increasing utility functions; this condition can be characterized in terms of <u>stochastic</u> <u>dominance</u> between distributions of payoffs.[2] Hadar and Russell (1969, 1971, 1974a,b, 1978) introduced the concept of <u>second-degree</u> <u>stochastic</u> <u>dominance</u> for consumers with increasing, risk-averse utility functions; this has become an important tool in the analysis of choice under uncertainty. This paper develops statistical tests for stochastic dominance. Section 2 reviews the concept of stochastic dominance, and makes a few minor extensions to Hadar and Russell's thorough characterization. Tests for first-degree and second-degree stochastic dominance are discussed in Sections 3 and 4, respectively. Section 5 discusses computation of the test statistics.

---

[1] This problem was suggested by Rulon Pope. I have benefited greatly from discussions with Chris Cavanagh, John Dagsvik, Joel Horowitz, Lindsey Klecan, and Peter Phillips. This research was supported in part by NSF Grant SES-8606349.

[2] One could go further and consider a full revealed preference test for the hypothesis of maximization of von Neumann-Morgenstern utility. The foundations for such analysis when prospects have <u>known</u> distributions are established in Green-Lau-Polemarchakis (1978), Varian (1983), and Green-Srivastava (1986). The statistical problem when only empirical distributions are observed has apparently not been considered.

2. Stochastic Dominance and Its Properties

Consider choice among asset portfolios. The returns from these portfolios are random variables whose desirabilities are described by their distributions, or prospects. I shall assume without loss of empirical generality that these returns are contained in the unit interval.[3] Let $\mathcal{F}$ denote the family of cumulative distribution functions on $[0,1]$; the elements of $\mathcal{F}$ can also be identified with the probability measures on $[0,1]$.

Assume decision-makers have von Neumann-Morgenstern utility functions on $[0,1]$ and rank portfolios by their expected utility $u(F) \equiv \int_0^1 u(x)F(dx)$.[4] Let $\mathcal{U}_1$ denote the family of all continuous, increasing utility functions from $[0,1]$ onto $[0,1]$.[5] Given a utility function $u \in \mathcal{U}_1$ and a set of feasible portfolios $\mathcal{A} \subseteq \mathcal{F}$, $F \in \mathcal{A}$ is (u-) optimal iff $u(F) \geq u(G)$ for all $G \in \mathcal{A}$.

Let $\mathcal{V}$ be a set of utility functions in $\mathcal{U}_1$, and define a binary relation $\succ_{\mathcal{V}}$ on $\mathcal{F}$: $F \succ_{\mathcal{V}} G$ iff $u(F) > u(G)$ for all $u \in \mathcal{V}$.[6] I will say that F $\mathcal{V}$-stochastically dominates G when $F \succ_{\mathcal{V}} G$, and will say that

---

[3] If returns are bounded, then they can be shifted and rescaled to lie in the unit interval without loss of generality. The assumption that returns are bounded is empirically harmless, and this assumption or more complex uniformity conditions are needed for the statistical results in this paper.

[4] I use the Lebesgue-Stieltjes definition of an integral, with

$$\int_0^1 u(x)F(dx) \equiv \lim_{J\to\infty} \sum_{j=1}^{J} u(j/J)F(\{x|(j-1)/J<u(x)\leq j/J\}).$$

This permits both continuous and discrete prospects. I repeatedly use integration by parts for such integrals: if $v(x)$ is continuous, then $\int_0^x v(y)F(dy) = v(x)F(x) - v(0)F(0+) - \int_0^x F(y)v(dy)$; see Dunford and Schwartz (1964, III.6.22). It is unnecessary to distinguish between a random variable X, giving the returns from a portfolio, and its distribution F. Thus, $u(F)$ and $\mathbf{E}_X u(X)$ are equivalent notations for the desirability of X.

[5] I assume that preferences satisfy the von Neumann-Morgenstern axioms in the form given by Arrow (1971, pp. 47-52). Then there exists a utility function over sure outcomes that is continuous and bounded, has the expected utility property for uncertain prospects, and is unique up to linear transformations. Without loss of generality, the utility can then be transformed so that its range is $[0,1]$.

[6] The same notation will be used for the random returns. Thus, for X and Y with respective distributions F and G, I write $X \succ_{\mathcal{V}} Y$ iff $F \succ_{\mathcal{V}} G$.

$F \in \mathcal{A}$ is $\mathcal{V}$-maximal if there is no $G \in \mathcal{A}$ satisfying $G \succ_{\mathcal{V}} F$.[7] When $\mathcal{V}$ equals $\mathcal{U}_1$, this is called first-degree stochastic dominance; I denote it $F \succ_1 G$, and refer to undominated prospects in $\mathcal{A}$ as first-degree-maximal.

Let $\mathcal{U}_2$ denote the subset of all weakly risk-averse (concave) utility functions in $\mathcal{U}_1$. $\mathcal{V}$-stochastic dominance for $\mathcal{V}$ equal to $\mathcal{U}_2$ is termed second-degree stochastic dominance, and is denoted $F \succ_2 G$. Undominated prospects using this criterion are called second-degree-maximal.

If sets of utility functions $\mathcal{V}$ and $\mathcal{T}$ are nested, $\mathcal{V} \subseteq \mathcal{T}$, then $F \succ_{\mathcal{T}} G$ implies $F \succ_{\mathcal{V}} G$, and the set of $\mathcal{V}$-maximal prospects in $\mathcal{A}$ is contained in the set of $\mathcal{T}$-maximal prospects in $\mathcal{A}$. Thus, a second-degree-maximal prospect is always first-degree-maximal. Then, one can nest the hypotheses of first-degree and second-degree maximality: second-degree maximality can be true only if first-degree maximality is true.

First- and second-degree stochastic dominance have convenient characterizations in terms of the distribution functions of the prospects. Hadar and Russell (1969) and Fishburn and Vickson (1978) establish the following result; I include a proof for completeness.

Theorem 1. *For* $F,G \in \mathcal{F}$,
(i) $F \succ_1 G$ *iff* $F \neq G$ *and* $F(x) \leq G(x)$ *for* $x \in [0,1]$,
(ii) $F \succ_2 G$ *iff* $F \neq G$ *and* $\int_0^x F(y)dy \leq \int_0^x G(y)dy$ *for* $x \in [0,1]$.

Proof: (i) Every function of the form $u(x) = \int_0^1 1(y<x)\psi(dy)$, where ψ is a continuous, increasing cumulative distribution function and 1(A)

[7] This is a definition of strict stochastic dominance; one could also consider weak dominance, $F \succsim_{\mathcal{V}} G$ iff $u(F) \geq u(G)$ for all $u \in \mathcal{V}$; or an intermediate case of strong dominance, $F \succeq_{\mathcal{V}} G$ iff $u(F) \geq u(G)$ for all $u \in \mathcal{V}$ with strict inequality for some $u \in \mathcal{V}$. If a prospect is optimal for some $u \in \mathcal{V}$, then no other feasible prospect can dominate it in the strict sense; if the prospect is uniquely optimal, then no other feasible prospect can dominate it in the weak sense. The theoretical hypothesis to be tested is that a chosen prospect $F \in \mathcal{A}$ is $\mathcal{V}$-dominated in the strict sense by a distinct, prespecified alternative $G \in \mathcal{A}$; this hypothesis is true iff the economic theory of choice is false. However, from a statistical point of view, the theoretically distinct hypotheses H_o: $G \succ_{\mathcal{V}} F$ or H_o: $G \succsim_{\mathcal{V}} F$ will induce the same test statistic and critical region, just as in the textbook case of testing the theoretically distinct null hypotheses H_o: $\theta \leq 0$ or H_o: $\theta < 0$ for the mean θ of a normal population.

is an indicator function that is one when A holds, and zero otherwise, is in $\mathcal{U}_1$. Conversely, $u \in \mathcal{U}_1$ can be represented in this form by taking $\psi(y) = u(y)$. This representation for $u \in \mathcal{U}_1$ yields $u(F) = \int_0^1\int_0^1 1(y<x)\psi(dy)F(dx) = \int_0^1(1-F(y))\psi(dy) = 1 - \int_0^1 F(y)\psi(dy)$. Therefore, $F \succ_1 G$ iff $\int_0^1 F(y)\psi(dy) < \int_0^1 G(y)\psi(dy)$ for all continuous, increasing cumulative distribution functions ψ. Taking ψ to be a sequence that approaches a discrete probability concentrated at x then gives (i).

(ii) Consider the function

$$u(x) = \lambda x + (1-\lambda)\int_0^1 r(y,x)\psi(dy)/\int_0^1 y\psi(dy), \tag{1}$$

where ψ is a cumulative distribution function, $r(y,x) \equiv \mathrm{Min}(x,y)$ is a "ramp" function, and $\lambda \in [0,1]$ is a constant. Since this expression is a non-negative mixture of continuous, concave, non-decreasing functions, it is continuous, concave, and non-decreasing. By construction, it maps [0,1] onto [0,1]. It is increasing in x if $\lambda > 0$ or if one is in the support of ψ. Therefore, any function u(x) of form (1) and increasing in x is in $\mathcal{U}_2$.

Conversely, consider $u \in \mathcal{U}_2$. Concavity implies that the one-sided derivatives of u exist; let u_0' and u_1' denote these derivatives at the boundaries, and let $u'(x)$ denote the right derivative at x. Note that $u_0' \geq 1 \geq u_1'$. If $u_0' = u_1'$, define $\lambda = 1$ and (arbitrarily) $\psi(x) = x$. Otherwise, define $\lambda = u_1'$ and $\psi(x) = (u_0' - u'(x))/(u_0' - u_1')$. The concavity of u implies ψ is non- decreasing, and the construction gives $\psi(0) = 0$ and $\psi(1) = 1$. Hence, ψ is a cumulative distribution function. The values of λ and ψ above when substituted in (1) yield the original function u. The demonstration for the case $u_0' > u_1'$ uses integration by parts to establish that the right-hand-side of (1) is $\lambda x + \mu[x - \int_0^x\psi(y)dy]$, with $\mu = (1-\lambda)/\int_0^1 y\psi(dy)$, and that $\int_0^1 y\psi(dy) = (1-u_1')/(u_0'-u_1')$. Then simplification gives the result.

To complete the proof of (ii), write $u \in \mathcal{U}_2$ in the form (1). Then

$$\begin{aligned} u(F) &= \lambda\int_0^1 xF(dx) + (1-\lambda)\int_0^1\int_0^1 r(y,x)\psi(dy)F(dx)/\int_0^1 y\psi(dy) \\ &= \lambda[1-\int_0^1 F(x)dx] + (1-\lambda)\int_0^1 \left\{\int_0^y xF(dx) + \int_y^1 yF(dx)\right\} \psi(dy)/\int_0^1 y\psi(dy) \\ &= \lambda[1-\int_0^1 F(x)dx] + (1-\lambda)\int_0^1 \left\{y - \int_0^y F(x)dx\right\} \psi(dy)/\int_0^1 y\psi(dy). \end{aligned}$$

Take $\lambda = 0$ and a sequence of ψ approaching a discrete probability concentrated at x to get (ii). □

By taking sets $\mathcal{V}$ of utility functions with properties beyond the axiom of risk aversion used in the definition of second-degree stochastic dominance, one could in principle develop a series of nested tests for these added properties. If a set $\mathcal{V}$ can be characterized by mixtures of "extremal" functions, such as the step and ramp functions appearing in the proof of Theorem 1, then it is only necessary to test satisfaction of the dominance condition for these extremal functions. For example, take $\mathcal{V}$ to be the family of utility functions generated by mixtures of constant absolute risk aversion (CARA) utility functions, $u(x) = (1-\alpha^x)/(1-\alpha)$ for $0 < \alpha < 1$. Then

(2) $$F \succ_{\mathcal{V}} G \text{ iff } \int_0^1 y^x F(dx) < \int_0^1 y^x G(dx) \text{ for } 0 < y < 1.$$

A theorem of Feller (1966, pp. 415-417) on Laplace transforms implies that the class of mixtures of CARA utility functions on $[0,\infty)$ coincides with the class of all infinitely differentiable utility functions with $u(0) = 0$, $u(1) = 1$, and $(-1)^{k-1}d^k u(x)/du^k > 0$, so that the derivatives alternate in sign. This completely monotone class includes, for example, the constant relative risk aversion utility functions $u(x) = x^\theta$ for $0 < \theta < 1$.[8] Thus, a test for maximality using the criterion (2) can be interpreted as a test of maximization of a completely monotone utility function.

If F in a set of feasible portfolios $\mathcal{A}$ is optimal for a utility u, then, for any set $\mathcal{V}$ containing u, F is $\mathcal{V}$-maximal. This result has a partial converse:

Theorem 2. *If $\mathcal{A} \subseteq \mathcal{F}$ is convex*[9]*, $\mathcal{V} \subseteq \mathcal{U}_1$ is closed, convex*[10]*, and equicontinuous*[11]*, and $F \in \mathcal{A}$ is $\mathcal{V}$-maximal, then there exists $u \in \mathcal{V}$ for which F is optimal.*

Proof: Consider the linear space $\mathcal{C}$ of all real continuous functions u on [0,1], with norm $\|u\| = \max_x |u(x)|$. Note that $\mathcal{U}_1 \subseteq \mathcal{C}$.

---

[8] The utility functions $u(x) = -x^\theta$ for $\theta < 0$ and $u(x) = \text{Log } x$ violate the boundedness condition implied by the von Neumann axioms (Arrow, 1971).

[9] Convexity of a set of cumulative distributions is satisfied if lotteries of the distributions are feasible.

[10] The families $\mathcal{U}_1$ and $\mathcal{U}_2$ are convex; the family of CARA utilities is not.

[11] A family of functions $\mathcal{V}$ is equicontinuous if, for each $\varepsilon > 0$, there exists $\delta > 0$ such that, for all $x,y \in [0,1]$ with $|x-y| < \delta$ and for all $u \in \mathcal{V}$, the inequality $|u(x) - u(y)| < \varepsilon$ holds.

Let $\mathcal{M}$ denote the Banach space of all regular, countably additive set functions defined on the Borel sets $\mathcal{B}$ in [0,1], with the norm of $G \in \mathcal{M}$ equal to $\sup_{B\in\mathcal{B}} |G(B)|$. Then, $\mathcal{M}$ is the space of continuous linear functionals on $\mathcal{C}$, and $\mathcal{F} \subseteq \mathcal{M}$. Give $\mathcal{M}$ its $\mathcal{C}$ topology. The set of probability measures $\mathcal{F}$ is compact in this topology (Billingsley, 1968, p. 37), implying that if $\mathcal{A} \subseteq \mathcal{F}$ is closed, then it is compact.

Define $\mathcal{D} = \{G\in\mathcal{M} | u(G) > u(F) \text{ for all } u \in \mathcal{V}\}$. Then, $\mathcal{D}$ is convex, and $\mathcal{D}\cap\mathcal{A} = \emptyset$ since F is $\mathcal{V}$-maximal. We show by contradiction that the point $G_o \in \mathcal{M}$ satisfying $G_o(B) = 0$ for $B \subseteq [0,1)$ and $G_o(\{1\}) = 3$ is interior to $\mathcal{D}$: Suppose $G_n \to G_o$, and suppose for each n there exists $u_n \in \mathcal{V}$ such that $u_n(G_n) \le u_n(F)$, so that $u_n \notin \mathcal{D}$. Since $\mathcal{V}$ is closed, bounded, and equicontinuous, it is compact, and u_n has a subsequence (retain notation) converging to some $u_o \in \mathcal{V}$. Then, $|u_n(G_n) - u_o(G_o)| \le |u_n(G_n) - u_o(G_n)| + |u_o(G_n) - u_o(G_o)|$. The first term on the right of this inequality is bounded by $\|u_n - u_o\| \cdot \|G_n\|$, which converges to zero for the subsequence u_n since G_n is bounded. The last term on the right converges to zero by weak convergence. Hence,

$$u_o(G_o) \leftarrow u_n(G_n) \le u_n(F) \to u_o(F).$$

But $u_o(G_o) = 3 > u_o(F)$ since $u_o(F) \le 1$, giving the contradiction.

Since $\mathcal{A}$ and $\mathcal{D}$ are disjoint, and $\mathcal{D}$ has a non-empty interior, a separating hyperplane theorem (Dunford and Schwartz, 1964, p. 417) implies the existence of $u_1 \in \mathcal{C}$ and a scalar α such that $\sup_{G\in\mathcal{A}} u_1(G) \le \alpha \le \inf_{H\in\mathcal{D}} u_1(H)$. Since $F \in \mathcal{A}$ is a boundary point of $\mathcal{D}$, the separating condition implies $\sup_{G\in\mathcal{A}} u_1(G) \le u_1(F)$. Hence, F is optimal for u_1. The condition $u_1(H-F) \ge 0$ for $H \in \mathcal{D}$ implies that u_1 is in the cone in $\mathcal{C}$ spanned by $\mathcal{V}$. The equicontinuity of the closed convex set $\mathcal{V}$ implies that it is compact. Therefore, a positive scalar multiple of u_1 is contained in $\mathcal{V}$. This proves the theorem. □

Stochastic dominance is a well-defined relation between the marginal distributions of random variables X and Y, even if these variables are not statistically independent.[12] However, the distributions of statistical tests for dominance will depend on the

[12] The presence of dependence among prospects does not alter the necessity of $\mathcal{V}$-maximality for the choice of a consumer with a utility function in $\mathcal{V}$. However, it may be more generally useful to consider <u>conditional</u> stochastic dominance -- given market history or market-wide uncertainty -- and the necessity of conditional maximality.

joint distribution of X and Y. The statistical tests in this paper are developed only for the simplest case of X and Y independent. This independence assumption is problematic in the application of dominance conditions to choice among asset portfolios. In the notation of Hadar and Russell (1973), in a market with m assets with returns X_i for i = 1,...,m, a portfolio is defined by a vector $p = (p_1,...,p_m)$ of non-negative shares that sum to one.[13] The return on the portfolio is the random variable $X = p_1X_1 +...+ p_mX_m$. Portfolios X and Y are independent only if they have no assets in common and if there is no market risk or correlated risk across assets. The statistical tests in this paper need to be extended to non-independent cases.

A second problem which may arise in applications concerns the form of the hypothesis to be tested. The simplest case, and again the one treated in this paper, is a test of the maximality of a chosen portfolio X against a preselected feasible alternative Y. However, it would often be of greater interest to test against a list of feasible alternatives. For example, when the prospects are portfolios of m assets, it might be reasonable to test X against a random selection of alternative portfolios, or against portfolios that are *ex post* optimal for selected utility functions. In addition to dependence, selection will enter the statistical distribution of such tests, and use of the test statistics developed in this paper would be inappropriate.

3. Testing First-Degree Stochastic Dominance

Suppose a chosen portfolio X with distribution F and an alternative portfolio Y with distribution G are statistically independent. The null hypothesis is that G first-degree stochastically dominates F. If the economic theory of choice by maximization of an increasing von Neumann-Morgenstern utility function is valid, then with sufficient data one should be able to reject this hypothesis. From Theorem 1, the null hypothesis is equivalent to $F \not\equiv G$ and $F(w) \geq G(w)$ for w in [0,1]. The probability of rejecting the null hypothesis when it is true (and the economic theory of choice is invalid) is greatest in the limiting case $F \equiv G$. I follow statistical convention in defining the significance level of a test of a compound null hypothesis to be the

[13] In a market that permits short positions, some components of p can be negative but will be bounded by margin requirements.

supremum of the rejection probabilities for all cases satisfying the null. This has the effect of making the null hypothesis H_o: $F(w) \geq G(w)$ for $w \in [0,1]$, against H_1: $F(w) < G(w)$ for some $w \in [0,1]$, with the significance level equal to the probability of rejecting H_o when $F \equiv G$. Suppose that random samples of returns $\mathbf{x} = (x_1,\ldots,x_n)$ from X and $\mathbf{y} = (y_1,\ldots,y_n)$ from Y are observed.[14]

If F and G are in parametric families, then stochastic dominance can be characterized in terms of parameter inequalities, and an efficient method of testing stochastic dominance is to test these inequalities.[15] A more challenging case occurs when the distributions F and G are not in parametric families. Define $F_n(x)$ to be the empirical distribution function formed from the X sample observations:

$$F_n(x) = \frac{1}{n}\sum_{i=1}^{n} \mathbf{1}(x_i \leq x) = \left(\text{fraction of X sample observations} \leq x\right),$$

where $\mathbf{1}(A)$ is an indicator that is one if A is true, zero otherwise. Similarly, define $G_n(y)$ to be the empirical distribution function formed from the Y sample observations.

For the hypothesis H_o: $F(w) \geq G(w)$ for $w \in [0,1]$, an obvious test statistic is the empirical analog

$$D_n^* = \max_{w\in[0,1]} D_n(w), \quad \text{with } D_n(w) \equiv \sqrt{n}[G_n(w) - F_n(w)]. \tag{3}$$

It is convenient in discussing the distribution of this and later statistics to consider the pooled observations from the X and Y samples. Let $\mathbf{z} = (z_1,\ldots,z_{2n})$ denote the <u>ordered</u> pooled observations, and define d_i to be an indicator that is +1 if z_i is from the Y sample, and -1 if z_i is from the X sample. Let $H_{2n}(z)$ denote the empirical distribution formed from the pooled observations, and note that $2nH_{2n}(z) = i$ implies $z_i \leq z < z_{i+1}$.

Define $D_{ni} = \frac{1}{\sqrt{n}}\sum_{j=1}^{i} d_j$. For $w \in [0,1]$, let $i = 2nH_{2n}(w)$. Then

[14] This sample may be visualized as a time-series of observations of returns on a portfolio. The assumption that it is a random sample from a fixed distribution rules out serial correlation, and excludes the possibility that the distribution of X shifts conditionally on market information and on portfolio transactions resulting from new information.

[15] For example, if F and G are in the parametric family $\{x^\theta \mid \theta > 0\}$, then $G \succ_1 F$ iff $\theta_F < \theta_G$.

$$D_n(w) = \frac{1}{\sqrt{n}} \sum_{j=1}^{2n} d_j 1(z_j \le w) \equiv D_{ni},$$

implying

(4) $$D_n^* = \max_{1 \le i \le 2n} D_{ni}.$$

This statistic is easy to compute using $D_{n,i+1} = D_{ni} + d_{i+1}/\sqrt{n}$; the maximum of D_{ni} is achieved at one of the n points from the Y sample. But D_n^* is the well-known Smirnov statistic (Durbin, 1973). Under the null hypothesis, the exact distribution of this statistic is[16]

(5) $$P(D_n^* > q\sqrt{n}) = (n!)^2/(n-k)!(n+k)!, \text{ where } k > nq \ge k-1$$

(i.e., k is the smallest integer greater than nq); see Gnedenko and Korolyuk (1961) and Durbin (1985). For n large, this has the limiting distribution

(6) $$P(D_n^* > q) \simeq e^{-q^2}(1 - (q/3)\sqrt{2/n} + O(1/n)).$$

This provides a simple and elegant test for first-degree stochastic dominance. A method for calculating the power of this test against alternatives of interest is discussed in Section 5.

The test statistic (4) has been used in a number of empirical studies of first-degree stochastic dominance; Porter (1978) provides a survey. In most of this literature, the empirical distributions of returns have been treated as exact.[17] An example is Kroll *et al* (1984). Apparently, the statistical distribution theory of such tests has been considered only recently; see Meyer and Rasche (1988).

4. A Test for Second-Degree Stochastic Dominance

Consider the null hypothesis that $G \succ_2 F$, where F is a chosen prospect and G is a feasible alternative. From Theorem 1, $G \succ_2 F$ iff $F \ne G$ and $\int_0^w F(y)dy \ge \int_0^w G(y)dy$ for all $w \in [0,1]$. The largest probability of rejecting the null hypothesis among the cases where it is true occurs in the limit where $F \equiv G$. As in the test for first-degree stochastic dominance, I include this limiting case in the definition

[16] This is the distribution of the test statistic for the least favorable limit under the null hypothesis, F = G.

[17] Joy and Porter (1974) use a sign test of the hypothesis $EY \ge EX$. This hypothesis is necessary, but not sufficient, for first-degree stochastic dominance.

of the null, so that I will test H_o: $\int_0^w F(y)dy \geq \int_0^w G(y)dy$ for all w in [0,1] against the alternative that $\int_0^w F(y)dy < \int_0^w G(y)dy$ for some w in [0,1], with the maximum rejection probability (significance level) occuring when $F \equiv G$. When F is second-degree maximal, I expect to be able to reject H_o. An obvious test statistic for this problem is the sample analog

$$(7) \qquad S_n^* = \operatorname*{Max}_{w\in[0,1]} S_n(w), \quad \text{with } S_n(w) \equiv \sqrt{n} \int_0^w (G_n(y) - F_n(y))dy.$$

Using the notation from the previous section for the pooled sample observations, define

$$(8) \qquad S_{ni} = \frac{1}{\sqrt{n}} \sum_{j=1}^{i} d_j(z_i - z_j).$$

This statistic satisfies the recursion

$$(9) \qquad S_{n,i+1} = (z_{i+1} - z_i)D_{ni} + S_{ni}.$$

For $w \in [0,1]$ and $i = 2nH_{2n}(w)$, implying $z_i \leq w < z_{i+1}$, one has

$$S_n(w) = \frac{1}{\sqrt{n}} \sum_{j=1}^{i} d_j(w - z_j) \equiv (w - z_i)D_{ni} + S_{ni}.$$

Since $D_{n,2n} = 0$, $S_n(w)$ is constant for $w > z_{2n}$, implying

$$(10) \qquad S_n^* = \operatorname*{Max}_{1\leq i\leq 2n} S_{ni}.$$

This statistic is easily computed using (9); the maximum is achieved at one of the points from the X sample. This statistic has again been used in the empirical literature on stochastic dominance, but without statistical analysis; see Porter (1978).

The distribution of the statistic S_n^* does not appear to have a tractable analytic form; I discuss some characterizations below. However, there is a simple computational method for calculating significance levels. When $F \equiv G$, so the probability of rejecting the null is maximum, every permutation of $\mathbf{d} = (d_1,\ldots,d_{2n})$ is equally likely, for any given **z**. Then, **d** and **z** are statistically independent, and the probability $Q_n(s|\mathbf{z})$ that S_n^* exceeds level $s > 0$, given H_{2n}, equals the proportion of the permutations of **d** yielding a value of the statistic exceeding s. (The unconditional probability $Q_n(s)$ of $S_n^* > s$ is then the expectation of $Q_n(s|\mathbf{z})$ in **z**.)

Let $S_n^* \equiv s_n^*(\mathbf{d},\mathbf{z})$ denote the test statistic for data $(\mathbf{d},\mathbf{z})$, calculated using (8) and (10). Let $\bar{S}_n^*$ denote the value of this statistic for the given sample. The significance level associated with $\bar{S}_n^*$, conditioned on $\mathbf{z}$, equals $Q_n(\bar{S}_n^*|\mathbf{z})$ and can be calculated by Monte Carlo methods: use (8) and (10) to calculate $s_n^*(\mathbf{d}',\mathbf{z})$ for a sample of permutations $\mathbf{d}'$ of $\mathbf{d}$, and find the frequency with which these simulated values exceed $\bar{S}_n^*$. Computation is discussed further in Section 5.

I give a series of results that partly characterize the asymptotic distribution of S_n^*. These do not provide a computationally convenient asymptotic approximation, but do provide some bounds.

Theorem 3. *Define* $\psi(w) = \int_0^w (w-z)F(dz)$, $\lambda(w) = \int_0^w (w-z)^2F(dz)$, $w \wedge v = \min(w,v)$, *and* $\rho(w,v) = 2(\lambda(w\wedge v) + |w-v|\psi(w\wedge v) - \psi(w)\psi(v))$. *Suppose the null hypothesis* $\int_0^w F(z)dz \geq \int_0^w G(z)dz$ *for* $w \in [0,1]$ *holds, with the least favorable case* $F \equiv G$. *Then, for* $w,v \in [0,1]$, $ES_n(w) = 0$, $ES_n(w)S_n(v) = \rho(w,v)$, $E(S_n(w) - S_n(v))^2 \leq 2(v-w)^2$, $S_n(w) \xrightarrow{d} N(0,\rho(w,w))$, *and there exists a sequence of random functions with the same finite-dimensional distributions as* S_n *that converge in probability to a Gaussian process on* $[0,1]$ *with mean zero and covariance function* $\rho(w,v)$.

Proof: Let $R_{Yn}(w) = \sum_{i=1}^{n} \max(w-y_i,0)/n$ and $R_{Xn}(w) = \sum_{i=1}^{n} \max(w-x_i,0)/n$. Then, $S_n(w) = \sqrt{n}(R_{Yn}(w) - R_{Xn}(w))$. Under the null hypothesis, $R_{Yn}(w)$ and $R_{Xn}(w)$ are independently and identically distributed, and $ER_{Yn}(w) = \psi(w)$. Therefore, $ES_n(w) = 0$. Further, for $v \geq w$,

$$\begin{aligned} nE[(R_{Yn}(w) - \psi(w))R_{Yn}(v)] &= \int_0^w (w-y)(v-y)F(dy) - \psi(w)\psi(v) \\ &= \int_0^w (w-y)^2F(dy) + (v-w)\int_0^w (w-y)F(dy) - \psi(w)\psi(v) \\ &= \lambda(w) + (v-w)\psi(w) - \psi(w)\psi(v). \end{aligned}$$

Hence,

$$ES_n(w)S_n(v) = 2(\lambda(w) + (v-w)\psi(w) - \psi(w)\psi(v)) \equiv \rho(w,v).$$

Next, for $v \geq w$,

$$E(S_n(v) - S_n(w))^2 = 2[\lambda(v)-\lambda(w)] - 4(v-w)\psi(w) - 2[\psi(v)-\psi(w)]^2.$$

But

$$\psi(v) - \psi(w) = (v-w)F(v) + \int_w^v (w-t)F(dt) = (v-w)F(w) + \int_w^v (v-t)F(dt),$$

implying $(v-w)F(v) \geq \psi(v) - \psi(w) \geq (v-w)F(w)$; and

$$\lambda(v) - \lambda(w) = 2(v-w)\psi(w) + (v-w)^2F(w) + \int_w^v (v-t)^2F(dt),$$

implying

$$2(v-w)\psi(w) + (v-w)^2F(w) \le \lambda(v) - \lambda(w) \le 2(v-w)\psi(w) + (v-w)^2F(v).$$

Substituting these expressions yields

$$2(v-w)^2[F(w)-F(v)^2] \le \mathbf{E}(S_n(v) - S_n(w))^2 \le 2(v-w)^2[F(v)-F(w)^2].$$

Thus, $\mathbf{E}(S_n(v) - S_n(w))^2 \le 2(v-w)^2$, and when F has a bounded density,

$$\mathbf{E}(S_n(v) - S_n(w))^2 = 2(v-w)^2\{F(w)(1-F(w)) + O(v-w)\}.$$

Since $S_n(w) = \sqrt{n}(R_{Yn}(w) - R_{Xn}(w))$ is the normalized sum of n independent, identically distributed random variables with zero mean and finite variance, a standard central limit theorem establishes, for any finite vector $(w_1,\ldots,w_k)$, that $(S_n(w_1),\ldots,S_n(w_k))$ converges in distribution to a multivariate normal with covariances $\rho(w_i,w_j)$. From the result $\mathbf{E}(S_n(v) - S_n(w))^2 \le 2(v-w)^2$, Chebyshev's inequality implies

$$\max_{w\le t\le v} P(|S_n(t)-S_n(w)| > \varepsilon) < 2|v-w|^2/\varepsilon^2.$$

Then, the final result follows from Billingsley (1968, Thm. 15.6). □

The next result gives bounds on the tail probabilities of S_n^*. These suggest the approximation $P(S_n^* > q) \simeq e^{-\alpha-\beta q^2}$ for large n and q, where α and β are constants that depend on the distribution F. Then, the computational method that uses random permutations to calculate the significance level for the sample statistic permits estimation of α and β for an application. This estimate can subsequently be used to approximate other critical levels.

Theorem 4. *Suppose the null hypothesis* $\int_0^w F(z)dz \ge \int_0^w G(z)dz$ *for* $w \in [0,1]$ *holds, with the least favorable case* $F = G$. *Then,*

$$3e^{-q^2/8} > P(S_n^* > q) > \frac{1}{4} e^{-q^2/\pi\sigma^2} + O(1/\sqrt{n}),$$

where $\sigma^2 \le 1$ *is the variance of* F.

Proof: The variance $\rho(w,w)$ of $S_n(w)$ has $\partial\rho(w,w)/\partial w = 4\psi(w)[1-F(w)] \ge 0$, and is maximized at $w = 1$. But $S_n(1) = \sqrt{n}(\bar{x} - \bar{y})$. $ES_n(1)^2 = 2\sigma^2$, where σ^2 is the variance of F, and the limit $S_n(1) \xrightarrow{d} N(0,2\sigma^2)$ imply

$$P(S_n^* > q) \ge P(S_n(1) > q)) = \Phi(-q/\sigma\sqrt{2}) + O(1/\sqrt{n})$$
$$\ge e^{-q^2/\pi\sigma^2}/4 + O(1/\sqrt{n}),$$

with the last inequality obtained from the bound $\Phi(-c) \ge (1/4)e^{-2c^2/\pi}$; see Abramowitz and Stegun (1964, 26.2.24).

The second inequality is obtained by a chaining argument. For each $i = 1,2,\ldots,$ partition $[0,1]$ into intervals of length 2^{-i} which have their centers at $w_{ik} \equiv (k-1/2)2^{-i}$ for $k = 1,\ldots,2^i$. For any $w \in [0,1]$, let $w_i \equiv w_i(w)$ be a center nearest w in the partition with intervals of length 2^{-i}. Then, $|w - w_i| \le 2^{-i-1}$ and $|w_{i+1} - w_i| \le 2^{-i-2}$. From this construction, $S_n(w) = S_n(w_1) + \sum_{i=1}^{\infty} [S_n(w_{i+1}) - S_n(w_i)]$. I will use Hoeffding's inequality for independent, identically distributed random variables Y_j which have $EY_j = 0$ and bound $|Y_j| \le \gamma$: $P(\sum_{j=1}^{n} Y_j/\sqrt{n} > t) \le e^{-t^2/2\gamma^2}$; see Pollard (1984). Observe that $S_n(w_1)$ is a normalized sum of $\max(w_1 - y_j,0) - \max(w_1 - x_j,0)$, and that $|\max(w-y_j,0) - \max(w-x_j,0)| \le |x_j - y_j| \le 1$. Then Hoeffding's inequality implies $P(S_n(w_1) > q/2) \le e^{-q^2/8}$. Next consider

$$Y_j = \max(w_{i+1}-y_j,0) - \max(w_i-y_j,0) - \max(w_{i+1}-x_j,0) + \max(w_i-x_j,0).$$

Then, $S_n(w_{i+1}) - S_n(w_i) = \sum_{j=1}^{n} Y_j/\sqrt{n}$. The Y_j are independent and identically distributed with $EY_j = 0$ and $|Y_j| \le |w_{i+1} - w_i| \le 2^{-i-2}$. Applying Hoeffding's inequality,

$$P(S_n(w_{i+1}) - S_n(w_i) > \sqrt{i}2^{-i-3}q) \le e^{-iq^2/8}.$$

Then,

$$\begin{aligned}
P(\max_{0\le w\le 1} S_n(w) > q) &\le P(\max_{0\le w\le 1} S_n(w_1(w)) > q/2) \\
&\quad + \sum_{i=2}^{\infty} P(\max_{0\le w\le 1} [S_n(w_{i+1}(w)) - S_n(w_i(w))] > \sqrt{i}2^{-i-3}q) \\
&\le P(S_n(w_{11}) > q/2) + P(S_n(w_{12}) > q/2) \\
&\quad + \sum_{i=2}^{\infty} \sum_{k=1}^{2^i} P([S_n(w_{i+1,k}) - S_n(w_{ik})] > \sqrt{i}2^{-i-3}q) \\
&\le 2 \max \{P(S_n(w_{11}) > q/2), P(S_n(w_{11}) > q/2)\} \\
&\quad + \sum_{i=2}^{\infty} 2^i \max_{k\le 2^i} P([S_n(w_{i+1,k}) - S_n(w_{ik})] > \sqrt{i}2^{-i-3}q) \\
&\le 2e^{-q^2/8}[1 + \sum_{i=0}^{\infty} 2^i e^{-iq^2/8}].
\end{aligned}$$

The first three inequalities hold because left-hand-side events are contained in the union of right-hand-side events. The last inequality is obtained by applying Hoeffding's inequality term by term. Finally, the right-hand-side of the last inequality exceeds one for $q^2 \le 8$ Log 4. Summing the geometric series for $q^2 > 8 \log 4$ yields the bound:

$$P(\max_{0\le w\le 1} S_n(w) > q) \le 3e^{-q^2/8}. \quad \square$$

Further characterization of the distribution of S_n^* is possible using the methods of Durbin (1985) for approximating first passage times; in this connection it is useful to note that (D_{ni}, z_i, S_{ni}) form a three-dimensional (inhomogeneous) Markov process in which D_{ni} and z_i are independent.

5. Computational Issues and Extensions

I consider first the question of computing the test statistic for second-degree stochastic dominance, and its significance level. The initial conditions $D_{n1} = d_1/\sqrt{n}$, $S_{n1} = 0$, and recursion formulas

(11) $$D_{n,i+1} = D_{ni} + d_{i+1}/\sqrt{n},$$

(12) $$S_{n,i+1} = (z_{i+1} - z_i)D_{ni} + S_{ni},$$

permit computation of $S_n^* \equiv s_n^*(d,z) = \max_{i\le 2n} S_{ni}$ with one pass through the sorted data. The significance level of the observed sample statistic $\bar{S}_n^*$ given z can be approximated by recalculating $s_n^*(d',z)$ for random permutations d' of d, and counting the percentage of values larger than $\bar{S}_n^*$. This can be done efficiently by drawing a random permutation d', and doing the calculation for d', its reflection -d', and all rotations of d' and -d'. The appendix gives a FORTRAN program for this calculation.

To test the accuracy of this approximation, I have carried out a Monte Carlo comparison. The first experiment assumes F is a uniform distribution; the second experiment assumes $F(w) = 1/2 + (w/4 - 1/8)^{1/3}$, which has a symmetric density tightly concentrated around $w = 1/2$. Both experiments assume a sample size $n = 100$.

Figure 1.1 gives the exact sampling distribution of S_n^* for the first experiment when the null hypothesis holds with $F \equiv G$; this calculation is based on 100,000 Monte Carlo draws. The statistic has

FIGURE 1. EXPERIMENT 1

1.1 Exact Probability of $S_n^* > q$ for the uniform distribution, and n = 100.

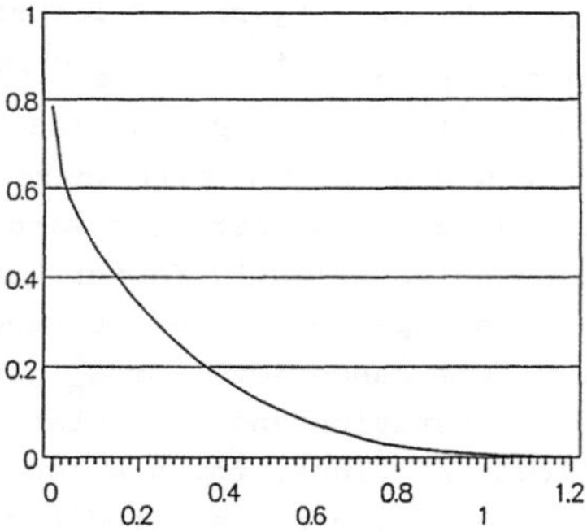

1.2 Approximation of Log Prob($S_n^* > q$) by $-\alpha - \beta q^2$

——— Exact

× × × Approximation

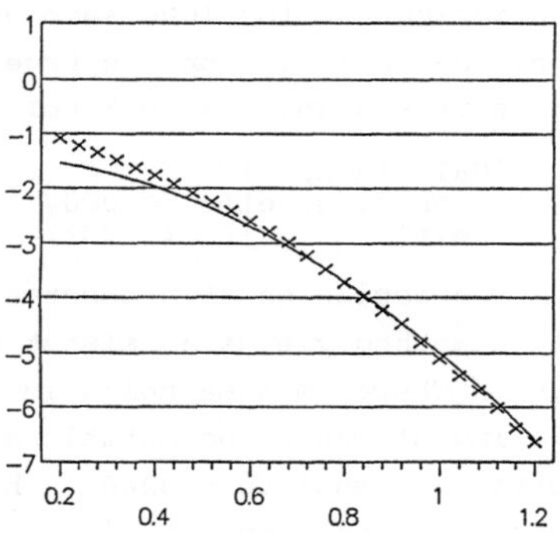

1.3 95 Percent confidence bounds on the exact significance level approximation using 10 random permutations

——— Exact

+ + + Bounds

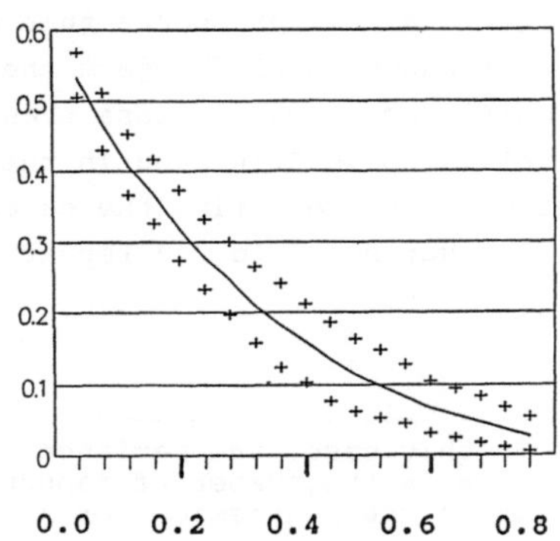

mean 0.1821, standard deviation 0.2328, a probability 0.2145 of equaling zero, median 0.0788, and critical levels 0.3550, 0.5330, 0.6828, and 0.9342 for significance levels 0.2, 0.1, 0.05, and 0.01, respectively. Figure 1.2 compares the exact distribution with the approximation $P(S_n^* > q) \simeq e^{-\alpha-\beta q^2}$ suggested by asymptotic analysis, with $\alpha = 1.3928$ and $\beta = 3.6105$ estimated by regressing $\log P(S_n^* > q)$ on one and q^2 in the tail where $0.1 \geq P(S_n^* > q)$. The fit is close for large q, although for this sample size the tail of the true distribution falls slightly faster than the approximation.

The experiment uses 10 random permutations of **d** in calculating the significance level of S_n^* given **z**, along with the reflection of each permutation and the rotations of each permutation and its reflection. Thus, for n = 100, a total of 10·2·200 = 4000 values of the statistic are evaluated for the significance level calculation. This takes about one minute on a fast personal computer. A Monte Carlo evaluation of the significance level calculated by this method was carried out for 1000 samples. A regression of the calculated significance levels on the true ones for the subset of the 1000 trials with a true significance level below 0.5 yields

$$\begin{bmatrix}\text{Calculated}\\ \text{Significance}\\ \text{Level}\end{bmatrix} = \underset{(0.002)}{0.0004} + \underset{(0.007)}{1.0072}\cdot\begin{bmatrix}\text{Exact}\\ \text{Significance}\\ \text{Level}\end{bmatrix}.$$

This regression has 510 observations and $R^2 = 0.973$. Thus, the permutation method yields an almost unbiased estimate of the significance level. There is some noise in the calculation from the Monte Carlo sampling of random permutations, with the standard error of the regression equal to 0.0240. This can be reduced by increasing the number of random permutations.[18]

Figure 1.3 compares the exact significance level with 95 percent confidence bounds on the permutation approximation. This figure suggests a test procedure that will closely approximate a five percent significance level: reject the null hypothesis when the calculated significance level is less than 0.025; accept it when the calculated level is above 0.10; and in the intermediate case, draw more permutations to refine the calculated significance level.

Figures 2.1 to 2.3 repeat these calculations for the second

[18] In this case, the variance of the regression is $0.000033 + 0.00543/\sqrt{k}$, where k is the number of random permutations drawn. Then, the standard error of the regression for k = 100 is 0.0094, and for $k = +\infty$ is 0.0058.

FIGURE 2. EXPERIMENT 2

2.1 Exact Probability of $S_n^* > q$ for $F(w) = 1/2 + (w/4 - 1/8)^{1/3}$, and $n = 100$.

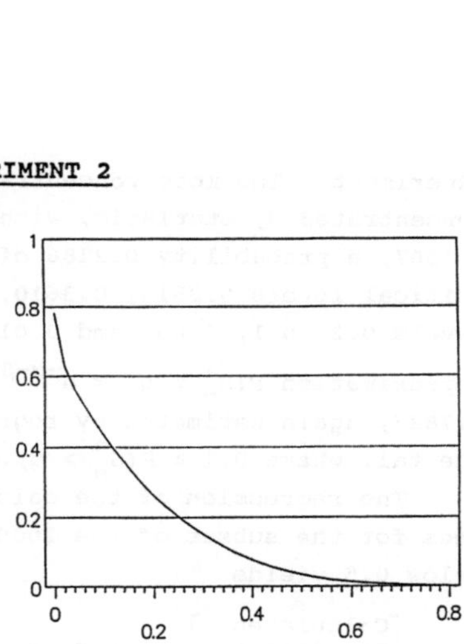

2.2 Approximation of $\text{Log Prob}(S_n^* > q)$ by $-\alpha - \beta q^2$

——— Exact

× × × Approximation

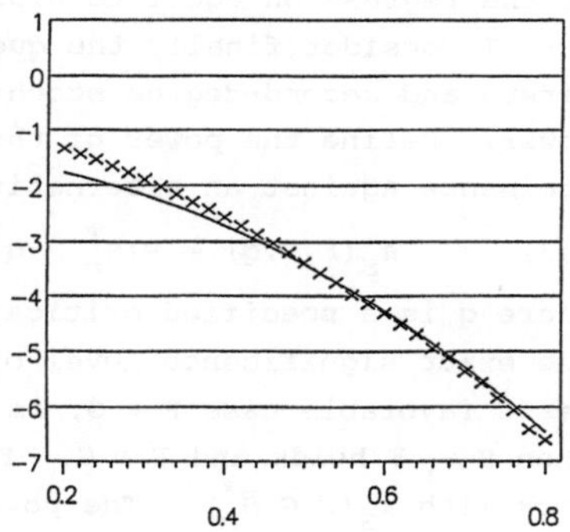

2.3 95 Percent confidence bounds on the exact significance level approximation using 10 random permutations

——— Exact

+ + + Bounds

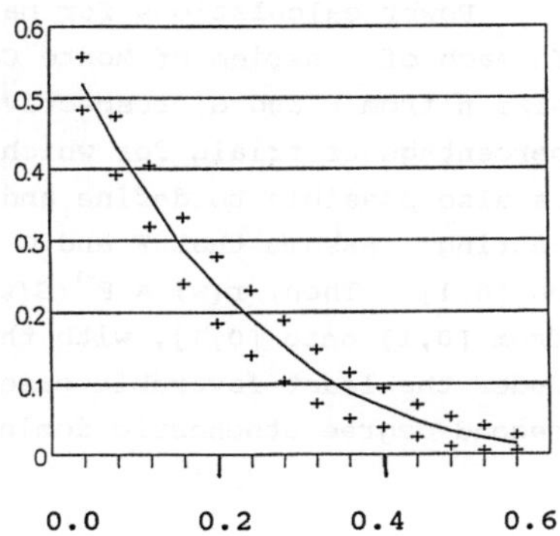

experiment. The more concentrated distribution of F yields a more concentrated S_n^* statistic, with mean 0.1294, standard deviation 0.1567, a probability 0.2186 of equaling zero, median 0.0672, and critical levels 0.2514, 0.3610, 0.4564, and 0.6367 for significance levels 0.2, 0.1, 0.05, and 0.01, respectively. The asymptotic approximation $P(S_n^* > q) \approx e^{-\alpha-\beta q^2}$ in Figure 2.2 has $\alpha = 1.4667$ and $\beta = 7.7827$, again estimated by regressing $\log P(S_n^* > q)$ on one and q^2 in the tail where $0.1 \geq P(S_n^* > q)$.

The regression of the calculated significance levels on the true ones for the subset of the 1000 trials with a true significance level below 0.5 yields

$$\begin{bmatrix}\text{Calculated}\\\text{Significance}\\\text{Level}\end{bmatrix} = \underset{(0.002)}{-0.0038} + \underset{(0.007)}{1.0093}\cdot\begin{bmatrix}\text{Exact}\\\text{Significance}\\\text{Level}\end{bmatrix}.$$

This regression has 503 observations, $R^2 = 0.978$, and a standard error of the regression equal to 0.0213.

I consider finally the question of the power of the tests for first- and second-degree stochastic dominance, and the calculation of power. Define the power of the test for second-degree stochastic dominance against an alternative with specified F,G as

$$(13) \qquad \pi_S(F,G,q) = P(S_n^* > q|F,G),$$

where q is a specified critical level. Then, $\pi_S(F,G,q)$ is equal to the exact significance level of S_n^* under the null hypothesis in the least favorable case $F \equiv G$, is large when $G \succ_2 F$ fails, and is small when $G \succ_2 F$ holds and $F \not\equiv G$. For computation, it is often useful to work with $\pi_S(F,G,\bar{S}_n^*)$. The power of the test for first-degree stochastic dominance is defined similarly as

$$(14) \qquad \pi_D(F,G,q) = P(D_n^* > q|F,G).$$

Power calculations for parametric F and G are straightforward: In each of a series of Monte Carlo trials, draw samples x and y of size n from F and G, respectively; calculate D_n^* or S_n^*; and count the percentage of trials for which the events in (13) or (14) occur. It is also possible to define and calculate power in a non-parametric setting. Assume that F and G are continuous and strictly increasing on [0,1]. Then, $r(w) \equiv F^{-1}(G(w))$ is a continuous, increasing mapping from [0,1] onto [0,1], with the inverse mapping $R(w) \equiv G^{-1}(F(w))$. Under the least favorable case of the null hypothesis for first- or second-degree stochastic dominance, r is the identity mapping. Alternative mappings that have $r(w) > w$ for some w violate first-degree stochastic dominance, and may violate second-degree stochastic dominance.

Consider the problem of calculating the power of the tests for a specified arithmetic mapping r when F and G are unknown, but are related by $F(r(w)) \equiv G(w)$. Then, the sample observations y_i and transformed sample observations $R(x_i)$ for $i = 1,\ldots,n$ can be pooled to form an empirical distribution estimate G_{2n} of G, while the observations x_i and transformed observations $r(y_i)$ for $i = 1,\ldots,n$ can be pooled to form an empirical distribution estimate F_{2n} of F. The power calculation now proceeds as follows: For a series of Monte Carlo trials, draw samples **x** and **y** of size n from F_{2n} and G_{2n}, respectively, and count the percentage of trials for which the events in (13) or (14) occur. To avoid problems with handling ties, one can work with smoothed versions of F_{2n} and G_{2n}: Letting $w_1,\ldots,w_{2n}$ denote the ordered, pooled observations from F obtained using the transformed data, define

$$F_{2n}^{-1}(p) = (2np-[2np])w_{[2np]+1} + ([2np]+1-2np)w_{[2np]},$$

where [x] is the integer formed by rounding down x, and $w_0 = 0$. G_{2n}^{-1} is defined analogously.

This paper has considered non-parametric test statistics for the null hypothesis that a prospect G first- or second-degree stochastically dominates a prospect F. I have shown that these statistics are feasible to compute, and that their exact significance level can be approximated by a practical Monte Carlo procedure. A method for calculating the power of the tests is also given. This paper leaves a number of questions for future research: What are the distributions of the test statistics when observations from F are not independent, or when there is dependence between the samples from F and G? What are appropriate test statistics, and what are their distributions, for the null hypothesis that F is first- or second-degree maximal in a <u>set</u> of feasible alternative prospects? What are appropriate test statistics for more restrictive forms of stochastic dominance, such as the form based on the class of completely monotone utility functions?

REFERENCES

Abramowitz, M. and I. Stegun, Handbook of Mathematical Functions. Washington: National Bureau of Standards, 1964.

Arrow, K., Essays in the Theory of Risk Bearing. Chicago: Markham, 1971

Billingsley, P., Convergence of Probability Measures. New York: Wiley, 1968.

Dunford, N. and J. Schwartz, Linear Operators, Vol. 1. New York: Interscience, 1964.

Durbin, J., Distribution Theory for Tests Based on the Sample Distribution Function. Philadelphia: SIAM, 1973.

Durbin, J., "The first passage density of a continuous gaussian process to a general boundary," Journal of Applied Probability **22** (1985): 99-122.

Feller, W., Probability Theory and Its Applications, Vol. 2. New York: Wiley, 1966.

Fishburn, P. and R. Vickson, "Theoretical foundations of stochastic dominance," in G. Whitmore and M. Findlay (eds.) Stochastic Dominance, Lexington: Lexington Books, 1978, 39-113.

Gnedenko, B. and V. Koroyuk, "On the maximum discrepancy between two empirical distributions," Selected Translations in Mathematical Statistics and Probability **1** (1961): 13-16.

Green, J., L. Lau, and H. Polemarchakis, "Identification of the von Neumann-Morgenstern utility function from asset demands" in J. Green and J. Sheinkman (ed) General Equilibrium, Growth, and Trade. New York: Academic Press, 1978, 151-161.

Green, R. and S. Srivastava, "Expected utility maximization and demand behavior," Journal of Economic Theory **38** (1986): 313-323.

Hadar, J. and W. Russell, "Rules for ordering uncertain prospects," American Economic Review **59** (1969): 25-34.

Hadar, J. and W. Russell, "Stochastic dominance and diversification," Journal of Economic Theory **3** (1971): 288-305.

Hadar, J. and W. Russell, "Diversification of interdependent prospects," Journal of Economic Theory **7** (1974): 231-240.

Hadar, J. and W. Russell, "Stochastic dominance in choice under uncertainty," in M. Balsch, D. McFadden, S. Wu (ed), Essays on Economic Behavior under Uncertainty, Amsterdam: North Holland, 1974, 134-150.

Hadar, J. and W. Russell, "Applications in economic theory and analysis," in G. Whitmore and M. Findlay (eds.) Stochastic Dominance, Lexington: Lexington Books, 1978, 295-333.

Joy, O. and R. Porter, "Stochastic dominance and mutual fund performance," Journal of Finance and Quantitative Analysis **9** (1974): 25-31.

Kroll, Y., H. Levy, and H. Markowitz, "Mean-variance versus direct utility maximization," Journal of Finance **39** (1984): 47-62.

Meyer, J. and R. Rasche, "Kolmogorov-Smirnov tests for the location and scale hypothesis with applications to portfolios of common stock," Michigan State University Working Paper, 1988.

Pollard, D., Convergence in Stochastic Processes, New York: Springer, 1984.

Porter, R., "Portfolio applications: empirical studies," in G. Whitmore and M. Findlay (eds.) Stochastic Dominance, Lexington: Lexington Books, 1978, 117-161.

Press, W., B. Flannery, S. Teukolsky, W. Vetterling, Numerical Recipes, Cambridge: Cambridge Univ. Press, 1986.

Varian, H., "Nonparametric tests of consumer behavior," Review of Economic Studies **50** (1983): 99-110.

APPENDIX

The FORTRAN routine given below calculates the test statistics for first- and second-degree stochastic dominance, and the significance level of the second statistic. Inputs are n = sample size from the distributions F and G; nper = number of random permutations used to calculate the significance level; and z = a 2×n array, the first row containing the pooled observations from F and G, and the second row containing an indicator that is +1 for observations from G and -1 for observations from F. (z need not be ordered). Program outputs are sd1 = test statistic D_n^*; sd2 = test statistic $\bar{S}_n^*$; and pct = significance level of sd2. The program requires randu, a function that returns a uniform random number, and sort, a subroutine that sorts a 2×m array b on its first column in ascending order. These routines can be found, for example, in Press *et al* (1985).

```
      subroutine sdom2(n,z,sd1,sd2,pct)        THE MAIN ROUTINE
      real*4 z(2,2000),zz(2,2000)
      parameter(nper=10)                       CONTROLS NUMBER OF PERMUTATIONS
      m=2*n
      call sort(m,z)                           ORDER THE POOLED DATA
      sd1=sd1f(m,z)                            THE TEST STATISTICS
      sd2=sd2f(m,z)
      na=0                  BEGIN THE SIGNIFICANCE LEVEL CALCULATION
      nb=0
      do 10 i=1,m           INITIALLY USE THE ORIGINAL DATA, ROTATED
       zz(1,i)=z(1,i)
       zz(2,i)=z(2,i)
   10 continue
      do 50 jj=1,nper       LOOP THROUGH RANDOM PERMUTATIONS OF d
       do 20 i=1,m              LOOP THROUGH ALL ROTATIONS
        call rotate(m,zz)
        sd21=sd2f(m,zz)
        if(sd21.gt.sd2) then       COUNT THE VALUES ABOVE AND BELOW sd2
          na=na+1
         else
          nb=nb+1
         endif
        call switch(m,zz)       REFLECTION REPLACING d WITH -d
        sd21=sd2f(m,zz)
        if(sd21.gt.sd2) then       COUNT THE VALUES ABOVE AND BELOW sd2
          na=na+1
         else
          nb=nb+1
         endif
        call switch(m,zz)          UNDO REFLECTION
   20  continue
       call permm(m,zz)            DRAW NEW RANDOM PERMUTATION
   50 continue
      pct=float(na)                CALCULATE SIGNIFICANCE LEVEL
      pct=pct/(pct+float(nb))
      return
      end
```

```
      function sd1f(m,b)          SUBROUTINE TO CALCULATE SD1 STATISTIC
      real*4 b(2,2000)
      dd=b(2,1)
      sd1=0.
      do 10 i=2,m
       dd=dd+b(2,i)
       if(dd.gt.sd1) sd1=dd
   10 continue
      sd1=sd1/sqrt(float(m)/2.)
      return
      end
c
      function sd2f(m,b)          SUBROUTINE TO CALCULATE SD2 STATISTIC
      real*4 b(2,2000)
      ss=0.
      dd=b(2,1)
      sd2=0.
      do 10 i=2,m
       ss=ss+dd*(b(1,i)-b(1,i-1))
       dd=dd+b(2,i)
       if(ss.gt.sd2) sd2=ss
   10 continue
      sd2=sd2/sqrt(float(m)/2.)
      return
      end
      subroutine permm(m,b)           SUBROUTINE TO RANDOMLY PERMUTE b
      real*4 b(2,2000)
      dimension istk(2000)
      do 5 i=1,m                  FORM STACK
       istk(i)=i
       b(2,i)=1.
    5 continue
      k=m/2                   SAMPLE FROM REMAINING STACK, REDUCE STACK
      do 15 i=1,k
       is=1+int((m-i)*randu(0))
       b(2,istk(is))=-1.
        do 10 j=is,m-i-1
        istk(j)=istk(j+1)
   10  continue
   15 continue
      return
      end
      subroutine rotate(m,b)          SUBROUTINE TO ROTATE 2ND ROW OF b
      real*4 b(2,2000)
      tmp=b(2,1)
      do 10 i=1,m-1
       b(2,i)=b(2,i+1)
   10 continue
      b(2,m)=tmp
      return
      end
      subroutine switch(m,b)          SUBROUTINE TO REFLECT 2ND ROW OF b
      real*4 b(2,2000)
      do 10 i=1,m
       b(2,i)=-b(2,i)
   10 continue
      return
      end
```

PART III
Applications

INSURANCE AND THE VALUE OF PUBLICLY AVAILABLE INFORMATION*

Marcel Boyer and Georges Dionne
Université de Montréal
and
Richard Kihlstrom
University of Pennsylvania

Introduction

A number of recent papers (e.g., Radner (1981, 1985), Townsend (1982), Rubinstein-Yaari (1983), Lambert (1983), Dionne (1983), and Rogerson (1985)) have studied the role of multi-period contracts in situations characterized by asymmetrically informed agents. In the circumstances envisaged by this literature, multi-period contracts perform no useful function when agents are equally well-informed.[1] The present paper considers a different set of circumstances and shows that multi-period contracts may be useful even when agents are symmetrically informed.

The particular contracts investigated here are insurance contracts. As we shall demonstrate, a series of one-period insurance contracts can be dominated by a single multi-period insurance contract. This occurs for informational reasons that are essentially the same as those discussed in Hirshleifer (1971). In the model we describe, the insured's past experience provides information about the risk of future losses. When the insurance contract is renegotiated every period as it is when short term contracts are used, the information obtained from past experience effectively eliminates insurance opportunities. The elimination of these opportunities can be avoided if the terms of the multi-period insurance contract are negotiated at the beginning of the first period and if both parties can, at that time, commit themselves to honor the contract in all periods. One way of achieving commitment from the insured is to require that he pay for

---

*We wish to acknowledge useful comments by J.-J. Laffont, C. Fluet and participants in Workshops at Universite de Toulouse and Université du Québec à Montréal. The Régie de l'assurance automobile du Québec provided financial support.

[1]For a detailed discussion of this point, see, in particular Townsend (1982).

insurance for all future periods when he agrees to the contract in the first period.

It should be noted that a series of short term contracts are essentially the same as a multi-period contract that provides for experience rating. Thus, our analysis can be viewed as a demonstration that multi-period insurance contracts which incorporate experience rating are dominated by contracts without experience rating.

There are, of course, conditions under which information may yield positive returns. Experience rating can be viewed as a decision to acquire information about the risk of loss. In the second section of the paper we assume that the insured uses information about the risk of loss to make more informed production decisions.[2] The information acquired by the insured is without explicit cost and is available to the insurer. We will illustrate the mechanism by which information generates positive returns. We will also isolate the factors that determine how the productive benefits generated by information compare to the insurance-reducing cost of information.[3]

A two-period model without production is described in Section 1. Section 2 introduces production. The results are summarized in the final section.

1. Insurance Without Production

Let us first present a simple one-period insurance contract. The formal analysis proceeds by assuming that the loss to the insured is financial. We refer to the insured as Individual B (the insurance buyer). The insurer is individual S (the insurance seller). When there is no loss, the insured's wealth is W_N^B. If a loss occurs, his wealth is reduced to W_L^B where, of course,

$$W_L^B < W_N^B.$$

If no insurance is provided, the insurer's wealth W^S is unaffected by the loss suffered by B.

---

[2]The concept of production we consider will be standard. However, one can interpret "production" as any welfare increasing activity which the individual may have and which could be adjusted when more information becomes available. See Palfrey and Spatt (1985) for the analysis of "care production" with incomplete information and learning.

[3]See Cooper (1984) for an analysis of a similar trade-off in a different context.

Both the insured and the insurer expect a loss to occur with probability μ which can be interpreted as the probability of the "average individual" in the market. The insured is assumed to be risk averse. He therefore maximizes the expected value of the strictly concave utility function u_B. When he has no insurance, his expected utility is

$$U^B(W_N^B, W_L^B) = (1 - \mu)u_B(W_N^B) + \mu u_B(W_L^B).$$

The insurer is assumed to be risk neutral. When he provides no insurance, his expected utility is simply W^S.

We assume that the price of insurance is actuarial. Specifically, we assume that there is a price p of coverage such that if c is the amount paid by S when B suffers a loss, i.e. c is the level of coverage net of premium, then pc is the premium paid by B if no loss occurs. Thus, if S sells B a policy that provides coverage c, then B's expected utility is

$$U^B(W_N^B - pc, W_L^B + c) = (1 - \mu)u_B(W_N^B - pc) + \mu u_B(W_L^B + c) \tag{1}$$

and S's expected utility is

$$W^S + (1 - \mu)pc - \mu c. \tag{2}$$

Equilibrium occurs when p is such that the c level that maximizes (1) is the same as that which maximizes (2).

This, of course, occurs when

$$p = (\mu/(1 - \mu)). \tag{3}$$

In this equilibrium, B is fully covered in the sense that

$$W_N^B - pc = W_L^B + c = E[W^B|\mu] = (1 - \mu)W_N^B + \mu W_L^B.$$

Since (3) implies that

$$(1 - \mu)pc - \mu c = 0, \tag{4}$$

then $W^S = W^S + (1 - \mu)pc - \mu c$, i.e., the insurer's utility is the same whether he supplies insurance or not. Thus S neither gains nor loses by providing coverage.

The equilibrium is described in the Edgeworth Box of Figure 1 where

X_N^S = S's wealth when B suffers no loss;

X_N^B = B's wealth when B suffers no loss;

X_L^S = S's wealth when B suffers a loss;

X_L^B = B's wealth when B suffers a loss.

M_o = initial situation

M_ϵ = equilibrium point.

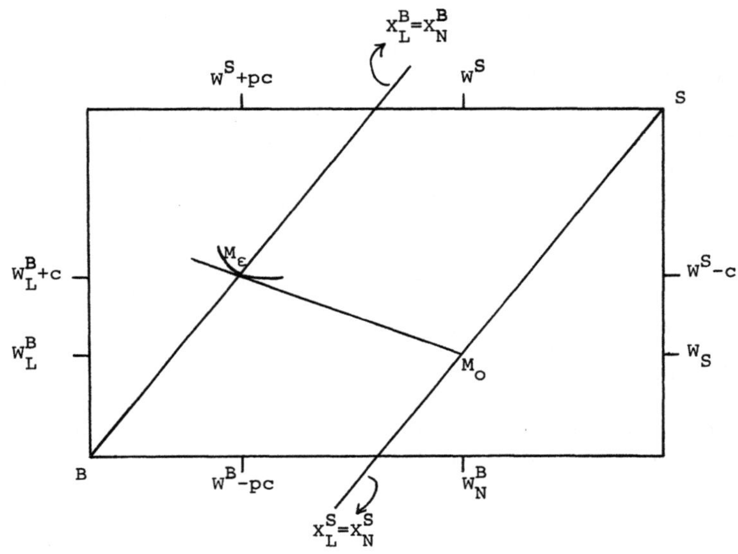

Figure 1

Let us now consider a two-period insurance contract. It can easily be shown that, without experience rating and for the same actuarial price of insurance in both periods, the insured will choose, <u>ex ante</u>, full insurance in each period in the sense that

$$W_{1N}^B - pc_1 = W_{1L}^B + c_1 = E[W_1^B|\mu] = (1 - \mu)W_{1N}^B + \mu\, W_{1L}^B$$

$$W_{2N}^B - pc_2 = W_{2L}^B + c_2 = E[W_2^B|\mu] = (1 - \mu)W_{2N}^B + \mu\, W_{2L}^B$$

where $W_{1N}^B = W_{2N}^B$ and $W_{1L}^B = W_{2L}^B$. Then $c_1 = c_2$. <u>Ex ante</u>, expected utility is equal to

$$u_B(E[W_1^B|\mu]) + \delta\, u_B(E[W_2^B|\mu])$$

where δ is a discount factor.

Suppose now that the information provided by B's past loss record is to be used by both parties before the insurance purchase in the second period. There are only two possible loss records that can be observed. These are denoted r_N and r_L. We interpret r_N as a good record and assume that the probability of a loss declines when r_N is observed. Formally, if $\mu(r_N)$ is the posterior probability of a loss when r_N is observed, then

$$\mu(r_N) < \mu.$$

Similarly, r_L is interpreted as a bad record that raises the probability of a loss. Thus,

$$\mu(r_L) > \mu$$

where $\mu(r_L)$ is the posterior loss probability after r_L is observed. The probability of observing r_N is ϕ. One important fact is that

$$\mu = \phi\mu(r_N) + (1 - \phi)\mu(r_L). \qquad (5)$$

After r_N has been observed, the equilibrium price of insurance will be

$$p(r_N) = \frac{\mu(r_N)}{1 - \mu(r_N)}\,. \qquad (6)$$

In this case, the equilibrium policy $c_2(r_N)$ will fully cover B in the sense that

$$W_{2N}^B - p(r_N)c_2(r_N) = W_{2L}^B + c_2(r_N) = E[W_2^B|\mu(r_N)]$$

$$= (1 - \mu(r_N))W_{2N}^B + \mu(r_N)W_{2L}^B.$$

Just as (3) implied (4), equation (6) implies that

$$(1 - \mu(r_N))p(r_N)c_2(r_N) - \mu(r_N)c_2(r_N) = 0 \qquad (7)$$

and that

$$W_2^S = W_2^S + (1 - \mu(r_N))p(r_N)c_2(r_N) - \mu(r_N)c_2(r_N).$$

Thus, in the equilibrium arrived at after both traders observe r_N, the insurer's expected wealth is W_2^S.

When r_L is observed, the equilibrium price will be

$$p(r_L) = \frac{\mu(r_L)}{1 - \mu(r_L)} \tag{8}$$

and B's income will be fully insured and will equal

$$W_{2N}^B - p(r_L)c_2(r_L) = W_{2L}^B + c_2(r_L) = E[W_2^B|\mu(r_L)]$$

$$= (1 - \mu(r_L))W_{2N}^B + \mu(r_L)W_{2L}^B.$$

Again (8) implies

$$(1 - \mu(r_L))p(r_L)c_2(r_L) - \mu(r_L)c_2(r_L) = 0, \tag{9}$$

so that S's expected utility will once more be

$$W_2^S = W_2^S + (1 - \mu(r_L))p(r_L)c(r_L) - \mu(r_L)c(r_L).$$

The two possible experience rating equilibria in period 2 M'_ϵ and M''_ϵ associated respectively with r_N and r_L are described in Figure 2. The equilibrium obtained without experience rating M_ϵ is also described in Figure 2 for purposes of comparison.

For B, the <u>ex ante</u> expected utility associated with experience rating is

$$u_B(E[W_1^B|\mu]) + \delta\{\phi\mu_B(E[W_2^B|\mu(r_N)]) + (1 - \phi)u_B(E[W_2^B|\mu(r_L)])\}$$

Since the insurance contracts in the first period are identical with and without experience rating, the comparison of welfare can be limited to the comparison of contracts in the second period. By Jensen's inequality,

$$\phi u_B(E[W_2^B|\mu(r_N)]) + (1 - \phi)u_B(E[W_2^B|\mu(r_L)])$$

$$< u_B[\phi E[W^B|\mu(r_N)] + (1 - \phi)E[W_2^B|\mu(r_L)]]$$

But (5) implies that $\phi E[W_2^B|\mu(r_N)] + (1 - \phi)E[W_2^B|\mu(r_L)] = E[W_2^B|\mu]$. Thus

$$\phi u_B(E[W_2^B|\mu(r_N)] + (1 - \phi)u_B(E[W_2^B|\mu(r_L)]) < u_B(E[W_2^B|\mu]) \tag{10}$$

Since the right-hand side of (10) is B's utility in the equilibrium associated with no experience rating in the second period, (10) asserts that B prefers that equilibrium to experience rating. Since S will have an <u>ex ante</u> expected utility of W_2^S with or without experience

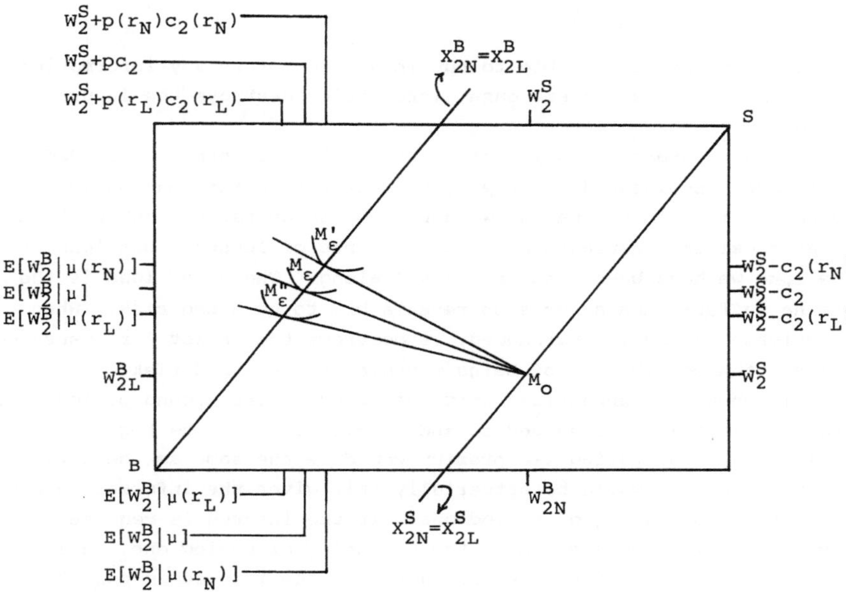

Figure 2

rating, he will not care whether experience rating is used or not. Thus, we have proved the following proposition:

<u>Proposition 1</u>: With public information and no production, it is socially preferable not to use experience rating.

In an insurance market, it is not particularly surprising that information reduces welfare. The point can be made most dramatically by assuming that information is perfect. In that case, no insurance policies will ever be issued. If it is discovered that no loss will occur, the insured will not want to buy insurance. If, on the other hand, it is discovered that a loss is sure to occur, the insurer will have no reason to provide insurance, since he knows that the premium will never be paid. The <u>ex ante</u> expected utility of each individual is the expected utility of the initial no-insurance position. Thus, B's utility is

$$U^B(W_N^B,\ W_L^B)$$

which, as Figure 1 makes clear, is less than the expected utility

$$U^B(W_N^B - pc,\ W_L^B + c)$$

he achieves when he is able to buy insurance before any information is revealed. In this extreme case, information destroys the insurance market.

When information is imperfect, the intuition can be extended. In that case, the insured who buys insurance before information is revealed, i.e. in the market without experience rating, can be thought of as receiving insurance against two kinds of losses. One loss is the loss we have been considering all along. The other loss is the one he suffers when experience reveals him to be a bad risk. When experience rating is introduced, it destroys the market for insurance against the possibility of being revealed to be a bad risk.

It should be emphasized that the terms of the second period insurance contract must be agreed to and committed to at the beginning of period one. The period two premium would be the same as the period one premium. It would be actuarially fair given the information available at the beginning of period one. If the insured is required to pay this period two premium at the beginning of period one, he is effectively committed to the contract. If the insured is permitted to delay payment of the period two premium until the end of period one, he would not be committed to accepting period two coverage for the period one premium. He would, indeed, refuse coverage on those terms if his period one experience revealed him to be a good risk. In that case he could obtain coverage elsewhere at the now lower actuarially fair rate. If the contract prohibits that option, he might simply prefer to refuse coverage and self insure.

2. Insurance With Production

In the preceding section, it was shown that both parties to the insurance contract prefer long term contracts that do not incorporate experience rating. This can be viewed as a decision not to acquire information about the risk of loss before negotiating the contract. In the context of the preceding section, information simply destroyed insurance possibilities.

Information may, of course, also yield positive returns. In the present section, we assume that the insured uses information about the risk of loss to make more informed production decisions. The introduction of this assumption yields a model that permits us to illustrate the mechanism by which information generates positive returns. It is also possible to indicate the factors that determine how the productive benefits generated by information compare to the insurance-reducing cost of information. Throughout this analysis, it is assumed that information acquired by one party is available to the other. It is also assumed that if one party is uninformed, the other is equally uninformed. We also assume that information is available without explicit cost. Thus, the only cost of information arises because its use can reduce insurance possibilities.

Let us introduce an example in which a firm purchases insurance to cover (commercial and/or political) export risks faced in foreign countries. Ex ante, the company and the insurer may be poorly informed about the probability of a loss but they may well know the average probability for all the firms in the country (μ). We assume that the insured cannot affect the loss probability. λ is a random variable ($0 \leq \lambda \leq 1$) which indicates the fraction of output produced that will be effectively delivered each year in the foreign countries (without commercial and political risks, $\lambda = 1$). The price of output is one. Since analytically, $E[\lambda|\mu]$ plays the same role as the price of output, it will be interpreted as a price and we will call it the "delivery value of an output."

We assume that the insured employs capital to produce the output that generates his revenues. If K is his capital input, $\lambda_N f(K)$ are his revenues when no loss is suffered and $\lambda_L f(K)$ are his revenues when a loss occurs. The size of the loss depends on the level of K chosen and K is public information. If we now let π be the cost of capital, then we can interpret W_N^B as $W_N^B = \lambda_N f(K) - \pi K$ and W_L^B can be expressed as $W_L^B = \lambda_L f(K) - \pi K$. Since $W_L^B < W_N^B$, we must of course also have $\lambda_L < \lambda_N$. The production function is assumed to have the usual properties, $f' > 0$, $f'' < 0$ and $f(0) = 0$.

We assume that the insurance market is the same as before. When there is no acquisition of information, the insurer will behave exactly as before, and the equilibrium price of insurance will still be given by (3). The insured will now choose c and K simultaneously so as to maximize[4]

$$U^B(\lambda_N f(K) - \pi K - pc, \lambda_L f(K) - \pi K + c).$$

In fact, the insured's problem can be considered in stages. We can, in particular, view him as first choosing K and then c. We can also

[4]Since under insurance, profits cannot be negative in this model, we assume that initial wealth is zero and that wealth is therefore equal to profits in order to simplify the presentation. (See Katz (1983) and Briys and Eeckhoudt (1985) for a discussion of this issue.)

follow the usual dynamic programming approach and analyze the choice of c on the assumption that K has already been chosen. By doing this, we can apply the preceding analysis to observe that, regardless of the K chosen, the insured will be perfectly insured and will receive an income equal to $E[\lambda|\mu]f(K) - \pi K$ where $E[\lambda|\mu] = \mu\lambda_L + (1 - \mu)\lambda_N$. The problem of choosing K will then simply be one of choosing K to maximize $E[\lambda|\mu]f(K) - \pi K$. Considering maximum profits as a function of the delivery value $E = E(\lambda|\mu)$ and of the cost of capital π, say $\psi(E, \pi)$, with

$$\psi(E, \pi) = \max_K Ef(K) - \pi K,$$

then B's equilibrium utility level will be, without the acquisition of information,

$$U_B(\psi(E[\lambda|\mu], \pi)). \tag{11}$$

As before, S's utility will be W^S.

With the acquisition of information, the analysis is analogous. In this case, when the information reveals r_N, the price of insurance is given by (6) and K and c are chosen simultaneously to maximize

$$(1 - \mu(r_N))u_B(\lambda_N f(K) - \pi K - p(r_N)c(r_N)) + \mu(r_N)u_B(\lambda_L f(K) - \pi K + c(r_N))$$

Once again we consider this problem in stages and observe that, for each K that he might choose, B will be completely insured and his income will be $E[\lambda|\mu(r_N)]f(K) - \pi K$. He will thus choose K to maximize $E[\lambda|\mu(r_N)]f(K) - \pi K$ and his utility will be $u_B(\psi(E[\lambda|\mu(r_N)], \pi))$. Again, S's utility equals W^S. By a similar argument, we observe that when the information reveals r_L, then B's equilibrium utility level will be $u_B(\Psi(E[\lambda|\mu(r_L)], \pi))$, and S's equilibrium utility level will be W^S again.

When there is acquisition of information, B's <u>ex ante</u> expected utility becomes

$$\phi u_B(\psi(E[\lambda|\mu(r_N)], \pi)) + (1 - \phi)u_B(\psi(E[\lambda|\mu(r_L)], \pi)). \tag{12}$$

We are now in a position to determine whether the acquisition of information is socially beneficial. As we have seen, the insurer is indifferent since his expected utility is W^S with or without the acquisition of information. The insured however will, in general, have a preference. He will prefer the acquisition of information if the *ex ante* expected utility computed in (12) exceeds the utility (11) obtained without it.

Before comparing (11) and (12) analytically, we observe that intuitively, the acquisition of information has two effects that operate in different directions. We have already seen that when there is no production, information reduces B's welfare by, in effect, partially destroying the insurance market. It should be noted that the welfare loss occurs because B is risk averse. Formally, the strict concavity of u_B is used to obtain (10) via Jensen's inequality. When there is production, the information can be used by B to improve on his choice of K. The effect produced by this use of information raises B's welfare. To observe this second effect in its most extreme form, we can eliminate the other effect, i.e. the welfare loss incurred because information destroys the insurance market, by assuming that B is risk neutral, i.e. that u_B is linear. In this case, B can effectively "self-insure" on the same terms that he is offered by the insurance market when it exists. Thus, even the complete elimination of the insurance market by the acquisition of information will not reduce B's welfare. Formally, when B is risk neutral, the *ex ante* expected utility associated with the acquisition of information is simply

$$\phi\psi(E[\lambda|\mu(r_N)], \pi) + (1 - \phi)\psi(E[\lambda|\mu(r_L)], \pi). \tag{12'}$$

In other words, when u_B is linear, (12) is replaced by (12'). And in this case, the utility associated with no information is simply

$$\psi(E[\lambda|\mu], \pi), \tag{11'}$$

the special form of (11) obtained when u_B is linear.

It is now possible to prove that information improves B's welfare when he is risk neutral by proving that (12') exceeds (11'). This is true because of Jensen's inequality, which can be applied because $\psi(E, \pi)$ is a strictly convex function. Since the delivery value E can be interpreted as the price of output if f(K) is interpreted as output, the convexity of ψ can be interpreted as the convexity of maximum profits as a function of the prices of output and input. It is, in fact, a well-known duality result that maximum profits are a convex function of those prices. The convexity of ψ and Jensen's inequality imply that (12') exceeds (11') and therefore that information raises B's welfare when B is risk neutral.

When B is risk averse, information will raise B's welfare if (12) exceeds (11). Because of Jensen's inequality, (12) exceeds (11) if $u_B(\psi(\cdot))$ is convex and (11) exceeds (12) if $u_B(\psi(\cdot))$ is concave. When

B is risk averse, u_B is strictly concave. When there is production, ψ is strictly convex. Thus, it is not clear whether $u_B(\psi(\cdot))$ is concave or convex or neither. The strict concavity of u_B, i.e. the risk aversion of B, causes B's welfare to fall when insurance markets are made less useful by the acquisition of information. The strict convexity of Ψ results in a welfare increase for B when information is acquired and used by B to improve his choice[5] of K. If the convexity of ψ outweighs the concavity of u_B in the sense that $u_B(\psi(\cdot))$ is strictly convex, then the gain from more appropriate production choices outweighs the loss from less effective insurance markets and information improves welfare in the sense that (12) exceeds (11).

From duality theory, we also know that--defining $\psi_i(\cdot)$ as the derivative of $\psi(\cdot)$ with respect to its i-th argument, $q(E, \pi)$ as the supply function and $K(E, \pi)$ as the demand function for input K--

$$\psi_1(E, \pi) = f(K(E, \pi)) = q(E, \pi)$$

$$-\psi_2(E, \pi) = K(E, \pi)$$

$$\psi_{11}(E, \pi) = q_1(E, \pi)$$

$$-\psi_{22}(E, \pi) = K_2(E, \pi)$$

$$-\psi_{21}(E, \pi) = K_1(E, \pi).$$

Since π is known with certainty, we can analyze the conditions under which information is valuable by simply differentiating $u_B(\Psi(E, \pi))$ twice with respect to E: the conditions under which information is valuable are the conditions under which $u_B(\Psi(E, \pi))$ is strictly convex with respect to E. The initial result of this differentiation is (13) where, for reasons of brevity and clarity, we do not write the arguments of Ψ,

$$(d^2/dE^2)[u_B(\psi)] = u_B''(\psi)\psi_1^2 + u_B'(\psi)\psi_{11}. \tag{13}$$

Equation (13) can be given a more useful expression as

$$(d^2/dE^2)[u_B(\psi)] = \xi\left[\frac{\psi_{11}E}{\psi_1} - R_R^{u_B}(\psi)\left(\frac{\psi_1 E}{\psi}\right)\right], \tag{14}$$

where $\xi = \dfrac{u_B'(\psi)\psi_1}{E} > 0$ and $R_R^{u_B}(\psi) = -\dfrac{u_B''(\psi)\psi}{u_B'(\psi)} > 0$. The term $R_R^{u_B}(\psi)$

---

[5]If K must be chosen <u>ex ante</u>, that is before r_L or r_N are known, then we are back to the first case without production. To generate a potentially beneficial information, it must be possible to adjust K afterwards.

is the Arrow-Pratt measure of the relative risk aversion of B evaluated at $\psi(E, \pi)$. It is the elasticity, computed at $\psi(E, \pi)$, of the marginal utility u'_B considered as a function of $\psi(E, \pi)$, and it measures the relative concavity of u_B at $\psi(E, \pi)$. Since $\psi_1 E/\psi$ is the E-elasticity of ψ, that is the elasticity of profits ψ with respect to the delivery value E, then the product $R_R^{u_B}(\psi)(\psi_1 E/\psi)$ which is positive, is the E-elasticity of $u'_B(\psi(E, \pi))$ as a function of E, and this term can be interpreted as a measure of the concavity of $u_B(\psi(E, \pi))$ with respect to E. The other term of (14) $\psi_{11}E/\psi_1$ is the E-elasticity of $\psi_1(E, \pi)$ and can be analogously interpreted as a measure of the convexity of ψ with respect to E.

Since ξ is positive, (14) can be interpreted as stating formally what we have already intuitively asserted to be the case, viz. that $u_B(\psi(\cdot))$ will be strictly concave (convex) if the concavity of u_B outweighs (is outweighed by) the convexity of ψ in the sense that u_B's concavity measure with respect to E, $R_R^{u_B}(\psi)(\psi_1 E/\psi)$, is larger (smaller) than ψ's convexity measure with respect to E, $\psi_{11}E/\psi_1$. Note that the concavity measure $R_R^{u_B}(\psi)(\psi_1 E/\psi)$ can be large for either of two reasons: because B is very risk averse in the sense that the relative risk aversion measure $R_R^{u_B}(\psi)$ is large, or alternatively because ψ is very responsive to E in the sense that the elasticity, $\psi_1 E/\psi$, of profits ψ with respect to price E, is large. Increases in either of these two terms can increase the welfare loss due to the fact that information reduces the effectiveness of insurance markets. On the other hand, the convexity measure $\Psi_{11}E/\Psi_1$ will be large when Ψ_1, the effect of E (which represents the expectation $E(\lambda|\mu)$) on maximum profits, is very responsive to variations in E; in other words, when the elasticity of the supply function $q(E, \pi)$ with respect to E is large.

It is useful to ask what conditions would make u_B more likely to be concave or convex in E. Consider (14) again. It can be rewritten as

$$(d^2/dE^2)[u_B(\psi)] = \xi \left[\frac{\psi_1 E}{\psi}\right]\left[\frac{\psi_{11}\psi}{\psi_1^2} - R_R^{u_B}(\psi)\right] \tag{15}$$

where $\xi \left[\frac{\psi_1 E}{\psi}\right] > 0$. From duality theory, we can rewrite the expression in the square brackets as $\left[\frac{\partial q}{\partial E}\ \psi/q(E, \pi)^2 - R_R^{u_B}(\psi)\right]$ or as $\left[\left(\frac{\psi}{I}\right)\eta - R_R^{u_B}(\psi)\right]$, where $I = q(E, \pi)E$ is the gross income or gross revenues of B, that is of the firm he controls, and η is the elasticity of the supply function $q(E, \pi)$ with respect to E, the delivery value of output. We can then rewrite (15) as follows:

$$(d^2/dE^2)[u_B(\psi)] = \xi \left[\frac{I}{\psi}\right]\left[\frac{\psi}{I}\eta - R_R^{u_B}(\psi)\right] . \qquad (16)$$

Therefore,

<u>Proposition 2A</u>: With production, the acquisition of information will be welfare increasing if the price elasticity of supply times the ratio of profits over gross revenues of the individual's firm is larger than the individual's relative risk aversion measured at the point of maximal profits.

Since by definition $R_R^{u_B}(\psi) = -\frac{u_B''(\psi)\psi}{u_B'(\psi)} = R_A^{u_B}(\psi)\psi$, where $R_A^{u_B}(\psi)$ is the Arrow-Pratt measure of absolute risk aversion evaluated at $\psi(E, \pi)$, (14) can be rewritten as

$$(d^2/dE^2)[u_B(\psi)] = \xi \left[\frac{\psi_{11}E}{\psi_1} - R_A^{u_B}(\psi)\psi_1 E\right] \qquad (14')$$

and (16) as

$$(d^2/dE^2)[u_B(\psi)] = \xi I \left[\frac{\eta}{I} - R_A^{u_B}(\psi)\right] . \qquad (16')$$

Therefore,

<u>Proposition 2B</u>: With production, the acquisition of information will be welfare increasing if the price elasticity of supply divided by the gross revenues of the individual's firm is larger than the individual's absolute risk aversion measured at the point of maximal profits.

To illustrate the above analysis, let us consider the following examples: $q = f(K) = K^\gamma$, $0 < \gamma < 1$, and $q = f(K) = AK - DK^2$, $0 < K < A/2D$. In the first case, one can easily get

$$q(E, \pi) = \left(\frac{\pi}{\gamma E}\right)^{-\frac{\gamma}{1-\gamma}}$$

$$K(E, \pi) = \left(\frac{\pi}{\gamma E}\right)^{-\frac{1}{1-\gamma}}$$

$$\eta = \frac{\gamma}{1-\gamma}$$

$$\frac{\psi}{I} = 1 - \gamma$$

Assuming that the individual's relative risk aversion measure is constant and equal to r--that is $u_B(\psi)$ is of the form ψ^{1-r}, $0 < r < 1$--then (16) becomes

$$(d^2/dE^2)[u_B(\psi)] = \xi\left(\frac{1}{1-\gamma}\right)[\gamma - r] \tag{17}$$

whose sign depends on the sign of $(\gamma - r)$.

Recall that γ is a measure of the concavity of the production function--γ being the elasticity of output with respect to K--in the sense that $-\frac{f''K}{f'} = 1 - \gamma$; but it is also a measure of the convexity of the profit function $\psi(E, \pi)$ with respect to E, since

$$\psi(E, \pi) = E\left(\frac{\pi}{\gamma E}\right)^{\frac{\gamma}{\gamma-1}} - \pi\left(\frac{\pi}{\gamma E}\right)^{\frac{1}{\gamma-1}} = E\left(\frac{E}{\pi}\right)^{\frac{\gamma}{1-\gamma}} \gamma^{\frac{1}{1-\gamma}} (\gamma^{\gamma} - 1)$$

and therefore $\frac{\psi_{11}E}{\psi_1} = \eta = \frac{\gamma}{1-\gamma}$. Since $\gamma \in (0,1)$, then the larger γ is, the less concave the production function is and the more convex the profit function is. Therefore,

<u>Proposition 3A</u>: Assuming that $f(K) = K^{\gamma}$, $0 < \gamma < 1$ and that the individual's relative risk aversion measure is constant, then the acquisition of information is more likely to be welfare increasing, the larger γ is.

Assuming on the other hand that the individual's absolute risk aversion measure is constant and equal to "a"--that is, $u_B(\psi)$ is of the form $-e^{-a\psi}$, $a > 0$--then (15) becomes

$$(d^2/dE^2)[u_B(\psi)] = \xi\left(\frac{1}{1-\gamma}\right)(\gamma - a\psi(\gamma)) \tag{18}$$

and (16')

$$(d^2/dE^2)[u_B(\psi)] = \xi I\left[\frac{\gamma}{1-\gamma}\,\gamma^{-\frac{\gamma}{1-\gamma}}\,E^{-\frac{1}{1-\gamma}}\,\pi^{\frac{\gamma}{1-\gamma}} - a\right] \tag{19}$$

whose sign depends on the sign of the expression in the square brackets. Therefore,

<u>Proposition 3B</u>: Assuming that $f(K) = K^{\gamma}$, $0 < \gamma < 1$ and that the individual's absolute risk aversion measure is constant, then the acquisition of information is more likely to be welfare increasing, the larger π is and/or the smaller E is.

Consider now the second example $q = f(K) = AK - DK^2$, $0 < K < A/2D$. One can get

$$q(E, \pi) = \frac{E^2A^2 - \pi^2}{4E^2D} = \frac{A^2 - \left(\frac{\pi}{E}\right)^2}{4D}$$

$$K(E, \pi) = \frac{EA - \pi}{2ED} = \frac{A - \left(\frac{\pi}{E}\right)}{2D}$$

$$\eta = \frac{2\pi^2}{E^2A^2 - \pi^2} = \frac{2\left(\frac{\pi}{E}\right)^2}{A^2 - \left(\frac{\pi}{E}\right)^2}$$

$$\frac{\psi}{I} = \frac{EA - \pi}{EA + \pi} = \frac{A - \left(\frac{\pi}{E}\right)}{A + \left(\frac{\pi}{E}\right)} .$$

Assuming that the individual's relative risk aversion measure is constant and equal to r, then (16) becomes

$$(d^2/dE^2)[u_B(\psi)] = \xi\left(\frac{I}{\psi}\right)\left[\frac{2\pi^2}{(EA + \pi)^2} - r\right] \tag{20}$$

whose sign depends on the sign of $\left[\frac{2\pi^2}{(EA + \pi)^2} - r\right]$, an expression which is homogenous of degree 0 in (E, π), decreasing with A and increasing with (π/E), that is increasing with π and decreasing with E. It is interesting to note that D plays no role in determining the sign of (20) although it does affect the concavity measure of the production function since

$$- \frac{f''K}{f'} = \frac{2DK}{A - 2DK}$$

an expression which decreases with A but increases with D: the larger D, the more concave the production function is at any $K < A/2D$. D is irrelevant to sign (20) because D has no effect on the convexity of the profit function ψ since

$$\frac{\psi_{11}E}{\psi_1} = \frac{2\pi^2}{E^2A^2 - \pi^2} = 2\,\frac{\left(\frac{\pi}{E}\right)^2}{A^2 - \left(\frac{\pi}{E}\right)^2}$$

an expression which is homogenous of degree 0 in (E, π), increases with (π/E) and decreases with A. Therefore,

<u>Proposition 4A</u>: Assuming that $f(K) = AK - DK^2$, $0 < K < A/2D$, and that the individual's relative risk aversion measure is constant, then the

acquisition of information is more likely to be welfare increasing, the larger π is, the smaller E is and/or the smaller A is.

Assuming on the other hand that the individual's absolute risk aversion measure is constant at "a", we can write the right hand side of (16′) as

$$\xi[I]\left[\frac{8D\pi^2E}{(E^2A^2-\pi^2)^2}-a\right] \tag{21}$$

The expression in the square brackets is positive if

$$\frac{8D\pi^2E}{(E^2A^2-\pi^2)^2}>a \tag{22}$$

and the left hand side of (22), say H(E), increases with D, decreases with A and increases with π, but may increase or decrease with E. It is discontinuous at $E=\frac{\pi}{A}$ and increasing without bounds when E approaches $\frac{\pi}{A}$ from either below or above. Therefore (21) will be satisfied for some interval (x, y) around $\frac{\pi}{A}$. Since E appears in the numerator, the subinterval above $\frac{\pi}{A}$ will be larger than the subinterval below $\frac{\pi}{A}$ as Figure 3 indicates.[6]

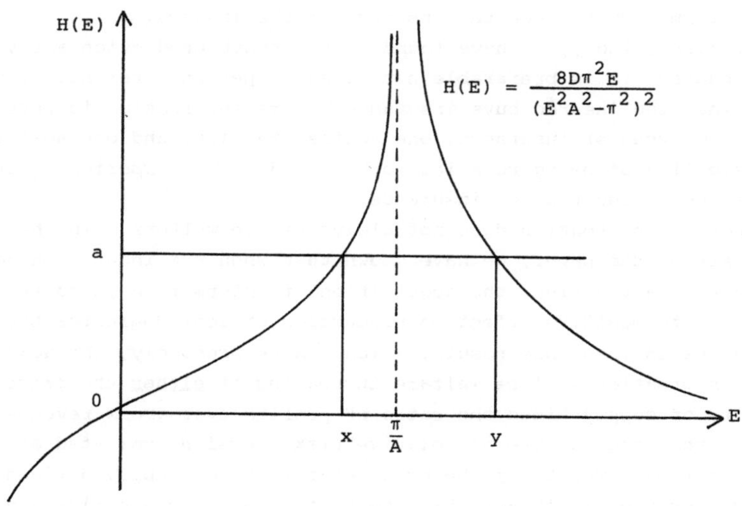

Figure 3

[6]The reader can easily check that $H(0)=0$, $H'(E)>0$ for $E<\pi/A$, $H'(E)<0$ for $E>\pi/A$ and that $H''(E)>0$ for $E>0$, $E\neq\pi/A$.

Therefore,

Proposition 4B: Assuming that $f(K) = AK - DK^2$, $0 < K < A/2D$ and that the individual's absolute risk aversion measure is constant, then the acquisition of information is more likely to be welfare increasing, the larger D is, the smaller A is, the larger π is and/or the closer E is to $\frac{\pi}{A}$.

It is interesting to note that f(K) is more concave at any given K, the larger D is and/or the smaller A is (but not vice-versa). But recall that with a quadratic production function, the convexity measure of the profit function, $\frac{\psi_{11}E}{\psi_1}$, is independent of D although it decreases with A. However, the larger D is, the smaller $\psi_1 E$ is and therefore the greater the convexity (or the smaller the concavity) measure of $u_B(\psi(E, \pi))$ with respect to E is, as one can see in (14').

Conclusion

In the first part of this paper, we have investigated the practice of experience rating by insurance companies in the presence of symmetric information between the insurer and the insured.

Not surprisingly, we have found that without production activities by the insured, it is preferable not to use experience rating. Intuitively, when the insured buys insurance before information is revealed, he buys two types of insurance, one against the loss and one against the possibility of being revealed to be a bad risk. Experience rating destroys the second type of insurance.

However, information does not always reduce welfare. In the second part of the paper, we have shown that when the insured engages in production activities, the acquisition of information increases welfare if its positive effect on production choices dominates the negative one on insurance possibilities. More precisely, the acquisition of information will be welfare increasing if either the price elasticity of supply times the ratio of profits over gross revenues is larger than the measure of relative risk aversion evaluated at the point of maximal profits or the price elasticity of supply divided by the gross revenues is larger than the measure of absolute risk aversion evaluated at the point of maximal profits.

We have also shown that with a Cobb-Douglass technology and constant relative risk aversion, the individual is more likely to acquire the information, the less concave his production function is. With constant absolute risk aversion, the individual is more likely to acquire the information, the larger the cost of capital (adjustable input) is and/or the smaller the delivery value (price) of output is. Note in the latter case that a more concave production function does not necessarily imply a preference for acquiring the information.

With a quadratic technology and constant relative risk aversion, the individual is more likely to acquire the information the larger the cost of capital is, the smaller the delivery value of output is and/or the smaller the intercept value (A) of the marginal product of capital function is. Note that a smaller A implies a more concave production function (but not vice-versa). With constant absolute risk aversion, the individual is more likely to acquire the information, the steeper the marginal production of capital function is, the smaller the intercept value of that function is, the larger the cost of capital is and/or the closer the delivery of output is to the ratio of the cost of capital over the intercept value of the marginal product of capital function.

References

Briys, E. and L. Eeckhoudt, "Relative Risk Aversion in Comparative Statics: Comment," American Economic Review 75 (March, 1985): 284-286.

Cooper, R., "Insurance, Flexibility and Non-Contingent Trades," Cowles Foundation Discussion Paper, No. 691, 1984.

Dionne, G., "Adverse Selection and Repeated Insurance Contracts," Geneva Papers on Risk and Insurance 8 (October, 1983): 316-333.

Hirshleifer, J., "The Private and Social Value of Information and the Reward to Inventive Activity," American Economic Review 61 (September, 1971): 561-575.

Katz, E., "Relative Risk Aversion in Comparative Statics," American Economic Review 73 (June, 1983): 452-454.

Lambert, R.A., "Long-term Contracts and Moral Hazard," Bell Journal of Economics 14 (Autumn, 1983): 441-453.

Palfrey, T.R. and C.S. Spatt, "Repeated Insurance Contracts and Learning," Rand Journal of Economics 16 (Autumn, 1985): 356-367.

Radner, R., "Monitoring Cooperative Agreements in a Repeated Principal Agent Relationship," Econometrica 49 (September 1981): 1127-1148.

________, "Repeated Principal-Agent Games with Discounting," Econometrica 53 (September, 1985): 1173-1199.

Rogerson, W.P., "Repeated Moral Hazard," Econometrica 53 (January, 1985): 69-77.

Rubinstein, A. and M.E. Yaari, "Repeated Insurance Contracts and Moral Hazard," Journal of Economic Theory 30 (June, 1983): 74-97.

Townsend, R.M., "Optimal Multiperiod Contracts and the Gain from Enduring Relationships Under Private Information," Journal of Political Economy 90 (December 1982): 1166-1187.

VERTICAL TRANSACTIONS UNDER UNCERTAINTY

J. Horen and S.Y. Wu*
U.S. Sprint Communications and
The University of Iowa

1. Introduction

Transactions between entities engaging in successive stages of production often take place outside the spot market. Some producers employ forward contracts to tie down price or quantity; others rely on some form of principal-agent arrangement; still others enter into joint stock ownership or even integrate vertically, thus, placing decision making in the hands of a single authority. These arrangements represent, in varying degrees, the producers' attempts to bypass the market. In a market-oriented economy, such practices require careful explanation. The purpose of this paper is to study how market uncertainties motivate these arrangements and to explain why one of these arrangements or a combination of them is chosen under a given set of market conditions.

The concern over vertical transactions is by no means new. Before proceeding, it is useful to summarize the relevant literature[1] and to establish our point of departure.

Literature Review

The bulk of this literature investigates vertical transactions under the conditions of certainty. A characteristic feature of decision under certainty is that the decision maker can make all of his decisions at once. He either uses the market fully or bypasses it altogether; there does not exist a midground. In a vertical exchange context, the producer's choice is strictly between spot exchange and vertical integration; contractual and agency arrangements are irrelevant under certainty because under certainty they yield the same result as the spot market case; partial integration is also irrelevant because the return from it is a linear combination of the returns from the first two cases and is, therefore, necessarily inferior to one of

*The authors wish to thank Professors David Baron, Roger Sherman and Charles Holt for their helpful comments on an early draft of this paper.

[1]For a detailed survey of this literature, see Kaserman (1978).

them. This being the case, the major concern in the literature naturally has been over the issues of vertical integration.

There are two motives attributed to vertical integration under certainty. The first is based upon the technical interdependence between stages of production. Vertical integration enables the producers in question to benefit from these technical economies. The second motive stems from the attempt to deal with monopoly power in the market place. Some writers stress that firms vertically integrate in order to amass and exert monopoly power (Burstein, 1960; Peltzman, 1969; Perry, 1978). Others claim that the firms will vertically integrate in order to circumvent the excessive monopoly power wielded by a trading partner (Wu, 1964; Klein, Crawford, and Alchian, 1978). Still others (Vernon and Graham, 1971; Warren-Boulton, 1974; Schmalensee, 1973) stress the point that if substitution among inputs in producing the final good is possible, then forward integration by the input monopolist will correct input distortion caused by monopoly pricing and, therefore, increase his profit.

The tradition of considering vertical integration as the only alternative to the spot market lingers even when uncertainty is brought into the picture. Here the presence of uncertainty offers another motive for firms to integrate vertically. Coase (1937) argues that market uncertainty inflicts a transaction cost on those who use the market. Coordination by authority for production will take place whenever the transaction cost under market coordination is less economical than internal coordination. Williamson (1971) invokes this argument to explain vertical integration. He states (p. 112) that:

> ... the substitution of internal organization for market exchange is attractive ... because what may be referred to broadly as 'transaction failures' in the operation of markets for intermediate goods.

Only recently has Carlton (1979) pointed out that uncertainty and transaction cost will also induce firms to use forward contracts to sell their products.

Points of Departure

Our treatment of vertical transactions follows the line taken by Blair and Kaserman (1978) treating vertical integration as a result of the firm's selection of its portfolio of activities. This paper differs from the existing literature in two major aspects. The first is related to the scope of the analysis and the second to the determinants of the vertical structure. These departures from the tradition are based upon the observation that under an uncertain market environment, where events unfold over time, the decision maker can no longer make all of his decisions at once. Because the timing of the sequentially received information is relevant to decision making, decisions of various types, e.g. production, sales, and pricing decisions, typically must also be made sequentially. The relationship between the time pattern of decision making and that of information revelation is by no means fixed; in fact, gains can be made by realigning the former against the latter. Two implications follow: First, realigning the two time patterns requires the support of an appropriate institutional arrangement. One alignment can be supported by the spot market, another by a contractual arrangement, and still a third, by vertical integration. Second, different alignments utilize the market to different degrees. Spot exchange utilizes the market fully, vertical integration bypasses the intermediate good market altogether, and contractual arrangements can be designed to bypass the intermediate good market in any degree that the contractual parties desire. For example, near one end of the spectrum, a buyer and a seller may contract on price and/or quantity and thus bypass the spot market. This arrangement, however, does not allow them to bypass the intermediate good market altogether because the market still determines the contractual price and/or quantity of the intermediate good. Towards the other end of the spectrum, firms may find it optimal to arrange something less than full integration. Partial vertical integration and the principal-agent arrangement (another contractual arrangement) are examples.

It is now evident that the scope of the producers' decision problem in the present context is broader than that discussed in the traditional literature which presents choices either between spot exchange and vertical integration or between spot exchange and contractual arrangement. In this paper, we include in the choice set not only the pure cases--spot exchange, contractual arrangement, and vertical integration--but also convex combinations of them.

Risk aversion and transactions cost are commonly recognized as uncertainty-related determinants of vertical exchange structure. In this paper, we also explore a third determinant, referred to as uncertainty management. When uncertainties are unveiled in stages, based upon the observation made above, we see that realigning the time pattern of decision making against that of information revelation will affect both the time at which a specific decision is made and the amount of information available in making this decision. The choice of the alignment between the two time patterns, therefore, affects the uncertainties faced by each of the trading partners and hence, their respective decision problem. The entrepreneur, in attempting to manage uncertainties, will base upon his risk attitude and opt for that alignment which is the most desirable. Because the alignment of the two time patterns and the vertical exchange structure are related, a vertical structure thus emerges as a consequence of the firm's attempt to select an optimal time pattern for making production, sales, and pricing decisions. This structure emerges despite the absence of transaction cost considerations.

Besides the introduction, this paper contains four additional sections. Section 2 presents the firms' decision problem corresponding to each exchange mode; its purpose is to study the relationship between a mode of exchange and its associated time pattern of decision making and to show how, in each case, the market uncertainty is distributed between the trading partners. On the basis of this analysis, we examine in section 3 the factors which determine a particular mode of exchange and the welfare implications of these outcomes. Since the selection of a single mode of exchange is, in general, not optimal from the viewpoint of the intermediate-good producer, we present in section 4 the optimal vertical structure with a combination of several modes of exchange, and discuss the implications of the results. Finally, in section 5, we make some concluding remarks.

2. Basic Models

The main objective of this section is to study how the vertical exchange arrangement affects the timing of final good producers' decisions and how this, in turn, affects the information available to and the uncertainties faced by each of the trading partners. This objective can best be accomplished by presenting models for the producer's decision problem associated with the three pure exchange modes: trading in the spot market, contracting both price and quantity in advance of production, and vertically combining.[2] The last arrangement includes partial vertical integration via either stock or asset acquisition.[3]

Some Simplifying Assumptions

Since the purpose of this paper is to investigate how uncertainties affect the choice of the vertical exchange mode, we need to purge from our analyses other structural determinants; that is, we need to

---

[2]Because the type of uncertainties involved do not include information asymmetry between the X- and Y-producers, there is no incentive for adopting the principal/agent type of arrangement.

[3]Under the simplifying assumptions adopted in this paper, the results derived from stock and asset acquisitions are identical.

select an analytical framework for which under certainty there would exist no incentive for the market participants to abandon the spot market. Our framework involves a final good Y which is produced competitively by firms using a fixed-coefficient production technology and an intermediate good X which is produced by a monopolist. It is well known that such a market structure satisfies the desired requirement (Vernon and Graham, 1971).

We assume that both the demand for Y and the cost of producing X are stochastic, that there exists a one-period production lag for all producers, and that all producers are risk averse. In order to keep the analyses tractable, we assume a very simple uncertainty structure. The market demand function for Y involves two random parameters, ϵ_1 and ϵ_2, revealed in successive periods. This assumption is intended to reflect the phenomenon that the producers gain knowledge about the market demand for Y with a mere passage of time. Regarding uncertainty in supply, we assume that any quantity of X can be produced, but the cost function contains a random parameter δ.

Based upon the assumed nature of the demand and cost uncertainties and the one-period production lag, there exists in the simplest setting three decision points referred to as periods 1, 2, and 3; δ and ϵ_1 are revealed in period 2 and ϵ_2 in period 3. The final-good producers may make their production decisions either in period 1 or in period 2. The intermediate-good producer, however, must make his production decision in period 1. Figure 1 depicts this sequence. The three modes of exchange to be examined in this paper represent all possible pure vertical structures under this simple market setting.

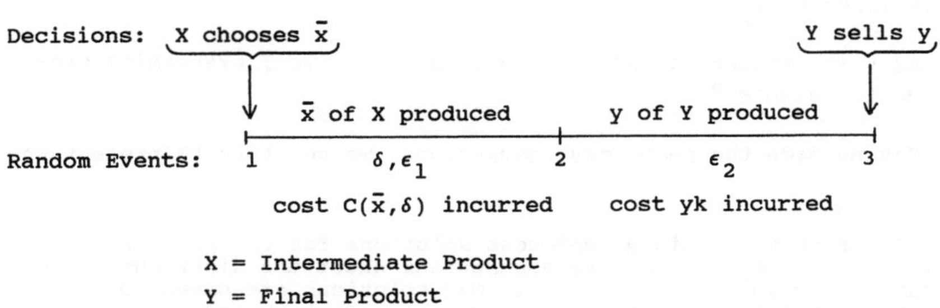

Figure 1. Vertical Transactions Scenario

In order to facilitate the computation and to obtain meaningful comparisons among results derived from the three vertical exchange regimes, we invoke two sets of simplifying assumptions:

<u>A1</u>. The demand function for the final good and the cost function for the intermediate good are, respectively, linear and quadratic with respect to quantity; and every agent's utility function exhibits the property of constant risk aversion. Specifically, we assume:

(i) The Final-Product Inverse Market Demand function:

$$G(y,\epsilon_1 + \epsilon_2) = \frac{y - a}{b} + \epsilon_1 + \epsilon_2$$

(ii) The intermediate good cost function: $C(x,\delta) = \frac{1}{2} cx^2 + \delta x$

(iii) The X-Producer's utility function: $U(\tilde{\pi}_x) = 1 - e^{-\alpha\tilde{\pi}_x}$

(iv) The Y-Producer's utility function: $V(\tilde{\pi}_y) = 1 - e^{-\beta\tilde{\pi}_y}$

where a, c, α, $\beta > 0$, $b < 0$. The X- and Y-producers' coefficients of risk aversion are denoted, respectively, by α and β and their profits, respectively, by $\tilde{\pi}_x$ and $\tilde{\pi}_y$. We assume that α is constant. The β is uniform for all Y-producers but is seen by X as random with mean $\bar{\beta}$ and variance σ_β^2. In addition, we assume that ϵ_1, ϵ_2 and δ are normally distributed with mean 0 and variance σ_1^2, σ_2^2 and σ_δ^2 respectively; ϵ_1 and ϵ_2 are mutually independent and β is independent of all other random variables.[4] Correlations are denoted by $\rho_1 = \text{corr}(\delta,\epsilon_1)$ and $\rho_2 = \text{corr}(\delta,\epsilon_2)$. We also assume that ϵ_2 can be written as $\epsilon_2 = E(\epsilon_2|\delta) + \eta = \bar{\epsilon}_2 + \eta$, where $E(\eta) = 0$, $\text{Var}(\eta) = \bar{\sigma}_2^2$, and η is independent of ϵ_1, $\bar{\epsilon}_2$ and δ. Thus, the knowledge of δ affects the mean but not the variance of ϵ_2.

<u>A2</u>. The sellers do not withhold outputs; i.e., everything produced is sold.[5]

Having made the necessary assumptions, we now turn to present the

---

[4]In order to obtain unambiguous solutions for the problems which are to follow, we need to make assumptions about the distributions of the random variables ϵ_1, ϵ_2 and δ. Our solutions are based upon the assumption that these variables are normally distributed. The same set of solutions can also be obtained by not making any assumptions about the distribution but instead assuming that the risks involved are small.

[5]This assumption enables us to circumvent computational difficulties associated with boundary conditions. For the cases which permit withholding, see Horen and Wu (1982). Generally, we found that relaxing A2 gives the X-producer more flexibility in exercising his monopoly power.

models which describe the three exchange modes. Before doing so, however, it is useful to state a mathematical lemma, proven in the appendix, which we shall apply later.

Lemma: If profit derived from Z is a random value of the form $\tilde{\pi} = CZ^2 + DZ + \tilde{\theta}Z$ where $\tilde{\theta}: N(0,\sigma^2)$ and the utility of profit is $W(\tilde{\pi}) = 1 - e^{-\gamma\tilde{\pi}}$, then the risk premium is given by

$$B(Z) = \frac{1}{2}\gamma Z^2\sigma^2$$

and the optimal Z satisfies

$$\frac{dB}{dZ} = \frac{d\bar{\pi}}{dZ}$$

that is, $\gamma\sigma^2 Z = 2CZ + D$.

Models Under Spot Market Arrangement

A spot market is characterized by the phenomenon that buyers take delivery of the commodity at the conclusion of an exchange. Based upon a one-period production lag, we summarize the sequence of market activities as follows: In period 1, the intermediate-good producer makes his production decision on the basis of his expectations about his demand and cost. In period 2, X is produced and the cost of producing it becomes known. Buyers of X also arrive at the market. On the basis of their expectations of the demand for Y, the Y producers reveal their demand for X. The price of X is now determined in the spot market. Simultaneously, the production decision for Y is also made. In period 3, Y is produced and its demand becomes known. This determines the price of Y. This market scenario serves as the basis for the following producers' decision problems:

Y-Producers' Decision Problem: Under this market scenario, the Y-producers must make their production decisions in period 2. Since the market demand for the final good is not known in period 2, in order to purchase X in the spot market, the Y-producers must base their demand for X on their expectations of the demand for their own product. Given these expectations, a risk-averse final-good producer will choose an amount of X which

$$\max_{x,y} \underset{<\epsilon_2>}{E} V(\tilde{p}y - wx - ky) \qquad (2.1a)$$

$$\text{s.t. } y = x \text{ and } x \geqq 0,$$

where V is the final-good producer's utility function, $\tilde{p} = G(y,\epsilon_1^o + \epsilon_2)$ the market price for the final product as seen in period

2, w the price of the intermediate product X, and k the marginal (average) cost associated with other cooperative factors. The notation "~" symbolizes that the variable in question is random in nature and the symbol "o" denotes the realized value of the random variable to which it is affixed. Note that this formulation is based upon the assumption that the commodity Y is competitively produced using a fixed-coefficient production technology. Without loss of generality, we assume that input-output ratio is 1, i.e., y = x. We also assume that $\frac{a}{b} + k < 0$, meaning that the highest possible expected price of Y (when y = 0) exceeds the marginal cost of producing Y.

We postulate that $V(\tilde{\pi}_y) = 1 - e^{-\beta\tilde{\pi}_y}$ and the Y-producers always know their common absolute risk aversion coefficient β. In the spot market case the X-producer, however, does not have this information until he deals with Y in period 2. Thus, the X-producer must view $\tilde{\beta}$ as a random variable in period 1.

Applying the Lemma to (2.1a) and substituting x, β, $(\tilde{p}y - wx - ky)$ and V for Z, γ, $\tilde{\pi}$ and W respectively, we obtain the Y-producer's risk premium as $B(x) = \frac{1}{2}\beta x^2\bar{\sigma}_2^2$ and his demand function for X as

$$w = \frac{x-a}{b} + \epsilon_1^o + \bar{\epsilon}_2 - k - \beta x\bar{\sigma}_2^2. \tag{2.2a}$$

In this derivation we treat the y in the market demand function $\tilde{p} = G(y, \epsilon_1^o + \epsilon_2)$ as a constant since the individual Y-producer cannot affect the total market quantity.

From (2.2a) we see that Y's expected utility of profit is maximized at where the input price w is equal to the Y producer's expected profit $\left(\frac{x-a}{b} + \epsilon_1^o + \bar{\epsilon}_2 - k\right)$ minus his marginal risk premium $(\beta x\bar{\sigma}_2^2)$. Since all final-good producers are assumed to be identical, the market demand function for X becomes

$$D(x, \tilde{\beta}, \epsilon_1) = \frac{x-a}{b} + \epsilon_1 + \bar{\epsilon}_2 - k - \tilde{\beta}x\bar{\sigma}_2^2. \tag{2.3a}$$

X-Producer's Decision Problem: Since we are assuming that X cannot be withheld, there is no need for the X-producer to make any decision in Period 2; he does, however, make the production decision in Period 1. At this time, the X-producer knows neither his cost nor his demand and must formulate expectations about both. The demand forecast for the intermediate-good producer is considerably more involved than the comparable problem for the final-good producers; it involves not only a forecast of the demand for the final product but also the final-good producer's utility function.

Based upon this expected demand function, the risk averse intermediate-good producer will select an output level which

$$\max_{x} \; \underset{<\tilde{\beta},\delta,\epsilon_1>}{E} \; U(\tilde{\pi}_x) \tag{2.4a}$$

s.t. $\tilde{\pi}_x = xD(x,\tilde{\beta},\epsilon_1) - C(x,\delta)$, (2.3a), and $x \geqq 0$.

Again, applying the Lemma to (2.4a) with x, α, $\tilde{\pi}_x$ and U for Z, γ, $\tilde{\pi}$, and W respectively, yields $B(x) = \frac{1}{2}\,\alpha x^2 \mathrm{var}(\epsilon_1 + \bar{\epsilon}_2 - \tilde{\beta}x\sigma_2^2 - \delta)$ and

$$\frac{2x-a}{b} - k - 2\bar{\beta}x\bar{\sigma}_2^2 = cx + \alpha x[\mathrm{Var}(\epsilon_1+\bar{\epsilon}_2-\delta) + 2x^2\bar{\sigma}_2^4\sigma_\beta^2] \tag{2.5a}$$

Thus, the X-producer's expected utility of profit is maximized when the expected marginal revenue $\left(\frac{2x-a}{b} - k - 2\bar{\beta}x\bar{\sigma}_2^2\right)$ equals the expected marginal cost cx plus X's marginal risk premium as seen in period 1. Finally, let x_s denote the quantity of X produced under the spot market regime; then from (2.5a), x_s satisfies

$$x_s = \frac{\frac{a}{b} + k \quad + (2\alpha\bar{\sigma}_2^4\sigma_\beta^2)(x_s)^3}{\{\frac{2}{b} - c - \alpha\,\mathrm{Var}(\epsilon_1+\bar{\epsilon}_2-\delta) - 2\bar{\beta}\bar{\sigma}_2^2\}} \;. \tag{2.6a}$$

From (2.6a) we see that the spot production x_s decreases as the coefficients of risk aversity α and $\bar{\beta}$ and the marginal production cost k increase. This result is intuitive.

Under the spot market regime the production policies for X and Y are determined sequentially. Equation (2.6a) determines the optimal quantity of X produced in period 1 as well as the quantity of Y to be produced in period 3. Upon the realization of β and ϵ_1, equation (2.3a) determines the price of X in period 2. The price of Y is determined by the market demand function for Y after the realization of ϵ_2 in period 3. Under the spot-market arrangement, the profit is determined in period 2 for the intermediate-good producer and in period 3 for the final-good producer.

<u>Models Under Contractual Arrangement</u>

Under the contractual regime, we assume that the final-good producers must negotiate in period 1 a contract with the intermediate-good producer regarding the price and the quantity to be exchanged in period 2. Since neither the demand for the final product nor the cost of producing the intermediate product are known at this time, these decisions must be made on the basis of the traders' expectations about them. According to the assumption A2 neither producer can withhold X or Y from the market in periods 2 and 3. The problems for both producers, thus, are reduced to determining in period 1 the price of X and the quantities of X and Y to be produced and exchanged. No decisions are required in period 2. In period 3, Y is produced and its demand revealed. This determines the price of Y.

The change in the decision time for the Y-producer not only affects his own decision problem but also drastically simplifies the problem for the intermediate-good producer.

Y-Producer's Problem: Under the contractual regime, since the Y-producer must make his production decision in period 1, he needs to forecast the final good demand in period 1 instead of in period 2. This clearly complicates his decision problem as compared to the spot market case. His problem now becomes

$$\max_{y, x_c} \; \underset{<\epsilon_1, \epsilon_2>}{E} \; \tilde{V}(\tilde{p}y - w_c x_c - ky) \tag{2.1b}$$

$$\text{s.t. } y = x_c$$

Note that the Y-producer, as compared to the previous case, now bears the demand uncertainty ϵ_1 in addition to ϵ_2. As in the previous case, both the individual and the market demand function for X can be obtained by applying the Lemma to (2.1b). The derived market demand for X, now seen as in period 1, becomes,

$$D_c(x) = \frac{x-a}{b} - k - \beta x \sigma^2 \quad \text{where} \quad \sigma^2 = \text{Var}(\epsilon_1 + \epsilon_2) = \sigma_1^2 + \sigma_2^2. \tag{2.3b}$$

X-Producer's Problem: The change in the Y-producer's decision time has also affected the X-producer's problem in a fundamental way. In negotiating a contract for X, the Y-producers must reveal their demand for X, represented by (2.3b), to the X-producer. This revelation eliminates the X-producer's burden of forecasting the demand for his own product and greatly simplifies his decision problem. Because (2.3b) involves no random elements, the X-producer's problem now involves only one stochastic element, δ; it becomes

$$\max_{x} \; \underset{<\delta>}{E} \; U(\tilde{\pi}_x) \tag{2.4b}$$

$$\text{s.t. } \tilde{\pi}_x = xD_c(x) - C(x,\delta), \quad (2.3b), \quad \text{and } x \geqq 0.$$

Again by applying the Lemma to (2.4b), we obtain

$$\frac{2x-a}{b} - k - 2\beta x \sigma^2 = cx + \alpha x \sigma_\delta^2, \tag{2.5b}$$

which states that the X-producer's expected utility of profit is maximized when the marginal revenue derived from X is equal to the marginal cost of producing X plus X's marginal risk premium. Note that the marginal revenue for X in period 1 is not seen as random as it was for the spot market case.

Now, let x_c denote the quantity of X produced under the contractual-exchange regime. From (2.5b) we can write the solution to (2.4b) as

$$x_c = \frac{\frac{a}{b} + k}{\frac{2}{b} - c - \alpha\sigma_\delta^2 - 2\beta\sigma^2} . \tag{2.6b}$$

Under the contractual exchange regime all non-trivial decisions are made in period 1. Equations (2.3b) and (2.6b) together determine, in period 1, the terms of the contract, i.e., the quantity x_c and price w_c of the intermediate good to be produced and delivered. Moving forward in time, we see that in period 2, x_c is produced and delivered; δ is revealed to the X-producer and thus determines his cost and profit. In period 3, the final good Y is produced. The revelation of ϵ_1 in period 2 and ϵ_2 in period 3 determines the final demand for Y and, hence, the price and the profit for the final-good producer.

Models Under Vertical Integration

When the intermediate-good producer integrates forward into the final-good stage of production, the integrated firm will act as a monopolist in the final-good market. The integrated firm must make its decision on the production of X in period 1. Because we assume that the producer does not withhold or discard any output, all X produced is employed in the production of Y. Thus, the production decision on Y is also trivially made in period 1. Since all production decisions are made at a time when the cost of X and the demand for Y are not known, the firm must do so on the basis of some expectations about ϵ_1, ϵ_2 and δ. This decision problem is simpler than the ones for the spot and contractual markets; the entrepreneur, in making the production decision on X, no longer needs to estimate the final-good producer's utility function as the function is now his own. The integrated firm now seeks to

$$\max_{x,y} \underset{\langle\delta,\epsilon_1,\epsilon_2\rangle}{E} U[y\tilde{G}(y,\epsilon_1 + \epsilon_2) - yk - C(x,\delta)], \tag{2.4c}$$

$$\text{s.t. } y = x, \text{ and } x \geqq 0.$$

Here, in contrast to the previous case, X bears all of the uncertainties ϵ_1, ϵ_2 and δ.

By applying the Lemma to (2.4c) and using $\mathrm{Var}(\epsilon_1 + \epsilon_2 - \delta) = \sigma^2 + \sigma_\delta^2 - 2\rho\sigma\sigma_\delta$, we obtain

$$\frac{2x-a}{b} - k = cx + \alpha x(\sigma^2 + \sigma_\delta^2 - 2\rho\sigma\sigma_\delta), \tag{2.5c}$$

where $\rho = \text{corr}(\delta_1, \epsilon_1 + \epsilon_2) = \rho_1\sigma_1\sigma_\delta + \rho_2\sigma_2\sigma_\delta$. Let x_I be the optimal quantity of X produced in period 1 under vertical integration, from (2.5c), we obtain the solution to (2.4c) as

$$x_I = \frac{\frac{a}{b} + k}{\frac{2}{b} - c - \alpha[\sigma^2 + \sigma_\delta^2 - 2\rho\sigma\sigma_\delta]} \quad . \tag{2.6c}$$

Moving forward in time, the cost of producing X is determined in period 2 after the revelation of δ. The price of the final product as well as the integrated producer's profit is determined in period 3 after the revelation of ϵ_1 in period 2 and ϵ_2 in period 3. In this problem there is no longer a need to determine the price of the intermediate product.

<u>Summary</u>

In this section, we have presented a set of models which describe the firms' decision problems under the various vertical exchange modes, and have established the proposition that: The vertical exchange mode affects the firms' decision time and the uncertainties faced by each of them; this, in turn, affects the producers' decision problems. In order to facilitate future reference, the uncertainties that X and Y face under the three modes of exchange are listed in Table 1.

TABLE 1

SUMMARY OF UNCERTAINTIES FACED BY X AND Y PRODUCERS

Mode of Exchange	Producer	
	X	Y
Spot	$\delta, \epsilon_1, \tilde{\beta}$	ϵ_2
Contract	δ	ϵ_1, ϵ_2
Vertical Integration	$\delta, \epsilon_1, \epsilon_2$	None

3. Selection of Vertical Structure

Because uncertainties faced by the producers differ under the various arrangements, the entrepreneur can choose an appropriate exchange arrangement and thereby change the market uncertainties. The relevant determinants of his choice are the nature and the degree of uncertainties existing in the market place, i.e., ϵ_1, ϵ_2, δ, σ_1, σ_2,

ρ_1 and ρ_2, and the risk attitudes of the decision makers, α and β.

In this section we state the conditions for pairwise comparison of the three exchange modes. We then examine two of the comparisons in detail.

Comparison Results

Under the simplifying assumptions A1 and A2, the necessary and sufficient conditions for the X-producer to choose one exchange arrangement over another can be derived from (2.6a), (2.6b), and (2.6c). They are summarized by the following theorems.[6]

Theorem 1: $$\left\{\begin{matrix} x_I > x_c \\ EU(\tilde{\pi}_x^I) > E(\tilde{\pi}_x^C) \end{matrix}\right\} \quad \text{iff } \frac{\beta}{\alpha} > \frac{1}{2} - \rho\,\frac{\sigma_\delta}{\sigma}\,.$$

Theorem 2: $$\left\{\begin{matrix} x_c > x_s \\ EU(\tilde{\pi}_x^C) > EU(\tilde{\pi}_x^S) \end{matrix}\right\} \quad \text{iff } \frac{\bar{\beta}}{\alpha} < \frac{1}{2} - \frac{\rho\sigma\sigma_\delta}{\sigma^2 - \bar{\sigma}_2^2} + (x_s)^3\sigma_\beta^2\,\frac{\bar{\sigma}_2^4\left(\frac{2}{b} - c - \alpha\sigma_\delta^2 - \bar{\beta}\sigma^2\right)}{\left(\frac{a}{b} + k\right)(\sigma^2 - \bar{\sigma}_2^2)}\,.$$

Theorem 3: $$\left\{\begin{matrix} x_I > x_s \\ EU(\tilde{\pi}_x^I) > EU(\tilde{\pi}_x^S) \end{matrix}\right\} \quad \text{iff } \frac{\bar{\beta}}{\alpha} > \frac{1}{2} - (x_s)^3\sigma_\beta^2\,\frac{\bar{\sigma}_2^2\left[\frac{2}{b} - c - \alpha\,\mathrm{Var}(\epsilon-\delta)\right]}{\frac{a}{b} + k}\,.$$

Likewise, the necessary and sufficient conditions for the Y-producer to choose one exchange arrangement over another is summarized by the following theorem:

Theorem 4: $$\{EV(\tilde{\pi}_y^C) > EV(\tilde{\pi}_y^S)\} \quad \text{iff } \frac{\beta}{a} < \frac{1}{2} - \frac{\rho\sigma\sigma_\delta}{\bar{\sigma}_2(\sigma - \bar{\sigma}_2)} + \frac{\sigma}{2\bar{\sigma}_2} + \frac{\alpha\sigma^2 + c - \frac{2}{b}}{2\alpha\sigma\bar{\sigma}_2}\,.$$

---

[6]The comparison conditions for the x's follow directly from (2.6a), (2.6b) and (2.6c). The comparison conditions for the EU's follow the fact that the equivalent profit for any exchange arrangement, given by $E(\tilde{\pi}_x) - B(x)$, can be shown to be an upside-down quadratic function of x going through the origin. Therefore, if one arrangement has a greater value of x at the mid-point of the inverted parabola (which is the optimal production) than that of another arrangement, the mid-point is also higher. This means that the equivalent profit and,therefore, the EU, is also higher.

In the rest of this section we make clear the implications of these theorems and state the conditions under which a choice of a mode of exchange is pareto superior. For brevity we limit the comparison to spot vs. contractual exchange and contractual exchange vs. vertical integration.

Spot vs. Contractual Exchange

Inspecting the conditions of Theorem 2, and noting the negativity of b and $\frac{a}{b} + k$, we find that, when σ_β^2 is sufficiently large, unless the equilibrium quantity x_s is very small, the inequalities in this theorem will always be satisfied. Since a small x_s is in itself undesirable, we may conclude that the producers will under this circumstance most likely not prefer the spot market arrangement.

The X-producer dislikes the spot market when σ_β^2 is large because he faces enormous amounts of uncertainties in that market, i.e., he must not only face the uncertainties represented by ϵ_1, and δ, but also that represented by $\tilde{\beta}$. Although the Y-producer faces less uncertainty in the spot market than under the contractual arrangement, his certainty-equivalent profit may be higher under the latter regime. A reduction in uncertainties to the X-producer caused by a switch from the spot market to the contractual arrangement may induce him to produce and sell a larger quantity to the Y-producer at a sufficiently lower price. All considered, we see that if $\sigma_\beta^2 >> 0$, then the spot market arrangement is unlikely to be chosen as a mode of exchange.

The choice between the spot and the contractual mode of exchange ceases to be one-sided if the Y-producer's utility function is known in Period 1, i.e., $\tilde{\beta} = \bar{\beta}$ and $\sigma_\beta^2 = 0$. The contractual exchange is preferred to the spot exchange if and only if

$$\frac{\beta}{\alpha} < \left(\frac{1}{2} - \rho \, \frac{\sigma \sigma_\delta}{\sigma^2 - \bar{\sigma}_2^2} \right) = \rho' \, \frac{\sigma_\delta}{\sqrt{\sigma^2 - \bar{\sigma}_2^2}} \, ,$$

where

$$\rho' \equiv \text{Corr}\,(\epsilon_1 + \bar{\epsilon}_2, \delta) = \frac{\rho \, \sigma}{\sqrt{\sigma^2 - \bar{\sigma}_2^2}} \, .$$

Let $(\sigma^2 - \bar{\sigma}_2^2)$ be interpreted as the variance in market demand as perperceived in period 1. Then this condition is analogous to that for the choice between the vertical integration and the contractual exchange given in Theorem 1. We defer our discussion about it to the next section. Here it is opportune to raise the question whether the realized mode of exchange is pareto superior among the possible choices, given that X is a monopolist.

Comparing Theorems 2 and 4, it can be shown with simple algebraic manipulation that when $\sigma_{\beta}^{2} = 0$, the X-producer's preference for the contractual mode of exchange is sufficient to guarantee that the Y-producers will prefer the same. The converse is, however, not true. Suppose that $\rho > 0$. There may exist a σ_{δ} sufficiently large which causes $\frac{\bar{\beta}}{\alpha} > \left(\frac{1}{2} - \rho \frac{\sigma\sigma_{\delta}}{\sigma^{2} - \bar{\sigma}_{2}^{2}}\right)$ and, thus, induces the X-producer to opt for the spot exchange. However, according to Theorem 4, the Y-producers may still prefer the contractual mode of exchange. Under this circumstance, a mutually agreeable exchange mode does not exist. If the X-producer has the power to impose his choice of the exchange mode on his trading partners, then the chosen mode is pareto inferior. It should be noted that since the Y-producer employs a fixed-coefficient production technology, the X-producer's choice of the vertical exchange mode is also favored by the consumer. According to Theorems 1-3, the X-producer's preferred arrangement yields the largest quantity of the final good. Since the market demand curve for Y is downward sloping, this quantity gives the lowest price for the consumer.

<u>Contractual Exchange vs. Vertical Integration</u>

According to Theorem 1, the X-producer will vertically integrate forward if, and only if, $\frac{\beta}{\alpha} > \left(\frac{1}{2} - \rho \frac{\sigma_{\delta}}{\sigma}\right)$.

If $\rho = 0$, we see that the X-producer will vertically integrate if and only if $2\beta > \alpha$. If this condition were $\beta > \alpha$, we should say that the X-producer found it advantageous to integrate forward because the Y-producers are too risk averse compared to his own risk attitude. Since a risk-averse entrepreneur will restrict output and thus reduce the employment of the factors of production, $\beta > \alpha$ implies that the Y-producers will demand X at a level too low to be consistent with the X-producer's risk attitude. In order to correct the impact of this inconsistency, the X-producer will integrate forward.

The condition $2\beta > \alpha$, however, implies that even if the final-good producer is less risk averse than the intermediate-good producer, there still may exist an incentive for the latter to vertically integrate. Vertical integration in this case reflects the advantage of portfolio diversification.

A positive ρ improves the likelihood for $\frac{\beta}{\alpha} > \left(\frac{1}{2} - \rho \frac{\sigma_{\delta}}{\sigma}\right)$ to hold. If $\rho > 0$ then increases (decreases) in the production cost for X are in general associated with increases (decreases) in the demand for Y and, hence, for X. Thus, the X-producer's profit is stabilized by vertical integration. In other words, vertical integration provides the X-producer a built-in insurance. The risk averse X-producer prefers this exchange mode and is willing to bear both demand and cost uncertainties. Moreover, when $\rho > 0$, the advantage of vertical integration is greater for $\sigma_\delta >> \sigma$. From the X-producer's point of view, a small σ implies that a greater benefit could be gained from the built-in insurance scheme relative to the additional risk ϵ_2; thus, when $\rho > 0$, the larger that σ_δ is relative to σ, the greater is the incentive for the X-producer to vertically integrate.

On the other hand, $\rho < 0$ dims the likelihood for $\frac{\beta}{\alpha} > \left(\frac{1}{2} - \rho \frac{\sigma_\delta}{\sigma}\right)$ and, thus, makes the contractual arrangement more desirable. A negative ρ means that increases (decreases) in the production cost of X are, in general, associated with a decrease (increase) in the demand for Y and, hence, X. This phenomenon implies that vertical integration destabilizes the X-producer's profit. The risk-averse X-producer will shun vertical integration and prefer portfolio specialization, i.e., he prefers to share the market uncertainties with the Y-producers. Again, this tendency is strengthened if $\sigma_\delta >> \sigma$. Contractual arrangement thus implies that the producers now specialize in risk bearing--the Y-producers bear the demand uncertainty ϵ, while the X-producer bears the cost uncertainty δ.

4. The Integrated Model

Thus far, we have demonstrated how the choice of the time pattern for decision making by the firm affects the vertical exchange structure and vice versa. For this purpose, it is necessary that we include in our analysis only the three pure exchange modes. In this section, we turn to explore the nature of an optimal vertical structure. In order to accomplish this goal, we need to present an integrated version of the choice problem where the X-producer can allocate his total production through a combination of the three pure exchange modes. This section is divided into three parts; the first is devoted to the presentation of the model, the second to the selection of an optimal vertical structure, and the third to the implications of the model.

The Model

We first formulate the integrated problem and then state conditions for its solution. Although the solution is less tractable than those for the three pure cases, we study it because it provides insight far beyond those of the separate problems.

For the integrated model we consider the following time scenario. In period 1, the X-producer chooses the total production $\bar{x}$ and, together with the Y producers, determines the contracted amount x_c and its price w_c. In period 2, δ and ϵ_1 are revealed; the X and Y producers jointly decide on the portion of the quantity $\bar{x} - x_c$ that will be exchanged in the spot market. Let us denote this quantity by x_s and its price by w_s. The remaining quantity x_I is retained by X to produce Y through the vertically integrated facilities.

As before, we assume that there is no withholding in any stage. To facilitate the computation that follows we further assume that $\sigma_\beta^2 = 0$.[7]

Y-Producer's Decision at Period 2: At period 2, the competitive Y-producer is committed to purchase the contracted amount x_c for the price w_c and faces the spot price w_s for the intermediate product X. He must choose to purchase the spot quantity x_s. His problem, then, is to

$$\max_{y_s, x_s} \underset{<\epsilon_2>}{E} V[(y_c + y_s)\tilde{G}(\bar{x}, \epsilon_1^o + \epsilon_2) - (x_c + x_s)k - w_s x_s - w_c x_c] \tag{4.1}$$

$$\text{s.t. } x_s = y_s,$$

$$\text{where } x_c = y_c.$$

By applying the Lemma, the first order conditions of (4.1) give the derived spot demand function

$$w_s = D_s(y_s, y_c, \bar{x}, \epsilon_1) = \frac{\bar{x}-a}{b} + \epsilon_1 + \bar{\epsilon}_2 - k - (y_c + y_s)\beta\bar{\sigma}_2^2 \tag{4.2}$$

X-Producer's Decision at Period 2: At period 2, the X producer has already chosen $\bar{x}$ and x_c and faces the derived demand given by (4.2). He must choose the spot quantity x_s and the quantity x_I so as to

$$\max_{\substack{x_s, x_I \\ x_I, x_s \geq 0}} \underset{<\epsilon_2>}{E} U[x_I\tilde{G}(\bar{x}, \epsilon_1^o + \epsilon_2) - kx_I + x_c w_c + x_s D_s(x_s, x_c, \bar{x}, \epsilon_1) - c(\bar{x}, \delta)] \tag{4.3}$$

$$\text{s.t. } \bar{x} = x_c + x_s + x_I, \text{ and (4.2).}$$

Again by applying the Lemma, the first order conditions of (4.3) give

---

[7]This assumption is not as restrictive as it appears at the first glance. Should X enter into a contractual arrangement with any of the Y-producers in period 1, because all Y-producers are identical, X gains the knowledge of β; hence $\sigma_\beta^2 = 0$.

$$x_I = \frac{2\bar{x}-x_c}{2\beta+\alpha}\,\beta \qquad (4.4)$$

$$x_s = \frac{\alpha\bar{x}-(\alpha+\beta)x_c}{2\beta+\alpha}\,. \qquad (4.5)$$

The optimal solution to (4.3) depends upon whether or not (4.4) and (4.5) represents a feasible solution with $x_s \geqq 0$ and $x_c \geqq 0$. We consider two cases for future reference.

Case A: $x_c \leqq \frac{\alpha}{\alpha+\beta}\,\bar{x}$. In this case, x_I and x_s in (4.4) and (4.5) are feasible and represent the optimal solution. The spot price is

$$w_s = \frac{\bar{x}-a}{b} + \epsilon_1 + \bar{\epsilon}_2 - k - \left(\frac{\alpha\bar{x}+\beta x_c}{\alpha+2\beta}\right)\beta\bar{\sigma}_2^2 \qquad (4.6)$$

Case B: $x_c > \frac{\alpha}{\alpha+\beta}\,\bar{x}$. Because the objective function in (4.3) is piece-wise concave as shown in Figure 2, the solution in this case is the nearest feasible point to that given by (4.4) and (4.5); that is,

$$x_I = \bar{x} - x_c \qquad (4.7)$$

$$x_s = 0. \qquad (4.8)$$

The spot price w_s is irrelevant.

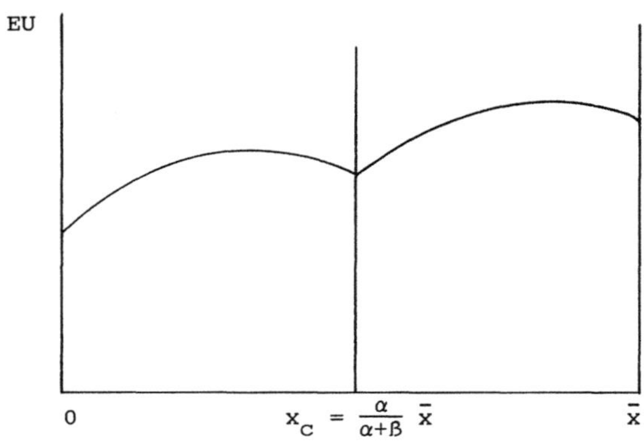

Figure 2. Integrated Model-Expected Utility as a Function of x_c

Y-Producer's Decision at Period 1: At period 1, the typical Y producer faces the contract price w_c. We also assume that the total production $\bar{x}$ is known. In anticipation of ϵ_1, ϵ_2, w_s and y_s, Y must choose to purchase the contracted amount so as to

$$\max_{y_c} \underset{<\epsilon_1,\epsilon_2>}{E} V[(y_c+y_s)\left(\frac{\bar{x}-a}{b} + \epsilon_1 + \epsilon_2\right) - (y_c+y_s)k - w_s y_s - w_c y_c], \tag{4.9}$$

where w_s is seen as random in period 1 and is given by (4.2), and $y_s = x_s$ is given by (4.5) or (4.8) depending on the value of x_c. Applying the Lemma to (4.9) yields the derived contractual demand[8]

$$w_c = D_c(y_c,\bar{x}) = \frac{\bar{x}-a}{b} - k - \beta(y_c\sigma^2 + y_s\bar{\sigma}_2^2). \tag{4.10}$$

X-Producer's Decision at Period 1: The X-producer faces the derived contractual demand curve and must choose the total production $\bar{x}$ and the contract sales x_c. The remainder $\bar{x}-x_c$ will be allocated in period 2 to the spot market and to integrated production. The decision is to

$$\max_{\bar{x},x_c} \underset{<\delta,\epsilon_1,\epsilon_2>}{E} U[x_I\left(\frac{\bar{x}-a}{b} + \epsilon_1 + \epsilon_2 - k\right) + x_c D_c(x_c,\bar{x}) + x_s D_s(x_s,x_c,\bar{x},\epsilon_1) - c(\bar{x},\delta)], \tag{4.11}$$

s.t. $x_c \leqq \bar{x}$,

(4.2), (4.4)-(4.5) or (4.7)-(4.8), and (4.10).

It is evident that the three exchange problems considered in Section 2 are embedded in the formulation given by (4.1), (4.3), (4.9), and (4.11). For example, if we restrict $x_I = x_c = y_c = 0$, then $x_s = y_s = \bar{x}$; (4.3) and (4.9) become trivial. In this case, (4.1) and (4.11) are identical to the spot market problems for X and Y.

The general solution to (4.11) is complicated because values of x_s and x_I in $\tilde{\pi}_x$ depend on $\bar{x}$ and x_c, as (4.4)-(4.5) and (4.7)-(4.8) show. In the remainder of this section we will discuss some interesting aspects of this solution.

Selection of Vertical Structure

We have presented a general model for the vertical exchange problem. There are eight cases embedded in this general model depending on the combination of the three variables being zero or positive. They are listed in Table 2.

---

8 Here we treat w_s, y_s, and w_c as constants with respect to y_c since the individual Y-producer's decision does not affect these variables.

TABLE 2

INTEGRATED MODEL--SPECIAL CASES

	x_c	x_s	x_I
Case 1	0	0	0
Case 2	0	+	0
Case 3	0	0	+
Case 4	0	+	+
Case 5	+	0	0
Case 6	+	0	+
Case 7	+	+	0
Case 8	+	+	+

Case 1 is clearly uninteresting; we exclude it from our discussion. Not all of the remaining cases are equally plausible, however. In this subsection, we examine the plausibility of each case and identify the conditions under which a particular case may prevail. In order to accomplish this objective, we normally compute the necessary and sufficient conditions for each case that could occur. Computing the sufficient conditions for any of these optimal solutions is complicated because it requires comparison of the objective values for all cases using the appropriate x's which are themselves complicated. Fortunately, we are able to list in Table 3 the necessary conditions for the optimal solutions, depending on the value of x_c.

Although contract, spot, and vertical integration are all basic components for the vertical exchange structure, they do not play a symmetric role in determining the final outcome. Because contractual arrangement must be made in period 1 while decisions on spot exchange and vertical integration can be made in period 2, it is convenient to present the seven non-trivial cases in two groups; the first does not include any contractual arrangement and the second does.

Thus, we first examine the necessary conditions for $x_c = 0$. We see in Table 3 that $x_c = 0$ if ρ is positive and σ_δ is large. That is, contract may not be desirable if final demand and production cost vary together and production cost uncertainty is high.[9]

[9]The reason is the same as that given in Section 3.

TABLE 3

OPTIMAL VALUES FOR INTEGRATED PROBLEM WITH NECESSARY CONDITIONS

Value of x_c	$\bar{x}$, x_c, x_I, x_s	Necessary Conditions
$x_c = 0$ (Case 4)	$x = \dfrac{\frac{a}{b} + k}{\frac{2}{b} - c - 2\beta\left[\frac{\alpha\bar{\sigma}_2}{\alpha+2\beta}\right]^2 - \alpha\left[\sigma_1^2 + Var(\bar{\varepsilon}_2) + \left(\frac{\alpha\bar{\sigma}_2}{\alpha+2\beta}\right)^2 + \sigma^2 - 2\rho\sigma\sigma_\delta\right]}$ $x_c = 0$ $x_I = \dfrac{2\beta}{\alpha + 2\beta}\bar{x}, \quad x_s = \dfrac{\alpha}{\alpha + 2\beta}\bar{x}$	(i) $\rho\sigma\sigma_\delta \geq \dfrac{\alpha^3 + \beta[2\sigma_1^2 - \bar{\sigma}_2^2 + 2Var(\bar{\varepsilon}_2)]}{\alpha + 2\beta}$
$0 < x_c < \dfrac{\alpha}{\alpha+\beta}\bar{x}$ (Case 8)	$\bar{x} = \dfrac{\left(\frac{a}{b} + k\right)C}{AC - B^2}, \quad x_c = \dfrac{-\left(\frac{a}{b} + k\right)B}{AC - B^2},$ $x_I = \dfrac{2\bar{x} - x_c}{\alpha + 2\beta}\beta, \quad x_s = \dfrac{\alpha\bar{x} - (\alpha+\beta)x_c}{\alpha + 2\beta}$ where $A = \dfrac{2}{b} - c - \dfrac{\alpha^2}{\alpha + 2\beta}\bar{\sigma}_2^2 - \alpha Var(\varepsilon_1 + \bar{\varepsilon}_2 - \delta)$ $B = \dfrac{\alpha(\alpha-\beta)}{\alpha + 2\beta}\bar{\sigma}_2^2 + \alpha[\sigma_1^2 + Var(\bar{\varepsilon}_2) - \rho\sigma\sigma_\delta]$ $C = \dfrac{3\beta^2 + 2\alpha\beta - \alpha^2}{\alpha + 2\beta}\bar{\sigma}_2^2 - 2\beta\sigma^2 - \alpha[\sigma_1^2 + Var(\bar{\varepsilon}_2)]$	(ii) $\rho\sigma\sigma_\delta < \dfrac{\alpha^3 + \beta[2\sigma_1^2 - \bar{\sigma}_2^2 + 2Var(\bar{\varepsilon}_2)]}{\alpha + 2\beta}$ and (iii) $\rho\sigma\sigma_\delta < \dfrac{\beta(\beta-5\alpha)}{(\alpha+2\beta)(2\alpha+\beta)}\bar{\sigma}_2^2 + \sigma^2$

Table 3--Continued

Value of x_c	$\bar{x}, x_c, x_I, x_s$	Necessary Conditions
$x_c = \frac{\alpha}{\alpha+\beta}\bar{x}$ (Case 6)	$\bar{x} = \dfrac{\frac{a}{b} + k}{\frac{2}{b} - c - 2\beta\left(\frac{\alpha\sigma}{\alpha+\beta}\right)^2 - \alpha\left\{\left(\frac{\beta}{\alpha+\beta}\right)^2[\sigma_1^2 + \mathrm{Var}(\bar{\varepsilon}_2)] + \sigma^2 - 2\left(\frac{\beta}{\alpha+\beta}\right)\rho\sigma\sigma_\delta\right\}}$ $x_c = \left(\frac{\alpha}{\alpha+\beta}\right)\bar{x}$ $x_I = \bar{x} - x_c$ $x_s = 0$	(iv) $\frac{\beta(\beta-5\alpha)}{(\alpha+2\beta)(2\alpha+\beta)}\bar{\sigma}_2^2 + \sigma^2 < \rho\sigma\sigma_\delta$ and (v) $\frac{\beta}{\alpha} \geq -\frac{1}{2}\rho\frac{\sigma_\delta}{\sigma}$
$\frac{\alpha}{\alpha+\beta}\bar{x} < x_c < \bar{x}$ (Case 6)	$\bar{x} = \dfrac{\left(\frac{a}{b} + k\right)R}{PR - Q^2}, \quad x_c = \dfrac{-\left(\frac{a}{b} + k\right)Q}{PR - Q^2}$ $x_I = \bar{x} - x_c, \quad x_s = 0$ $P = \frac{2}{b} - c - \alpha(\sigma^2 + \sigma_2^2 - 2\rho\sigma\sigma_\delta)$ $Q = \alpha(\sigma^2 - \rho\sigma\sigma_\delta)$ $R = -(\alpha + 2\beta)\sigma^2$	(vi) $\frac{\sigma^2}{\alpha+\beta} < \frac{\sigma^2 - \rho\sigma\sigma_\delta}{\alpha+2\beta} < \frac{\sigma^2}{\alpha}$

Table 3--Continued

Value of x_c	$\bar{x}$, x_c, x_I, x_s	Necessary Conditions
$x_c = \bar{x}$ (Case 5, Pure Contract)	$\bar{x} = \dfrac{\frac{a}{b} + k}{\frac{2}{b} - 2\beta\sigma^2 - c - \alpha\sigma^2}$ $x_c = \bar{x}$ $x_I = 0, \quad x_s = 0$	(vii) $\frac{\beta}{\alpha} < -\frac{1}{2}\rho\frac{\sigma_\delta}{\sigma}$

In general, as we show below, a vertical structure without contractual arrangement always implies a combination of spot exchange and vertical integration (Case 4); in other words, spot exchange by itself (Case 2) or vertical integration alone (Case 3) is never optimal. It can be shown that when $x_c = 0$, in (4.3) the intermediate good producer's profit function, as seen in period 2, is comprised of three components: the random term caused by vertical integration, the risk premium that must be paid to Y in order to entice him to participate in the spot exchange, and a component independent of x_I; that is,

$$\tilde{\pi}_x = x_I(\epsilon_2 - \bar{\epsilon}_2) - (\bar{x} - x_I)^2 \beta \bar{\sigma}_2^2 + A \tag{4.12}$$

where A is a constant with respect to x_I. A small increase in x_I will yield a marginal increment in the expected profit equal to $2\beta\bar{\sigma}_2^2(\bar{x}-x_I)$. However, this increase in x_I will also expose X to a greater risk in the final good market. The minimum return that X must receive in order to entice him to accept this risk is $\alpha x_I \bar{\sigma}_2^2$. Consequently, the intermediate good producer will commit to greater vertically integrated activities if

$$M = 2\beta\bar{\sigma}_2^2(\bar{x} - x_I) - \alpha\bar{\sigma}_2^2 x_I > 0. \tag{4.13}$$

When x_I is small, then M always increases with an increase in x_I; therefore, x_I can never be zero. On the other hand, x_I can never be equal to $\bar{x}$ either. When x_I approaches $\bar{x}$, M becomes negative, which implies that a decrease in x_I will always contribute to profit. Thus, if $x_c = 0$, then neither pure spot exchange nor vertical integration is ever optimal. This outcome is analogous to a well known theorem in portfolio theory: A risk averse investor who has the option to choose among a combination of a riskless asset (spot exchange in this case) and an uncertain investment with a higher mean (vertical integration in this case) will never choose either of the extremes.

There are four cases associated with $x_c > 0$. Which one of these cases will prevail is dependent upon the size of x_c relative to the total quantity of X produced. In order to facilitate the discussion, it is convenient to recall that the X-producer's utility function represented by (4.3) is piece-wise concave with respect to x_c, as shown in Figure 2. The kink takes place at $x_c = \frac{\alpha}{\alpha+\beta}\bar{x}$. This point will serve as a reference point for the ensuing discussion.

Recall that x_s and x_I both must be positive when x_c is equal to zero. Since x_s and x_I are functions of x_c and $\bar{x}$ and these functions are continuous in their arguments, as x_c rises above zero the values of x_s and x_I must remain positive. In fact, x_s and x_I are both positive as long as $x_c < \frac{\alpha}{\alpha+\beta}\bar{x}$, an increase in x_c causes both x_s and x_I to decrease, i.e., both x_s and x_I are decreasing functions of x_c. Moreover, x_I cannot become zero before x_s does. This can be seen by observing that when contractual arrangement is a part of the vertical exchange structure, the X-producer's profit function, as seen in period 2, is

$$\tilde{\pi}_x^* = x_I(\epsilon_2 - \bar{\epsilon}_2) - (\bar{x} - x_I)(\bar{x} - x_I - x_c)\beta\bar{\sigma}_2^2 + A^*, \qquad (4.14)$$

where A^* again is a component independent of x_I. The marginal net gain derived from vertical integration now becomes

$$M^* = \beta\bar{\sigma}_2^2\,[2(\bar{x} - x_I) - x_c] - \alpha x_I\bar{\sigma}_2^2. \qquad (4.15)$$

From (4.15), it is evident that if $x_I = 0$, then $M^* > 0$ always. Thus, a small increase in x_I will always increase the X-producer's profit. This conclusion, therefore, implies that case 7 can never prevail.

Since x_I cannot become zero before x_s does, as x_c increases, eventually x_s will first become zero. This occurs when $x_c = \frac{\alpha}{\alpha+\beta}\bar{x}$. The necessary conditions for the solution of x_c and x_I to be optimal are given as (iv) and (v) in Table 3. When these conditions are satisfied, case 6 emerges.

Case 6 occurs not only when $x_c = \frac{\alpha}{\alpha+\beta}\bar{x}$; it prevails as long as $\bar{x} > x_c > \frac{\alpha}{\alpha+\beta}\bar{x}$. The necessary condition for the existence of the optimal values for x_I and x_c in this case is different from those of the previous one; it is listed as (vi) in Table 3.

Although a pure spot arrangement and pure vertical integration will never be chosen when the entrepreneur can choose a convex combination of the three pure forms of exchange, it is possible that the total output of the intermediate good producer be sold entirely on contract. The necessary condition for this case (Case 5) to occur is $\frac{\beta}{\alpha} < -\rho\,\frac{\sigma_\delta}{\sigma}$ as shown in Table 3. Recalling that in section 3 we observed that the intermediate-good producer will prefer contractual arrangement over vertical integration whenever $\frac{\beta}{\alpha} < \frac{1}{2} - \rho\,\frac{\sigma_\delta}{\sigma}$. Comparing the two conditions $\frac{\beta}{\alpha} < -\rho\,\frac{\sigma_\delta}{\sigma}$ and $\frac{\beta}{\alpha} < \frac{1}{2} - \rho\,\frac{\sigma_\delta}{\sigma}$, we can see that there exists a discrepancy between them. This discrepancy can be explained by the fact that the choice in section 3 is among the three pure vertical exchange modes, while the choice here is among all convex combinations of them. We know that if the pure contractual arrangement is optimal among all convex combinations, then it is optimal among the three pure exchange modes, and that the converse is not true. Accordingly $\frac{\beta}{\alpha} < -\rho \frac{\sigma_\delta}{\sigma}$ implies $\frac{\beta}{\alpha} < \frac{1}{2} - \rho \frac{\sigma_\delta}{\sigma}$.

Welfare Implications

In the previous section, we derived the X-producer's preferred structure. In this section we shall examine whether this choice is consistent with the consumers' welfare.

Let the vertical structure of a market be described by a triplet $\lambda = (\lambda_s,\lambda_c,\lambda_I)$ where λ_s, λ_c, and λ_I, respectively, denote the proportion of $\bar{x}$ that is distributed through the spot market, contractual arrangement and vertically integrated production, and $\lambda_s + \lambda_c + \lambda_I = 1$. From (4.11), we can write explicitly

$$\tilde{\pi}_x = (x_c+x_s+x_I)\left(\frac{\bar{x}-a}{b} - k\right) - \frac{1}{2} c\bar{x}^2 - \beta(x_c+x_s)(x_c\sigma^2 + x_s\sigma_2^2) + \epsilon_1(x_I+x_s) + \epsilon_2 x_I - \delta\bar{x} \tag{4.16}$$

The vector value of λ emerges simultaneously with the X-producer's resolution of his production-sales problem, which can be summarized as:

$$\max_{\bar{x},x_c} \; \underset{<\delta,\epsilon_1>}{E} \; \max_{x_s,x_I} \; \underset{<\epsilon_2>}{E} \; U(\tilde{\pi}_x) \tag{4.17}$$

$$\text{s.t. (4.16) and } x_c + x_I + x_s = \bar{x}.$$

Let the resultant vertical structure be $\lambda^o = (\lambda_s^o,\lambda_c^o,\lambda_I^o)$, $\lambda_s^o + \lambda_c^o + \lambda_I^o = 1$, and the total quantity of X produced be $\bar{x}^o$. We shall compare λ^o to the λ that maximizes consumer welfare. Before proceeding, it is important to note that in the present context the X-producer can potentially inflict welfare losses to the society both by being a monopolist in X and by choosing a vertical structure. Our present concern is strictly related to the latter.

In order to examine this welfare issue, we need to establish an appropriate objective for the consumer. Suppose that the X-producer is restricted by a regulator to produce x_s, x_c, and x_I in the proportion λ_s, λ_c, and λ_I. The X-producer's choice problem now becomes:

$$\max_{\bar{x}} \; \underset{<\delta,\epsilon_1,\epsilon_2>}{E} \; U(\tilde{\pi}_x) \tag{4.18}$$

$$\text{s.t. (4.16), where } \lambda_s + \lambda_c + \lambda_I = 1.$$

Let $Q(\lambda_s,\lambda_c,\lambda_I)$ be the value of $\bar{x}$ that solves this problem. From the society's point of view, it prefers a vertical structure $\lambda^* = (\lambda_S^*, \lambda_C^*, \lambda_I^*)$, $\lambda_S^* + \lambda_C^* + \lambda_I^* = 1$, which maximizes Q. Therefore, it seems reasonable for us to adopt the following welfare criterion: the X-producer's choice of the vertical structure does not impair social welfare whenever $\bar{x}^* \le \bar{x}^o$.

In order to make the necessary welfare judgment on the basis of this criterion, we first examine the X-producer's equivalent profit function $F(\bar{x}) = E\tilde{\pi}_x - \frac{1}{2}\alpha\, \mathrm{Var}(\tilde{\pi}_x)$. It can be shown that $F(\bar{x})$ has the form $A\bar{x}^2 + B\bar{x} + C$ with $A < 0$ and B independent of λ. Since the solution for $\bar{x}$ under this circumstance is $-B/2A$, it is evident that the λ which maximizes $\bar{x}$ also maximizes $F(\bar{x})$. In other words, the welfare maximizing problem is equivalent to

$$\max_{\bar{x}, x_C, x_I, x_S} \; \underset{\langle\delta, \epsilon_1, \epsilon_2\rangle}{E} \; U(\tilde{\pi}_x) \tag{4.19}$$

s.t. (4.16)

Furthermore inspecting the solutions of (4.17) given in Table 3, we see that both the optimal values of x_S and x_I are independent of δ and ϵ_1. Consequently,

$$\max_{\bar{x}, x_C} \; \underset{\langle\delta, \epsilon_1\rangle}{E} \; \max_{x_S, x_I} \; \underset{\langle\epsilon_2\rangle}{E} \; U(\tilde{\pi}_x) = \max_{\bar{x}, x_C, x_S, x_I} \; \underset{\langle\delta, \epsilon_1, \epsilon_2\rangle}{E} \; U(\tilde{\pi}_x). \tag{4.20}$$

This equality implies that the problems represented by (4.17) and the welfare maximizing problem are equivalent, i.e., the $\bar{x}$ associated with λ^o is the same as that associated with λ^*. We, therefore, may conclude that the vertical structure chosen by X is consistent with maximizing welfare.

5. Summary and Conclusions

As stated in the introduction, the main purpose of this paper is to investigate the impact of market uncertainties on the vertical structure of the firm and the market. We provided an explanation as to how a particular vertical structure emerges under a given market environment and examined its welfare implications.

We presented models describing three pure modes of exchange in order to study the impact of the time pattern of decision on the choice of the exchange mode under a given market environment. In the process of achieving this goal, it became apparent that even in the absence of any technical advantages associated with vertical integration and any uncertainty-related transaction costs, the firm might still opt to sidestep the market and vertically integrate.

Since, in general, it is not optimal for X to select a vertical structure merely from the pure modes of exchange, we presented a general model which permits vertical structure as a convex combination of the three pure exchange modes. It was discovered that spot exchange and vertical integration in their pure form are never optimal. The same is true for a mixture of contractual and spot arrangements. The remaining combinations are, however, possible. Table 3 lists the necessary conditions for each of these cases to prevail.

Since X is the dominant party choosing the vertical structure, it is important to know under what circumstance his choice is consistent with the choice which maximizes consumer's welfare. A criterion was introduced to identify such circumstances. Based upon this criterion, we see that under the assumed market environment, the vertical structures chosen by the X-producer does not yield any anti-social effect.[10]

There has been more controversy among economists and lawyers regarding the welfare implications of vertical mergers than for any other anti-trust issues. Some writers stress that vertical mergers create efficiency, increase output, and therefore are incapable of injuring consumer welfare. Others, however, insist that vertical mergers may foreclose buying or selling outlets to rivals, distort input employment and, thus, harm competition.[11] The present analysis suggests that these controversies, perhaps, are not focused on the right issues. Vertical integration should not be viewed as either good or bad per se; this paper suggests that from the society's point of view the relevant consideration ought to be whether a vertical-structure represents the optimum mix of market arrangements.

Appendix

Proof of Lemma, Section 2

By definition, B should satisfy

$$EW(\tilde{\pi}) = W(\bar{\pi} - B). \qquad (A.1)$$

---

[10] This welfare conclusion is a consequence of the assumption that the market uncertainties are exogenously given. This conclusion may not hold if some of the market uncertainties are generated endogenously.

[11] For these controversies, see Bork (1969), Greenhut and Ohta (1979), Hay (1973), Perry (1975), Peltzman (1969), Schmalensee (1973), Warren-Boulton (1974), and Wu (1964).

Substituting for π and W and taking the expectation over θ,

$$\frac{1}{\sigma\sqrt{2\pi}} \int_\theta \exp[-\gamma(CZ^2 + DZ + \theta Z) - \theta^2/2\sigma^2]d\theta = e^{-\gamma(CZ^2+DZ-B)}. \quad (A.2)$$

Using $\frac{1}{\sigma\sqrt{2\pi}} \int_\theta \exp\left[-\frac{1}{2\sigma^2}(\theta + \sigma^2\gamma Z)^2\right]d\theta = 1$ gives

$$e^{-\gamma(CZ^2+DZ - \frac{\sigma^2\gamma}{2} Z^2)} = e^{-\gamma(CZ^2+DZ-B)}, \quad (A.3)$$

which, in turn, yields

$$B = \frac{1}{2}\gamma Z^2\sigma^2. \quad (A.4)$$

Finally, by (A.1), the optimal Z should maximize $W(\bar{\pi} - B)$. This Z should satisfy $0 = \frac{d}{dz} W(\bar{\pi} - B)$, which implies $\frac{d}{dZ}\bar{\pi} = \frac{d}{dZ} B$. Q.E.D.

References

Arrow, K.J., "Vertical Integration and Communication," Bell Journal of Economics, Vol. 6 (Spring 1975): 173-183.

Balch, M. and S. Wu, "An Introduction to Economic Behavior Under Uncertainty," in Essays on Economic Behavior Under Uncertainty, eds. M. Balch, D. McFadden, and S. Wu. North Holland, 1974.

Baron, D.P., "Price Uncertainty, Utility and Industry Equilibrium in Pure Competition," International Economic Review, Vol. 11 (October 1970): 463-480.

Blair, R.D. and D.L. Kaserman, "Uncertainty and Incentive for Vertical Integration," Southern Economic Journal (July 1978): 266-272.

Burstein, M.L., "A Theory of Full-Line Forcing," Northwestern University Law Review, Vol. 55 (March/April 1960): 62-95.

Carlton, D.W., "Vertical Integration in Competitive Market Under Uncertainty," Journal of International Economics, Vol. 27, No. 3 (March 1979).

________, "Contracts, Price Rigidity and Market Equilibrium," Journal of Political Economy (October 1979): 1034-1062.

Coase, R.H., "The Nature of the Firm," Economica, Vol. 4 (November 1937): 386-405.

Greenhut, M.L. and H. Ohta, "Vertical Integration of Successive Oligopolists," American Economic Review, Vol. 69 (March 1979): 137-141.

Hay, G.A., "An Economic Analysis of Vertical Integration," Industrial Organization Review, Vol. 1 (1973): 188-198.

Horen, J. and S. Wu, "Partial Vertical Integration," mimeographed, 1982.

Kaserman, D.L., "Theories of Vertical Integration: Implications for Anti-Trust Policy," The Anti-Trust Bulletin (1978): 483-510.

Klein, B., R.C. Crawford and A.A. Alchian, "Vertical Integration, Appropriate Rents and the Competitive Contract Process," Journal of Law and Economics (October 1978): 297-326.

Peltzman, S., "Issues in Vertical Integration Policy," in Public Policy Toward Mergers. Goodyear, 1969.

Perry, M.K., "The Theory of Vertical Integration by Imperfectly Competitive Firms," Center for Research in Economic Growth, Memorandum No. 197, Stanford University, 1975.

________, "Price Discrimination and Forward Integration," Bell Journal of Economics, Vol. 9 (Spring 1978): 209-217.

Schmalensee, R., "A Note on the Theory of Vertical Integration," Journal of Political Economy, Vol. 81 (March/April 1973): 442-449.

Shavell, S., "Risk Sharing and Incentives in the Principal and Agent Relationship," Bell Journal of Economics, Vol. 10 (Spring 1975): 163-172.

Spence, A.M., "The Economics of Internal Organization: An Introduction," Bell Journal of Economics, Vol. 6 (Spring 1975): 163-172.

Vernon, J.M. and D.A. Graham, "Profitability of Monopolization by Vertical Integration," Journal of Political Economy, Vol. 79 (September/October 1971): 924-925.

Warren-Boulton, F.R., "Vertical Control with Variable Proportions," Journal of Political Economy, Vol. 82 (July/August 1974): 783-802.

Williamson, O.E., "The Vertical Integration of Production: Market Failure Considerations," American Economic Review, Vol. 61 (May 1971): 112-123.

Wu, S.Y., "The Effects of Vertical Integration on Price and Output," Western Economic Journal, Vol. 2 (1964): 117-133.

________, "An Essay on Monopoly Power and Stable Price Policy," American Economic Review, Vol. 69 (March 1979): 60-72.

OPTIMAL TARIFFS AND QUOTAS UNDER UNCERTAIN INTERNATIONAL TRANSFER

Takao Itagaki*
Institute of Socio-Economic Planning
University of Tsukuba
1-1-1 Tennodai
Tsukuba City, Ibaraki 305, Japan

1. Introduction

Developing countries face various sorts of uncertainties. Some of them have been investigated in the literature.[1] It is well known that many developing countries receive foreign aids or gifts in one form or another: they are either financial or real. Amounts of such transfers, however, are often not known with certainty in advance, because usable funds in donor countries are not sure owing to uncertain economic conditions such as production or consumption, or uncertain political decision processes in those countries. On the other hand, there exists some time lag between the formulation of trade policies and their implementation in developing countries. In such a case the policy-makers of the developing countries have the problem that they must decide optimal levels of trade policies before the amounts of transfer to receive are known. This paper addresses the issue of the optimal tariffs and quotas when a developing country faces uncertainty about the amount of transfer to receive.

The paper assumes a market economy in which producers and consumers in the developing country maximize profits and utilities respectively after uncertainty is resolved. The problem of uncertainty is thus for the policy-maker of the developing country. In this paper the international transfer to this country is made in the form of its importable goods. This setting fits best many developing countries confronting the shortages of imports of foods, oil or other strategic goods. The international transfer is made either by a third country or an international organization, which is different from the country

---

*The author would like to thank Professor Hiroshi Ohta of Kobe University of Commerce for comments.

[1]For example, Batra (1975) and Newberry and Stiglitz (1981) deal with commodity price risk faced by developing countries, and analyze the consequences of its stabilization.

against which the recipient country sets the optimal tariffs or quotas.[2]

Major results obtained are summarized as follows. While under a plausible assumption about the foreign offer curve the optimal tariff for a large country under certainty about the positive amount of transfer is lower than under no transfer, for a small country the best policy is the zero tariff even under a positive transfer. Under uncertainty the optimal tariffs may be lower or higher than $E\{1/(\epsilon^* - 1)\}$, where ϵ^* is the import elasticity of the foreign country, both for risk-averse and a risk-neutral large country. However, the optimal tariff for a risk-averse large country is higher than that for a risk-neutral large country. For a small country the best policy is to set the tariff rate at the zero level under both risk neutrality and risk aversion. As for the optimal quotas, a risk-neutral country sets the quota level such that the expected implicit tariff rate is equal to $1/(\epsilon^* - 1)$, while a risk-averse country sets it such that the expected implicit tariff rate is lower than $1/(\epsilon^* - 1)$. In terms of quantities, the risk-averse countries set greater quotas than the risk-neutral countries both for a large and a small country, which means that the risk-averse countries are less protectionist than the risk-neutral countries. The results contrast sharply to those for the tariff.

Section 2 analyzes the optimal tariffs, and Section 3 investigates the optimal quotas. In Section 4 a summary is given.

2. The Optimal Tariffs

The developing country concerned is assumed to export the first goods and import the second goods. Their foreign and domestic prices are denoted by p_i^* and p_i $(i = 1,2)$, respectively. Let X_i and D_i denote the country's output and consumption of the first and the second goods, respectively. Furthermore, let A be the volume of the second goods transferred to the country, say, in the form of aid. A is random when the government formulates the optimal trade policies. Denoting the spendable income of the country under a tariff by Y, it is written as

---

[2] Our setting of international transfer differs from the usual treatment of the transfer problem in two ways: first, while in the usual case a transfer is defined as one of purchasing power, in this paper it takes the form of the transfer of the goods, and second, while in the former case the transfer problem is considered between the transferee and the transferor, in our case the problem is considered between the transferee and a country independent of the transfer process itself. As an example of recent contributions on bilateral transfer we can mention Bhagwati, Brecher and Hatta (1983).

$$Y = p_1X_1 + p_2X_2 + tp_2^*M_2 + p_2A, \tag{1}$$

where t is the ad valorem tariff rate and M_2 is the import of the second goods from the foreign country. M_2 is equal to

$$M_2 = D_2 - X_2 - A. \tag{2}$$

Dividing (1) by p_1, we get

$$y = X_1 + pX_2 + tp^*M_2 + pA, \tag{3}$$

where $y = Y/p_1$, $p = p_2/p_1$, and $p^* = p_2^*/p_1 = p_2^*/p_1^*$. Under the tariff regime p is equal to $(1 + t)p^*$ ex post.

Let $U = U(p, y)$ be the indirect utility function, which represents the maximum utility attained at the domestic relative price p and the income y. The objective of the policy-maker is to maximize the expected indirect utility.

In order to find an optimal tariff we differentiate the expected indirect utility function $EU = EU(p, y)$ with respect to t. Then we get

$$\frac{dEU}{dt} = E\left\{U_p \frac{dp}{dt} + U_y\left(\frac{dX_1}{dt} + p\frac{dX_2}{dt} + X_2\frac{dp}{dt} + p^*M_2 + tp^*\frac{dM_2}{dt} + tM_2\frac{dp^*}{dt} + A\frac{dp}{dt}\right)\right\},$$

where $U_p = \partial U/\partial p$ and $U_y = \partial U/\partial y$. Making use of $dX_1/dt + pdX_2/dt = 0$ from the ex post efficient production by producers, and also Roy's identity $U_p + U_yD_2 = 0$, we get

$$\frac{dEU}{dt} = EU_y\left\{-M_2\frac{dp}{dt} + p^*M_2 + t\left(p^*\frac{dM_2}{dt} + M_2\frac{dp^*}{dt}\right)\right\} \ . \tag{4}$$

The next step is to obtain expressions of dp^*/dt, dp/dt and dM_2/dt. For this purpose let us write the import demand functions of this developing country, which we shall call the home country, and of the foreign country respectively as

$$M_2 = M_2(p^*, t, A), \tag{5}$$

and

$$M_1^* = M_1^*\left(\frac{1}{p^*}\right) . \tag{6}$$

In international equilibrium the imports of the two countries are equal:

$$p^* M_2 = M_1^*. \tag{7}$$

From (5) and (6) we have

$$\frac{dM_2}{dt} = \frac{\partial M_2}{\partial p^*} \frac{dp^*}{dt} + \frac{\partial M_2}{\partial t}, \tag{8}$$

and

$$\frac{dM_1^*}{dt} = - \frac{1}{p^{*2}} \frac{\partial M_1^*}{\partial (1/p^*)} \frac{dp^*}{dt}. \tag{9}$$

Differentiating (7) with respect to t, we get

$$p^* \frac{dM_2}{dt} + M_2 \frac{dp^*}{dt} = \frac{dM_1^*}{dt}. \tag{10}$$

Substituting (8) and (9) into (10), and arranging, we get

$$\left\{ p^* \frac{\partial M_2}{\partial p^*} + M_2 + \frac{1}{p^{*2}} \frac{\partial M_1^*}{\partial (1/p^*)} \right\} \frac{dp^*}{dt} = -p^* \frac{\partial M_2}{\partial t}.$$

Making use of (7), and solving the above equation for dp^*/dt, we obtain

$$\frac{dp^*}{dt} = \frac{p^* \eta}{(1 - \epsilon^* - \epsilon)t}, \tag{11}$$

where

$$\epsilon^* = - \frac{(1/p^*)}{M_1^*} \frac{\partial M_1^*}{\partial (1/p^*)} \quad \text{and} \quad \epsilon = - \frac{p^*}{M_2} \frac{\partial M_2}{\partial p^*}$$

are respectively the import demand elasticities of the foreign and the home countries with respect to the foreign relative price p^*, and

$$\eta = - \frac{t}{M_2} \frac{\partial M_2}{\partial t}$$

is the import demand elasticity of the home country with respect to t with p^* constant. η is assumed to be positive.

The following is immediate from $p = (1 + t)p^*$ and (11):

$$\frac{dp}{dt} = \frac{(1 + t)p^* \eta}{(1 - \epsilon^* - \epsilon)t} + p^*. \tag{12}$$

Moreover, substituting (11) into (8), and arranging, we finally get

$$\frac{dM_2}{dt} = - \frac{M_2 \eta}{t} \left(\frac{1 - \epsilon^*}{1 - \epsilon^* - \epsilon} \right). \tag{13}$$

Lastly, to obtain the solution for t, we substitute (11), (12) and (13) into (4), and equate the resulting equation to zero. After some manipulation we have

$$E\left\{\frac{U_y p^* M_2 \eta(\epsilon^* - 1)}{(1 - \epsilon^* - \epsilon)t}\left(t - \frac{1}{\epsilon^* - 1}\right)\right\} = 0 \tag{14}$$

The above equation is written as

$$t - E\left(\frac{1}{\epsilon^* - 1}\right) + \frac{\text{cov}\,\{B,\, t - 1/(\epsilon^* - 1)\}}{EB} = 0, \tag{15}$$

where cov denotes the covariance, and

$$B = \frac{U_y p^* M_2 \eta(\epsilon^* - 1)}{(\epsilon^* + \epsilon - 1)t}\,. \tag{16}$$

In the above derivation of (15), we note that U_y, p^*, M_2, η, ϵ^* and ϵ are all random. This is due to randomness of A: the latter causes relative price, production, income, consumption, import and export of the home country to be random. The last two in turn make p^* and ϵ^* random.

The situation is illustrated in Figure 1. Let us suppose free trade. Of in Figure 1 is the offer curve of the foreign country, while Oh and Oh' are the two offer curves of the home country corresponding to two different values of A. Suppose that A is increased at a constant p^*. It is seen from (2) that $\partial M_2/\partial A = m_2 - 1$, where m_2 is the marginal propensity to consume the second goods. Normally $m_2 < 1$. Hence M_2 decreases as A rises. Then home export of the first goods, $M_1 = X_1 - D_1$, also decreases owing to the balance of trade constraint. Thus, Oh' shows the home offer curve corresponding to a higher value of A than that for Oh.

Since the true value of A is not known <u>ex ante</u>, the exact location of the home offer curve is not known. Hence, the equilibrium levels of trade, p^*, p and so forth are not known. The situation is the same even under a tariff, although, as is well known, it shifts each of the home offer curves leftwards.

<u>(i) The Optimal Tariffs under Certainty</u>

Suppose that the amount of the transfer to be received is known with certainty, and the policy-maker maximizes the indirect utility. Then it is easy to see from (14) that the optimal tariff is equal to $1/(\epsilon^* - 1)$, which is a familiar formula in the theory of the tariff. But, it should not mean that the optimal tariff rate under a positive

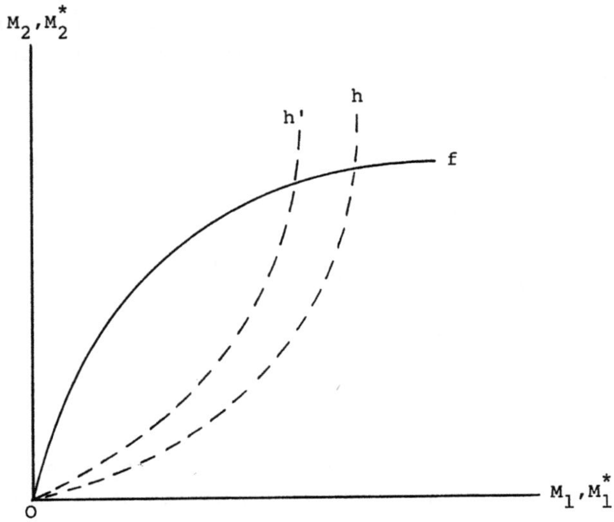

Figure 1

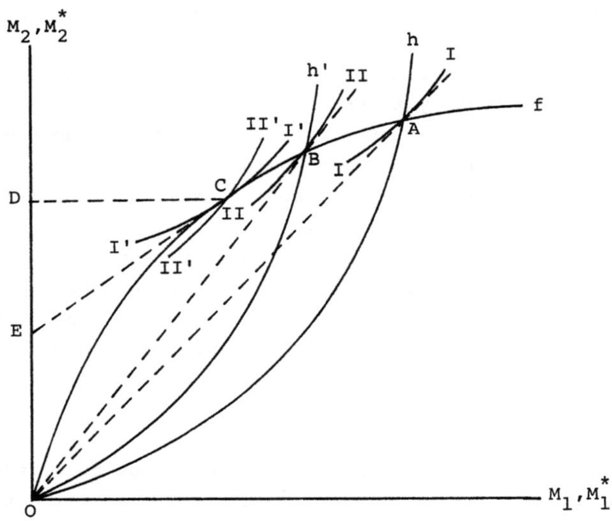

Figure 2

A is equal to that under A = 0. This can be shown as follows. In Figure 2 Oh is the home offer curve under A = 0, and Oh' is that under a positive A. In free trade equilibria trade indifference curves I I and II II are tangent to the foreign relative price lines at A and B in the respective cases. A crucial point here is that the two trade indifference curves I I and II II belong to different families. Point C provides the optimum for the home country under A = 0, where a home trade indifference curve I'I' is tangent to the foreign offer curve. ϵ^* in the formula of the optimal tariff under A = 0, $1/(\epsilon^* - 1)$, is given by the ϵ^* at that point, i.e., OD/OE.

It is pointed out that the trade indifference curve under the positive A which passes through point C intersects I'I' and the foreign offer curve like II'II'. A simple proof of this statement is given as follows. We showed that the home offer curve under a higher positive amount of A is a shrunk one of the home offer curve under a lower amount of A, which includes A = 0. Such is possible only when a trade indifference curve under a positive A intersects a trade indifference curve under A = 0 like I'I' and II'II' in Figure 2. This means that the optimum for the home country under a positive A is located southwest from C on the foreign offer curve. In the normal case elasticities of import demand of the foreign country increase as we move from C toward the origin, which we shall assume in the following, we can conclude that the optimal tariff rate under a positive A is lower than under A = 0.

At the extreme, however, if the country concerned is small compared with the foreign country, which means that $\epsilon^* = \infty$ everywhere on the foreign offer curve, we see that the optimal tariff is zero, which is identical to the well-known proposition of the tariff, and to which the usual explanation for free trade is applied.

(ii) The Optimal Tariffs under Uncertainty

Let us turn back to the case of uncertainty. We first examine the sign of the third term of the left-hand side of (15). In EB, $\epsilon^* + \epsilon - 1 > 0$ for the Marshall-Lerner condition for stability of international equilibrium. Following the familiar argument for the optimum tariff we can also deduce that the optimum is attained at the range of $\epsilon^* > 1$ even under the expected utility maximization, because the expected utility at the range of $\epsilon^* > 1$, which may be represented by a trade indifference curve around that range of the foreign offer curve, is greater than that at the range of $\epsilon \leq 1.^*$ A similar deduction leads us to believe that even under uncertainty the optimal tariff for a large country is positive ($t > 0$). All this means that $EB > 0$.

Let us consider that the home country is risk-neutral. Suppose that A is increased. Then, as was indicated earlier, the home offer curve shifts leftwards. The international equilibrium point moves also leftwards, and in "the normal case," ϵ^* increases. Then $t - 1(\epsilon^* - 1)$ increases. Noting in (3) that $M_2 = D_2 - X_2 - A$, the coefficient of A is p^*, and hence y increases as A rises. For risk neutrality, however, U_y in B of (16) is constant.[3] We see that p^* and M_2 decrease in the elastic portion of the foreign offer curve as the home offer curve shifts leftwards as a result of rises in A. Moreover, changes in ϵ and η are not known definitely. All this implies that B may increase or decrease. Consequently, the covariance in (15) may be positive or negative, and the optimal tariff in (15) may be lower or higher than $E\{1/(\epsilon^* - 1)\}$.[4] Only when ϵ and η change such that $\eta(\epsilon^* - 1)/(\epsilon^* + \epsilon - 1)$ decrease as A rises, is the covariance negative, and $t > E\{1/(\epsilon^* - 1)\}$.

Even for risk aversion, for which U_y decreases as A rises, the covariance may have either a positive or a negative value. Hence $t \gtrless E\{1/(\epsilon^* - 1)\}$. An interesting question is which is more protective between risk neutrality and risk aversion. Since as A rises U_y decreases for risk aversion while it is constant for risk neutrality, the covariance in the former case is smaller than the covariance in the latter case, and hence, other things being equal, the optimal tariff under risk aversion is higher than that under risk neutrality.[5]

An economic explanation of this result is given as follows. We can point out first that even under uncertainty the gains from the tariff for a large country in the form of improvements of terms of trade and the losses from decreases in imports will appear regardless of the attitudes toward risk, although these are measured in the expected terms. In the comparison of risk neutrality and risk aversion we should recognize that randomness of the transfer causes consumption of the second goods, $D_2 = M_2 + X_2 + A$, also to be random. The risk-averse country is more concerned about risky consumption of the second goods than the risk-neutral country. However, the former

---

[3]For this definition of risk neutrality and that of risk aversion below, see, for example, Turnovsky (1974) and de Meza (1987).

[4]Since $1/(\epsilon^* - 1)$ is a convex function of ϵ^*, from Jensen's inequality $E\{1/(\epsilon^* - 1)\} > 1/(E\epsilon^* - 1)$.

[5]This is contrasted with the result of de Meza (1987) of the optimal tariff under uncertain terms of trade that risk aversion may raise or lower the optimal tariff compared with risk neutrality.

country cannot reduce risk itself by means of a tariff: not only the transfer A but also home production X_2 and import M_2 are still random. The only response or the only thing that the risk-averse country can do is to reduce the expected amount of consumption of the second goods, and it requires a higher tariff.

Up to now in this section we have considered that the developing country is a large country. Now suppose that this country is small compared with the foreign country. Then the foreign offer curve becomes a straight line having the slope of $1/p^*$. This implies that regardless of values of A and of the locations of the home offer curve, values of p^* and ϵ^* ($= \infty$) are certain. This in turn implies that the covariance in (15) is zero, and we have an important conclusion that the optimal tariff is zero for a small country regardless of the attitudes toward risk, which is in a sharp contrast to the results for the case of a large country.

Since in the case of a small country the foreign relative price is known with certainty, the domestic relative price $p = (1 + t)p^*$ is known with certainty as well. Hence the production and consumption decisions or their levels are also known <u>ex ante</u>. Thus, the policy-maker of this small country does not in effect face the problem of uncertainty. Under such a situation the free trade or zero tariff policy is optimum both under risk neutrality and risk aversion. Randomness of the transfer A is adjusted by adjustments in <u>ex post</u> import M_2 under free trade.

3. The Optimal Quotas

Now suppose that the government of the developing country determines the level of imports before the true value of the transfer is known. A crucial difference from the tariff is that when the government fixes M_2, it simultaneously determines the foreign relative price p^*, since the foreign offer curve itself is known with certainty. The import licenses are sold to importers in a competitive manner at the price of $p - p^*$, when the actual volume of the transfer and the domestic relative price p are known.[6]

The spendable income under the quota in terms of the first goods is written as

---

[6]The following analysis may cover the case in which the government itself engages in trade, and determines levels of imports.

$$y = X_1 + pX_2 + (p - p^*)M_2 + pA, \qquad (17)$$

where $(p - p^*)M_2$ are the quota revenues.

The optimal M_2 is determined so as to maximize the expected indirect utility $EU(p, y)$. After A is actually realized, domestic production and consumption are determined so as to equate $D_2 - X_2$ to $M_2 + A$. In that process the domestic relative price is determined.

Differentiating $EU(p, y)$ with respect to M_2, and making use of $dX_1/dM_2 + pdX_2/dM_2 = 0$ and Roy's identity, we get

$$\frac{dEU}{dM_2} = EU_y\left\{(p - p^*) - M_2 \frac{dp^*}{dM_2}\right\}. \qquad (18)$$

On the foreign offer curve $(M_2/p^*)(dp^*/dM_2) = 1/(\epsilon^* - 1)$. Equating (18) to zero, letting $\tau = (p - p^*)/p^*$, which is known as the implicit tariff rate in the literature (see Bhagwati (1965)), and arranging, we obtain

$$\frac{dEU}{dM_2} = EU_y p^* \left(\tau - \frac{1}{\epsilon^* - 1}\right) = 0.^7 \qquad (19)$$

Noting that p^* and ϵ^* are non-random, we get from (19)

$$E\tau = \frac{1}{\epsilon^* - 1} - \frac{\text{cov}\,(U_y, \tau)}{EU_y}. \qquad (20)$$

Let us check the sign of cov (U_y, τ). When A rises, p becomes lower in the home market and hence τ becomes lower. On the other hand, when A increases, y increases (note that arranging the right-hand side of (17), the coefficient of A is p^*). Hence, while U_y is constant for risk neutrality, U_y decreases for risk aversion. Thus, cov (U_y, τ) is zero for risk neutrality, and it is positive for risk aversion. These imply that

$$E\tau = \frac{1}{\epsilon^* - 1} \quad \text{for risk neutrality,}$$

and

$$E\tau < \frac{1}{\epsilon^* - 1} \quad \text{for risk aversion,} \qquad (21)$$

that is, the expected implicit tariff rate is equal to $1/(\epsilon^* - 1)$ for risk neutrality, and it is lower than $1/(\epsilon^* - 1)$ for risk aversion.

---

[7] From this it is easy to see that the optimal quota under certainty is given such that the implicit tariff rate τ is equal to $1/(\epsilon^* - 1)$.

Since we see from (19) or (20) that at the optimum under risk neutrality, $E\tau = 1/(\epsilon^* - 1)$, $dEU/dM_2 = p^* \text{cov}(U_y, \tau) > 0$ under risk aversion, the optimal quota under risk aversion is greater than that under risk neutrality. This is true for a small as well as a large country. The situations are illustrated in Figure 3, where the home country is considered to be large. While the foreign offer curve Of is known with certainty, the location of the home offer curve is not known <u>ex ante</u> as before, which depends on the realized value of A. The optimal quota levels are such as OD for the risk-neutral country and OC for the risk-averse country. The equilibrium terms of trade are given by the slopes of OB and OA in the respective cases. However, the equilibrium home relative price is not known <u>ex ante</u> because of randomness of A and the home offer curve.

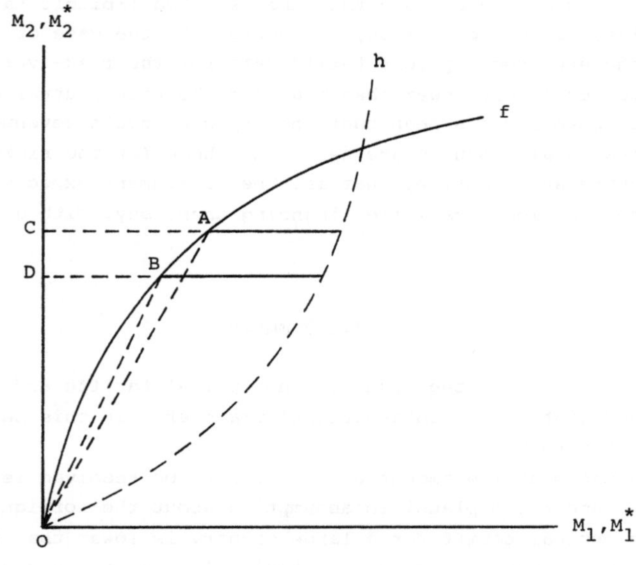

Figure 3

When ϵ^* increases as M_2 decreases along the foreign offer curve, in (21) the ϵ^* relevant to risk aversion is smaller than the ϵ^* relevant to risk neutrality. Hence in this case we cannot compare the levels of the expected implicit tariff rates between risk neutrality and risk aversion.

The above results are in sharp contrasts to those for the optimal tariff: in contrast to the tariff a risk-averse country employs a less protectionist policy than a risk neutral country. An economic explanation is given as follows. In the case of the quota, the risk-averse country facing uncertain consumption of the second goods, $D_2 = M_2 + X_2 + A$, can and does substitute more imports, which are surely determined, for the uncertain supply by home production X_2 through increasing M_2 and thereby lowering the expected home relative price of the second goods. This is the economic explanation.

The above explanation is also valid for a small country. Unlike a tariff p and hence X_i and D_i $(i = 1,2)$ are random even for a small country. When $\epsilon^* = \infty$, we see from (20) or (21) that while the risk-neutral small country sets the quota level such that the expected implicit tariff rate is zero, or $Ep = p^*$, the risk-averse small country sets the quota level such that the expected implicit tariff rate is negative, or $Ep < p^*$. Thus, in contrast to the case of a large country the expected implicit tariff rate for the risk-averse small country is definitely lower than that for the risk-neutral small country. The above results mean that the expected quota revenues for the risk-neutral small country are zero, and those for the risk-averse small country are negative, that is, the government expects to pay rewards to the importers while financing them, say, with a lump sum tax.

4. Summary

We have analyzed the issue of the optimal tariffs and quotas under uncertainty about international transfer. In this section we summarize the results.

When the positive amount of transfer to be received is known with certainty, under the plausible assumption about the foreign offer curve the optimal tariff for a large country is lower than that under no transfer. However, the optimal tariff is zero for a small country. Under uncertainty the optimal tariffs for a large country may or may not be higher than $E\{1/(\epsilon^* - 1)\}$ both under risk neutrality and risk aversion. The optimal tariff for a risk-averse large country is higher than that for a risk-neutral large country. For a small country the zero tariff is optimum regardless of the attitudes toward risk.

The results for the optimal quotas are quite in contrast with those for the optimal tariffs. The optimal quotas under risk aversion are greater than those under risk neutrality both for a large and a small country. While levels of the expected implicit tariff rates are not comparable between a risk-averse and a risk-neutral large country, the expected implicit tariff rate for a risk-averse small country is lower than that for a risk-neutral small country, and in particular it is negative.

References

Batra, R.N., The Pure Theory of International Trade under Uncertainty. New York: John Wiley & Sons, 1975.

Bhagwati, J.N., "On the Equivalence of Tariffs and Quotas," in R.E. Baldwin, et al., Trade, Growth, and the Balance of Payments: Essays in Honor of Gottfried Haberler. Chicago: Rand McNally & Company, 1965, 53-67.

Bhagwati, J.N., R.A. Brecher, and T. Hatta, "The Generalized Theory of Transfers and Welfare: Bilateral Transfers in a Multilateral World," American Economic Review 83 (September 1983): 606-618.

de Meza, D., "The Optimum Tariff and Quota When the Terms of Trade are Random," Oxford Economic Papers 39 (June 1987): 412-417.

Newberry, D.M.G., and J.E. Stiglitz, The Theory of Commodity Price Stabilization: A Study in the Economics of Risk. Oxford: Clarendon Press, 1981.

Turnovsky, S.J., "Technological and Price Uncertainty in a Ricardian Model of International Trade," Review of Economic Studies 41 (April 1974): 201-217.

INVESTMENT, CAPITAL STRUCTURE AND COST OF CAPITAL: REVISITED

Yoram Kroll and Haim Levy
The Hebrew University, Jerusalem and
The University of Florida, Gainesville

Introduction

The relevance of capital structure for a firm's valuation is an unresolved issue (see [10], [7], [16], [4], [8], [17], [9], [15], [13], [14], and others). In a series of papers, Modigliani and Miller conclude that in a world without taxes, capital structure does not matter, but with corporate tax they reach the conclusion that the larger the proportion of debt the larger is the value of the firm (see Modigliani and Miller, [11], [12], [13]). However, Miller [10], in his presidential address has shown that under certain assumptions, with corporate and personal taxes, once again that capital structure does not matter.

In a completely different framework, in a world of no taxes, Hirshliefer [5] has shown that investors who maximize the utility from consumption $U(C_1, C_2)$ are indifferent to the capital structure chosen by the firm. Though the relevant cost of capital appropriate for discounting cash flows is provided by Modigliani and Miller as well as by Hirshliefer, some confusion arises in the treatment of certain cash flows. In particular, it is sometimes not clear whether r or (1-T)r should be used as the discount rate, r being the risk-free interest rate and T the corporate tax (see [1], [2]).

The purpose of this paper is threefold: First, in Section 1, we analyze Modigliani and Miller's as well as Miller's arguments in Hirshliefer's framework. This is mainly a graphical exposition which yields the main results in a very simple way. In Section 2 we show that Modigliani and Miller's analysis is incomplete. Namely, it is a comparative static analysis which does not take into account the fact that change in the capital structure induces a change in the optimum production, hence the impact of debt on the value of the firm is greater than the one proposed by them. Section 3 analyzes the firm's cost of capital when there is a constraint on the amount of borrowing. In Section 4 we analyze more thoroughly the impact of bankruptcy expenses which induces increasing cost of borrowing and leads to an interior optimum capital structure. Concluding remarks are given in Section V.

1. Capital Structure and the Value of the Firm: Graphical Exposition

A. A World Without Taxes

Consider a two-period model.[1] The firm's production function is $C_2 = f(I)$, where C_2 is the consumption in the second period and I is the investment. Having a wealth of W in the first period and consumption of C_1, the production function can also be rewritten as $C_2 = f(W-C_1)$, since by definition $W-C_1 = I$. We first assume, like Hirshliefer, a complete certainty, or alternatively, that f(I) is the production function in terms of the certainty equivalent. Namely, each project has its cash flow X (a random variable) and the appropriate certainty equivalent X^*, where $EU(W+X) = U(W+X^*)$, U being the individual utility function and W is the initial wealth. Since not all individuals have the same preferences, we may end up with many certainty equivalent production functions stemming from one basic uncertain production function, and the number of these functions can be as large as the number of the stockholders. However, in our analysis we can pick one certainty equivalent function and the same analysis (e.g. the impact of debt on valuation) holds also for all other certainty equivalent production functions. In short, the following analysis is invariant to the production function that we start with. Thus, for simplicity only, we assume a representative stockholder with a given certainty equivalent production function. In Section 5 we deal with uncertainty more explicitly.

Like Modigliani and Miller, we assume that individuals, as well as firms, borrow and lend at the same riskless interest rate r. Figure 1 illustrates Hirshliefer's investment-consumption analysis. The straight line with a slope of $-(1+r)$ is an iso-present value line. Maximizing the present value of the consumption (C_1, C_2) will maximize the individual's utility. Thus, the firm's optimum production strategy is to invest I^*. All projects with an Internal Rate of Return (IRR) greater than r are accepted and all projects with IRR smaller than r are rejected (compare the slope on the production function with the slope of the straight line). If the firm decides to borrow or

---

[1]This does not impose a constraint on the model and the analysis can be extended to more than two periods. However, the graphical exposition beyond 3-periods is impossible.

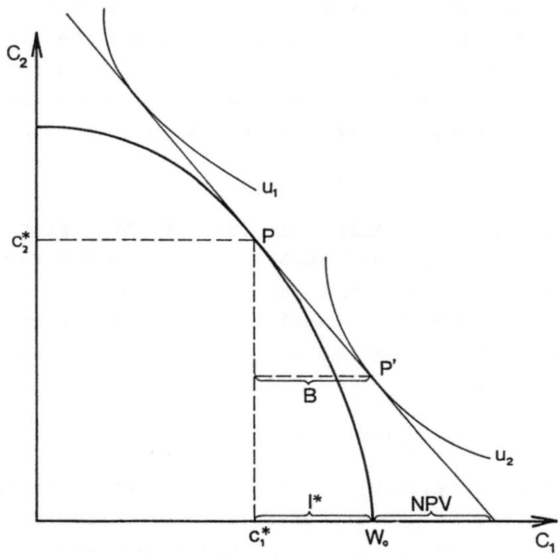

Figure 1

lend money, it moves from point P along the iso-present value line. Since individuals can also move along the same line, "homemade" leverage is as good as the firm's leverage and hence $V_L = V_U$ where V_L at V_U stand for the values of levered and unlevered firms, respectively.

Before we turn to the corporate tax case, note that

$$V_L = V_U = W_0 + NPV$$

where NPV is the net present value of all accepted projects. This value is also given by

$$V_L = V_U = PV(C_1^*, C_2^*) = C_1^* + C_2^*/(1+r)$$

where (C_1^*, C_2^*) are the cashflows (dividends) given by the optimum production at point P.

This analysis illustrates the Separation Theorem in a world with no taxes which states that the firm should stop at point P on the production function, and the way the firm finances the investment does not matter. If, for example, the firm borrows the amount B and some stockholders do not like it, they can "undo" the leverage by lending this amount and moving back from point P' to point P (see Figure 1).

Moreover, if some investors have strong preferences for future consumptions (see U_1), they can lend money and move along the straight line until their utility from consumption is maximized. So far, this is Hirshliefer's separation analysis, and there is nothing new in our analysis though it serves as a good starting point for the following post-tax analysis.

B. A World With Corporate Tax But Without Personal Taxes

Suppose now that a firm is exposed to a corporate tax of T percent of its net income. In such a case, the production function is a post-tax production function; namely, if C_2^B is the before-tax future cashflow corresponding to investment I, ($C_2^B = f(I)$), then the post-tax future cashflow C_2 will be:

$$C_2 = (1-T)[C_2^B-I] + I = (1-T)C_2^B + TI \tag{1}$$

Note that (for simplicity only) we assume that the whole investment is depreciated. However, if not all of it is depreciable we simply deduct the relevant part for tax purposes. Financial expenses are not deducted from the cashflow since they are taken into account indirectly by the discounting process. The effective interest rate that the firm pays on its borrowing is (1-T)r, while stockholders can borrow and lend at r. This discrepancy in the effective interest rate for firms and individuals induces the well-known benefit of debt.

Figure 2 illustrates the post-tax production function and the impact of leverage on the value of the firm. First note that if the firm is unlevered, the optimum production point is P, where the production function is tangent to the iso-present value line with a slope of -(1+r). (See line 1. For simplicity the minus sign is omitted from all figures.) In the case of the unlevered firm the strategy of stopping at point P maximizes the stockholders' present value of consumption and hence maximizes their utility. Note that r and not (1-T)r is the relevant slope of the iso-present value line since individuals borrow and lend on their account, hence r and not (1-T)r is the relevant discount rate.

Suppose now that the firm which stops at point P borrows the amount B. Since interest is tax-deductible, it will pay the lender in the future an after tax amount of B_F (the subscript F stands for future payment) given by:

$$B_F = B[1 + (1-T)r] \tag{2}$$

Hence, the stockholders obtain the cashflow (C_1^{**}, C_2^{**}) which is the

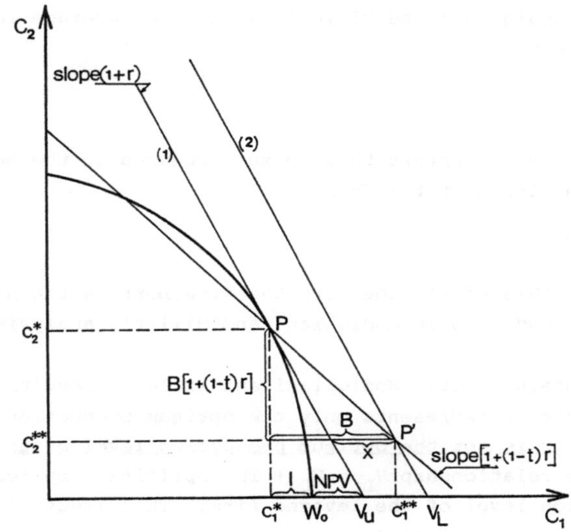

Figure 2

cashflow due to production and borrowing decisions of the firm (see Figure 2). Since the firm borrows at (1-T)r, it moves along the line whose slope is only -(1 + (1-T)r), namely from point P to point P'. Do stockholders benefit from this leverage? The answer is positive. They can borrow and lend at r, hence move from point P' to any point along the iso-present value line (2) which has a slope of -(1+r). The intercept of this line with the horizontal axis is the value of the levered firm. The horizontal distance between line (2) and (1) represents the gain from the leverage. Let us calculate this gain which we denote by X (see Figure 2). Note that

$$\frac{-B[1 + (1-T)r]}{B - X} = -(1+r)$$

Hence

$$B + B(1-T)r = B(1+r) - X(1+r)$$

Hence

$$X = \frac{BTr}{1+r}$$

This is exactly Modigliani and Miller's gain from leverage for a one-period case, namely:

$$V_L = V_U + \frac{Btr}{1+r} \tag{3}$$

In the perpetuity context this formula reduced to the well-known Modigliani and Miller post-tax formula[2]

$$V_L = V_U + BT \tag{4}$$

Obviously, under this model, the more the firm borrows the higher will be V_L, hence it leads, as in Modigliani and Miller's analysis to a corner solution.

While we obtain exactly Modigliani and Miller's results, it can be noted that point P represents only the optimum production of the unlevered firm, it is not the optimum production level of the levered firm. Thus, the relationship $V_L = V_U + TB$ implicitly implies a non-optimal production level of the levered firm. This issue will be further elaborated in Section 2.

C. Corporate and Personal Taxes

Let us incorporate personal taxes. We analyze first the pre-1986 tax reform, when the capital gain tax rate T_g was lower than the personal income tax rate, T_p. As before, T denotes the corporate tax rate, T_p the personal tax rate on income, T_g the personal capital gain tax and $T_g \le T_p$. We assume first that the firm wishes to minimize the tax payment, hence it pays all its future cashflow as capital gain subject to the tax rate T_g. Thus, the after-tax production function is of the form:[3]

$$C_2 = (C_2^B - I)(1-T)(1-T_g) + I \tag{5}$$

where C_2^B is the before-tax cashflow and I is the investment, (which is all assumed to be depreciable). The firm's after-tax cost of borrowing is given by $(1-T)(1-T_g)r$. This is the discount rate since each dollar borrowed reduces the stockholders future net income by $(1-T)(1-T_g)r$. If the firm chooses to lend money, the after all taxes income due to the lending transaction is $(1-T)(1-T_g)r$. Thus, the minimum required

[2]Note that $\sum_{t=1}^{\infty} \frac{BTr}{(1+r)^t} = BT$.

[3]If the firm pays some of its income as dividend and some as capital gain, an average tax rate of T_g' should replace T_g, where $T_g' > T_g$.

rate of return by the firm on investment is $(1-T)(1-T_g)r$. The individuals, on the other hand, borrow and lend at the after-tax rate $(1-T_p)r$, since interest income (or expenses) are subject to personal tax T_p.

Let us assume first that T_p and T_g are constant across all individuals and $T_p > T_g$. Figure 3 illustrates the relationship between the value of the levered and unlevered firm in this scenario. The iso-present value line which tangents to point P has a slope of $-[1 + (1-T)(1-T_g)r]$. Let us assume that the firm borrows \$B and will return the loan in the second period, hence the net cashflow in the second period will be reduced by $B_F = B[1 + (1-T)(1-T_g)r]$. This financial transaction switches the firm from point P to point P′. Does this leverage increase the value of the firm? The answer is strictly a function of the relationship between T_p, T_g and T. If $(1-T)(1-T_g) < (1-T_p)$ leverage increases the value of the firm and vice versa. To see this note that without leverage, stockholders get the cashflows (C_1^*, C_2^*), and since their after tax cost of capital is $(1-T_p)r$, the value of the unlevered firm is given by point V_U which is the intercept of the line whose slope is $-[1 + (1-T_p)r]$ with the horizontal axis. Let us assume that this line is steeper than the line whose slope is $-[1 + (1-T)(1-T_g)r]$, hence showing a gain from leverage. The value of the levered firm which borrows B is given by the intercept of line (3) which is parallel to line (2) but passes through the new point available to stockholders, P′. The gain from leverage is given by X which is the distance between lines (3) and (2). Let us calculate this value. We employ, as before, the following relationship:

$$\frac{-B[1 + (1-T)(1-T_g)r]}{B - X} = -[1 + (1-T_p)r]$$

Hence $B[1 + (1-T)(1-T_g)r] = B[1 + (1-T_p)r] - X[1 + (1-T_p)r]$ which finally yields

$$X = \frac{Br[(1-T_p) - (1-T)(1-T_g)]}{(1 + (1-T_p)r)} \tag{6}$$

Extending the analysis to a case of perpetuity we have

$$\sum_{t=1}^{\infty} \frac{Br[(1-T_p) - (1-T)(1-T_g)]}{[1 + (1-T_p)r]^t} = \frac{Br[(1-T_p) - (1-T)(1-T_g)]}{(1-T_p)r}$$

hence the relationship of the value of the levered and unlevered firm is given by

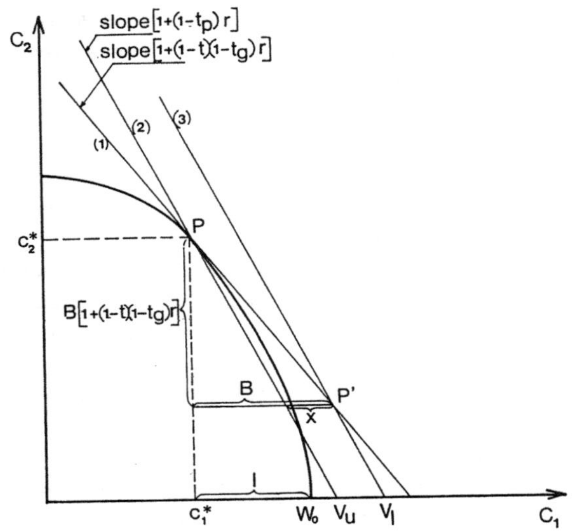

Figure 3

$$V_L = V_U + B\left[1 - \frac{(1-T)(1-T_g)}{1-T_p}\right] \qquad (7)$$

Using Modigliani and Miller's arbitrage argument, this is precisely the formula obtained by Arditti, Levy and Sarnat [1] (ALS) and the one employed by Miller [10]. The benefit or loss due to leverage is a function of the sign of the terms within the squared brackets which appears on the right-hand side of equation (7).

Miller [10] claims that in equilibrium, at the margin we must have

$$(1-T_p) = (1-T)(1-T_g)$$

which implies that the terms in the squared brackets are equal to zero. Hence, with corporate and personal taxes capital structure does not matter. Let us see Miller's argument in Hirshliefer's framework.

First recall that Miller assumes many investors with various tax brackets. Thus, in Hirshliefer's framework it implies many lines with slopes $-[1 + (1-T_p)r]$ when T_p is no longer treated as constant. The whole industry borrows initially from investors with low T_p, but as long as $(1-T)(1-T_g) < (1-T_p)$, it is worthwhile for the firms to borrow more. Thus, industry will continue to borrow from individuals with higher tax brackets. Hence T_p increases, until at the margin $(1-T_p) = (1-T)(1-T_g)$.[4] In terms of Figure 3, as T_p increases, the line (2) and (3) will be flatter until it will be tangent to the production curve at point P. Hence, in equilibrium lines (1) and (2) will coincide and there is no benefit due to leverage. Since the marginal investor determines the equilibrium market interest rate which is unique for all borrowers and lenders, Miller claims that those investors who are characterized by a lower T_p than the value of T_p of the marginal lender, enjoy a "bondholder surplus".

After the 1986 tax reform we have $T_p = T_g$. Yet, since capital gain tax is paid only with the realization of the income, the effective tax rate T_g is lower than the effective rate T_p, as caused by a tax deferral. Hence the pre-1986 tax reform analysis still holds, though the difference between T_p and T_g shrinks.

Miller's presidential address renewed the debate on the role that capital structure plays in determining the value of the firm (see for example [4], [14], [8]). We do not join this debate but show rather ALS results as well as Miller's argument in a simple graphical Hirshliefer's investment-consumption framework.

2. The Interrelationship Between Production and Capital Structure

Modigliani and Miller [11] and virtually all studies which followed their paper as well as textbooks, assume explicitly or implicitly that the net operating income of the levered and unlevered firm is identical. Under this assumption Modigliani and Miller obtain that $V_L = V_U + TB$. However, this comparative statistics framework analyzes a case where one firm is at the optimum production and the other is not. For example, if the unlevered firm is at the optimum production point, then, in order to achieve the well-known relationship

---

[4]To be more precise, Miller assumes that $T_g = 0$. Under this assumption there is no benefit due to leverage when $T_p = T$. The analysis can be generalized to the case $T_g > 0$ as done above. Also note that if $(1-T_p) > (1-T)(1-T_g)$, the stockholders will be better off by switching money from equity to debt. By switching $1 of income from equity income to debt income, the stockholder loses $(1-T)(1-T_g)$ as capital gain, but gets an income (from the debt) of $(1-T_p)$. Thus, as long as $(1-T_p) > (1-T)(1-T_g)$, the industry will borrow more, T_p will increase, and this borrowing by the industry will stop exactly at the point $(1-T_p) = (1-T)(1-T_g)$.

$V_L = V_U + TB$, we must assume that the levered firm is not at the optimum production point.[5]

Figure 4 illustrates the relationship between the value of the levered and unlevered firms. Point P on the production line reports the optimum production of the unlevered firm whose value is V_U^*. Line (2) which passes through this point, but with a slope of $-[1 + (1-T)r]$, yields the value V_L. Consider the specific case where the firm borrows B (the maximum possible borrowing) and pays in the future all its cashflow in return for the principal and the post-tax interest.

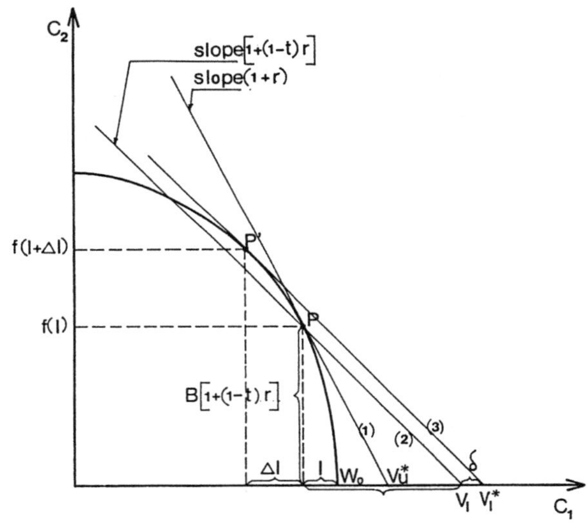

Figure 4

[5]A similar argument is given by Hite [6], who analyzes the borrowing policy as part of the multifactors optimization problem of the firm. Hite assumes that the firm borrows small amounts, such that the probability of bankruptcy is zero. Thus, borrowing can be only at the riskfree rate and the optimal capital structure cannot be analyzed through Hite's framework. In Sections 4 and 5 we will assume that the amount of borrowing is either externally constrained or that, due to positive probability of bankruptcy and the existence of cost of bankruptcy, the cost of borrowing for the borrowers is an increasing function of the amount borrowed. Our analysis leads to interior optimum capital structure.

As we have shown above, in this case we have $V_L = V_U + TB$. However, the levered firm is not in equilibrium, since with a cost of capital of $(1-T)r$, the firm should increase its production up to point P′ by additional investment of I. The implied value of the levered firm will be V_L^* and $V_L^* > V_L$ (see Figure 4). Thus, with corporate taxes there is no separation between the production and financial decision. The decision to borrow money simultaneously determines the firm's cost of capital (which is $(1-T)r$ rather than r), which, in turn, determines the optimum production. Hence, when we compare the value of the levered firm to the value of the unlevered firm, when both are at the optimum production level, the relationship $V_L = V_U + TB$ no longer holds.

Denoting by V_L^* the value of the firm at the optimum production we have

$$V_L^* = V_U^* + TB + \delta = V_L + \delta \quad \text{(see Figure 4)} \tag{8}$$

Of course, $\delta > 0$ and its magnitude is a function of the slope of the production function. To be more specific, in our case of maximum borrowing, we have:

$$\frac{-[f(I+\Delta I) - f(I)]}{\Delta I + \delta} = -[1 + (1-T)r] \quad \text{(see Figure 4)}$$

Hence

$$\delta = \frac{f(I+\Delta I) - f(I)}{[1 + (1-T)r]} - \Delta I \tag{9}$$

From (9) we learn that the addition to the value of the levered firm, in comparison to what is claimed by Modigliani and Miller, is the NPV due to the additional investment ΔI which is induced by the borrowing.

When Modigliani and Miller and other researchers analyze the capital structure issue they want to isolate all other parameters by holding "all other factors constant". To be more specific, Modigliani and Miller assume that the two firms (or the same firm in two alternative states) are characterized by the same EBIT which they denote by X. In our analysis we assume that the two firms face the same production function so that both firms have the same physical opportunities to invest, but are allowed to move along this production function. Since the decision to raise debt interacts with the decision on the selection of the physical activities, we have additional gain δ which does not appear in the Modigliani and Miller analysis. Thus, Modigliani and Miller measure only a partial gain from leverage with no change in the investment level, while incorporating δ we measure the whole benefit from leverage due to a cheaper debt as well as the additional projects taken.

Recall, that in a world of no taxes or in a world of corporate and personal taxes, the previous Modigliani and Miller or Miller analyses are unchanged. In a world of no taxes we have a separation between production and financial decisions, and in a world of corporate and personal taxes, Miller's argument holds in the situation where $(1-T_p) = (1-T)(1-T_g)$, hence there is no change in the optimum production point due to leverage, and we obtain $\delta = 0$.

Of course, what is left to the readers' judgment is to decide whether it is more logical to assume that the production function (physical projects available) should be held constant, or that the production level (i.e., a point on this production function) should be held constant in debt issue analyses. We believe that if there is an interrelation between the financial decision and the physical activities, we should hold the physical opportunities constant, but let the firm choose the optimum point on the production function.

In principle, when we analyze two states of the same firm (with and without leverage), the production function (i.e., available projects) should be held constant, but the firm can change the number of accepted projects as it wishes.

3. An Imperfect Market: A Constraint on the Amount Borrowed

We have seen that the firm's cost of capital is r in the absence of taxes and $(1-T)r$ when corporate tax is taken into account and the firm employs an extreme leverage. In this section we analyze the determination of the firm's optimum production and the firm's cost of capital in cases where the firm is allowed to borrow at r but there is a restriction on the amount borrowed. The restriction can be determined externally, i.e., by regulation or by lenders, or it may even be determined internally by the firm's management. For example, it may be that due to agency costs the management may decide not to have more than a given proportion of debt in its capital structure, even though from the stockholders' point of view increasing the proportion of debt is desirable. In this section, we assume that such a constraint on borrowing exists, and analyze its economic consequences.

Suppose that the unlevered firm's cashflows is given by (C_1, C_2). The maximum amount that the firm can borrow is

$$B^* = C_2/[1 + (1-T)r]$$

Namely, the firm has a future cashflow of C_2 which should suffice in the future to pay the principle B, and the post-tax interests. In this case of maximum borrowing, the firm's cost of capital is $(1-T)r$ (see Section 1). Now, suppose that there is a constraint that only $B = \alpha B^*$ is borrowed when $0 \le \alpha \le 1$. What is the optimum investment I and what is the appropriate discount rate in this case?

In order to answer these questions, let us choose the level of investment which maximizes the present value of consumption which is denoted by Y:

$$Y \equiv (W-I) + \alpha B^* + \frac{(1-\alpha)C_2(I)}{1 + r} \tag{10}$$

To see that this is the present value of consumption note that if W is the initial wealth, then (W-I) is the initial wealth less the investment which is available for distribution in the first period. Since αB^* is borrowed, this sum is also available for distribution in the first period. In the second period the cashflow due to investment I, is $C_2(I)$. However, the firm has to pay for the borrowed money in the future α of C_2.

$$\alpha B^*[1 + (1-T)r] = \alpha C_2(I)$$

Recall that $B^*[1 + (1-T)r]$ is the after tax cashflow $C_2(I)$, hence what is left for distribution in the second period is only $(1-\alpha)C_2(I)$. The stockholders' appropriate discount rate is r, thus the contribution to the present value of this term is $(1-\alpha)C_2/(1+r)$. Rewriting Y we obtain:

$$Y = (W-I) + \alpha C_2(I)/[1 + (1-T)r] + (1-\alpha)C_2(I)/(1+r) \tag{11}$$

Taking the derivative of Y with respect to I and equating to zero yields:

$$-1 + C_2'(I)\left[\frac{\alpha}{1 + (1-T)r} + \frac{(1-\alpha)}{1+r}\right] = 0$$

Hence the marginal return on production (IRR) at the optimum point is given by $C_2'(I)$

$$C_2'(I) = \frac{1}{\frac{\alpha}{1 + (1-T)r} + \frac{1-\alpha}{1+r}} = \frac{(1+r)[1 + (1-T)r]}{\alpha(1+r) + (1-\alpha)[1 + (1-T)r]}$$

which can finally be rewritten in the form

$$C_2'(I) = \frac{(1+r)[1 + (1-T)r]}{(1+r) - (1-\alpha)Tr} \tag{12}$$

Equation (12) states that the firm should produce until the after-tax return on production $C_2'(I)$ will be given by the right hand side of equation (12). Since all terms on the right hand side are known parameters, for a given α, the optimum production can be determined. Note the following extreme cases:

(1) For $\alpha = 1$, the firm borrowed the maximum possible amount and we obtain, as expected, $C_2'(U) = 1 + (1-T)r$.

(2) For $\alpha = 0$, we have no borrowing, and equation (12) reduces to $C_2'(I) = 1+r$. For any $0 < \alpha < 1$ we obtain at the optimum point,

$$1 + (1-T)r < C_2'(I) < I + r$$

Denoting by $1 + \rho = C_2'(I)$, we can determine that the appropriate discount rate, ρ, is between r and $(1-T)r$ and is a function of the constraint on borrowing given by the parameter α. Note that the α on borrowing is given as a proportion on the maximum available borrowing, where this maximum is determined by the future cashflow of the firm discounted by $(1-T)r$. This proportion is different from the traditional one which is given as a percent of the value of the firm. These two different approaches yield two different values for the firm's cost of capital. For example, if $r = 10\%$, $T = 60\%$ and $\alpha = 70\%$ we obtain from equation (12) $\rho = 5.73\%$. If we use the traditional Weighted Average Cost of Capital (WACC) equation and we assume that debt is 70% out of the value of the firm (an assumption which is different from the one which assumes that 70% of future cashflow is committed to debt services), then we obtain WACC = 5.8%. Thus, the two methods do not yield the same cost of capital.

Moreover, employing the traditional WACC has a profound difficulty; the value of the firm is determined by the discounted future cash flow of the firm. However, in order to use the WACC as the discounting factor one should know first the value of the firm.

Therefore, we have two variables which are dependent; we cannot solve for the value of the firm without knowing the cost of capital, but by the same token we cannot solve for the cost of capital without knowing first the value of the firm. Our approach which defines leverage as a proportion of future cashflow is free of this complexity.

This difficulty is resolved in our approach since the discounting factor is determined by the proportion of future cashflow which is committed to after tax debt services (see equation (12)), and this amount is given from the production function. A graphical presentation of our proposed process is given in Figure 5.

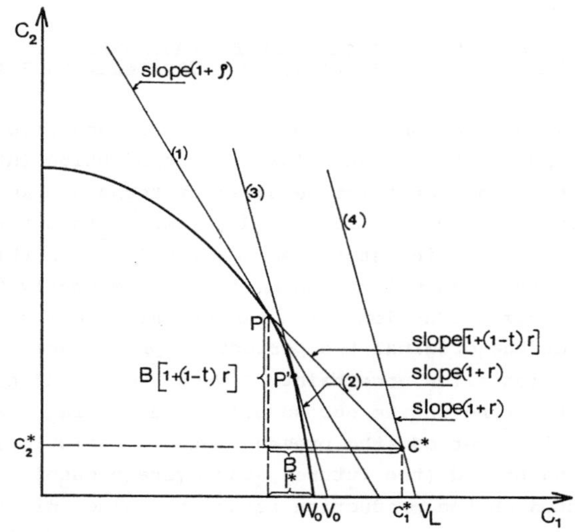

Figure 5

In case the firm does not employ leverage, the optimum production is P′ and V_0 is the value of the unlevered firm (see Figure 5, line 3, whose slope is $-(1+r)$). Suppose now that the firm borrows $B = \alpha B^*$. For a given α one can employ equation (12) to solve for the appropriate discount rate ρ and produce until $C_2'(I) = 1 + \rho$, namely the optimum production is at point P and the optimum investment is I (see line 1, whose slope is $-(1+\rho)$). The firm borrows $B = \alpha B$ and hence provides the stockholders with point C , i.e., the cashflows (c_1^*, c_2^*). The present value of this cashflow determines the value V of the levered firm:

$$V_L = PV(c_1^*, c_2^*) = c_1^* + c_2^*/(1+r)$$

The horizontal distance between lines (4) and (3) is the additional value due to leverage. As in the previous case, the gain from leverage is due to the tax shelter of the interest payment as well as the change in the optimum production due to the reduction in the firm's cost of capital from r to ρ. Thus, the value of the levered firm is given by $V_U + TB + \delta$ when δ is the net present value of the additional accepted projects due to the shift from point P′ to point P (see Section 2).

4. Extensions: Uncertainty, Increasing Cost of Borrowing and Equity and Internal Optimum Capital Structure

In the previous sections we avoided a direct analysis of uncertainty by reducing the future cashflows from production into certainty equivalent terms. Since certainty equivalent terms are subjective and vary among individuals, we, in turn, had to assume that there is a "representative" average investor (see Section 1).[6] In this section we drop the certainty equivalent assumption, consequently C_2, the future cashflow from production, is a random variable whose mean is $\bar{C}_2$. Note that the original two periods graphical analysis of Hirshliefer does not allow uncertainty. Thus, we extend this original analysis by considering in the second period the average cashflow $\bar{C}_2$. Namely, in the first period (the present), the cashflow C_1, is certain and in the second period (the future), the average cashflow $\bar{C}_2$ rather than C_2 is plotted on the production frontier. Since different levels of average cashflows in the future might also include different levels of risk, one should be careful and take the effects of risk into consideration, when comparing the various points on this production frontier. Our way of considering this risk will be by assuming that individuals can transfer cashflows from one period to another at market prices, which include risk premiums. The firm can also borrow at a rate of $r(C_2,\alpha)$. This rate of borrowing increases with the level of uncertainty which is due to the production selection (C_2), as well as the proportion α of borrowing. Note that the firm can also lend money at a rate r_L which might be independent of C_2 and α. However, we will show that under reasonable tax assumptions it is not optimal for the firms to lend money. Thus, under this assumption, in equilibrium the firms borrow and individuals might borrow or lend. Also note that the increase in interest rate due to increase in the amount of

[6] Alternatively, to the "certainty equivalent" assumption, it was possible to determine the production frontier in terms of the average cashflow of production less the insurance premium which insures this average cashflow.

borrowing is consistent with the increased probability of bankruptcy.[7] We also assume that the stockholders opportunity cost $K(C_2, \alpha)$ of shifting consumption (risky cashflows) from one period to another, is a function of both the "operating" risk involved with the selection of a specific level of C_2 and the financial risk associated with α. These two assumptions are depicted in Figure 6.

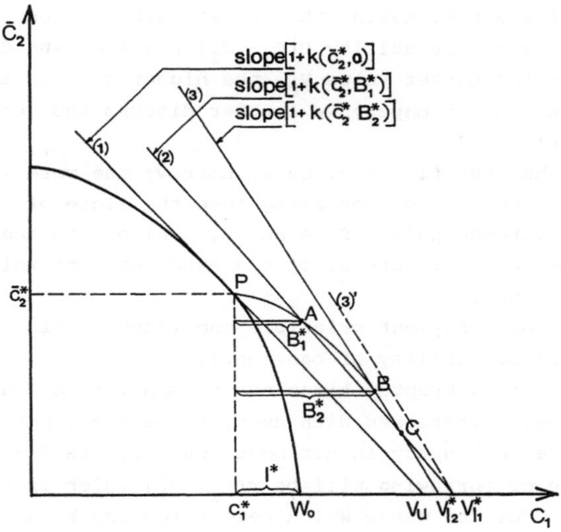

Figure 6

Suppose the firm decides to invest I^* reaching point P on the production frontier (see Figure 6). If the firm decides not to borrow the available cashflows for the individuals is C_1^* in the present period and the average of $\bar{C}_2^*$ in the future period; from this point the individuals can exchange, along line (1), the cashflow in the first period with the <u>average</u> cashflow in the second period at a <u>constant</u> market price of $K(C_2^*, 0)$. This exchange rate is given by the slope of line (1). We assume that the amount which the individual exchanges as well

---

[7]Hite [6], who also analyzed the effect of borrowing on optimal production, limited his analysis to small risk with zero probability of bankruptcy, thereby limiting his analysis to the case of constant cost of borrowing at the <u>risk free</u> market rate.

as the direction of the exchange (borrowing or lending) do not affect the market price K. This is reasonable under the assumption that the individuals are relatively "small" and can be price-takers in the market. Thus, the personal transformation lines (like line (1)) are straight lines. The point at which the personal transformation line cuts the horizontal axis C_1, gives the present value (V_U) of the point $P(C_1^*, \bar{C}_2^*)$.[8] The stockholder's goal is to maximize the present value, since by maximizing this value he (or she) maximizes the utility from consumption. For example, having the market value V_U, one can lend money at r to maximize the utility $U(C_1, C_2)$ where C_1 and C_2 are certain. The higher the market value V_U, the higher will be the achieved $U(C_1, C_2)$. (Later in the paper, we further discuss and demonstrate this point (see Figure 7)).

Assume now that the firm decides to borrow; the more it borrows the higher is the interest on borrowing (see the slope of the curved lines which pass through points P, A and B). Also note that the cost of borrowing depicted in Figure 6, is the expected cost which includes the following elements:

(a) The cost of repayment principle and interest times one, minus the probability of bankruptcy.

(b) The cost of bankruptcy times the probability of bankruptcy.

The cost of borrowing increases with debt, since the lenders are risk averters and since bankruptcy is not costless. If the firm borrows B_1^* the marginal rate of borrowing will be $r(\bar{C}_2^*, B_1^*)$ which is equal to the slope, at point A, of the curve which passes through P, A, B. From point A the individuals can transform $\bar{C}_2$ with C_1 at a price of $K(\bar{C}_2^*, B_1^*)$ along the straight line (2). This line cuts the horizontal axis C_1 at the point V_{L1}^* which determines the present value of point A. Since, in our example, $V_{L1}^* > V_U$, we can conclude that the firm gains from borrowing the amount of B_1^*. If the firm borrows the amount B_2, the appropriate personal transformation line is (3). This line passes through B and cuts the horizontal axis at V_{L2}^*. Also note that in our example $V_{L2}^* < V_{L1}^*$ which means that the firm is better off by borrowing only B_1^* rather than B_2^*. Note that in our example lines (2) and (3) intersect at point C (see Figure 6). Thus, to the left of this point line (3) is above line (2). However, this does not mean that being on line (3) is more desirable than being on line (2) since the financial risk on (3) is higher. In order to clarify this point let us consider

---

[8] Note that if K is not constant, as we assumed, and lines like (1) are not straight, then one can have conflicting results between present values and future values and the optimum depends on the personal preferences of the individuals (see Hirshliefer [5]).

being on the intersection point C. The individual can obtain this point either when the firm borrows only B_1^* and the individual transforms future average cashflow for present cashflow along line (2), or when the firm borrows B_2^* and the individual transforms future average cashflow for present cashflow along line (3). In both cases, being at point C means the same present cashflow and the same <u>average</u> future cashflow. However, being at this point through line (3) means that risk is higher (the slope of line (3) is steeper than the slope of line (2)). Thus, though point C can be obtained in two ways, the more desirable one is that the firm borrow only B_1^* and the individuals transform along line (2). In other words, point C provides the same <u>average</u> vector of consumption, but a lower risk is attached to the consumption vector achieved by line (2), hence it dominates the average consumption vector achieved through line (3).

In our case, the higher present value is V_{L1}^* and borrowing B_1^* is preferable to borrowing B_2^*.[9] Thus, our example demonstrates optimum interior capital structure. Note that in the previous analysis in Section 3 we only assumed external constraints on the amount of borrowing, but we did not derive internal solution for capital structure.

Before we turn to more rigorous analyses, recall that in order to use the risk-free borrowing and lending opportunity by individuals the two periods risk analysis should be transformed again into certainty equivalent terms. Figure 7 exhibits this transformation. Suppose the firm produces up to point P and borrows up to A. The appropriate risky discounting factor $-(1 + K(\alpha))$ is the slope of line (1). This line crosses the horizontal axis at the point V_L. From point V_L we can draw the risk-free line (2) with a slope of $-(1+r_F)$. The distance between line (2) and the horizontal axis represents the certainty equivalent values of future cashflows. For example, the distance between the horizontal axis and A′ is the certainty equivalent of point A.

So far, we have shown a possible interior optimum capital structure. In the following analysis we calculate explicitly the optimum capital structure and the optimum investment strategy. As a result of this optimization, we derive the cut-off rate to a firm which, in

---

[9] The proof that corporate leverage of B_1^* is preferable to leverage of B_2^* is as follows: Suppose the firm borrows B_1^*. Therefore the present value as well as the market value of point A is V_{L1}^*. Since $V_{L1}^* > V_{L2}^*$, the individual can sell his holdings in A and buy holdings in B at the price $k(C_2, B_2)$. This transaction causes a movement from line (2) to line (3′) which is parallel to line (3) and thus is preferred over line (3) which passes through B (see Figure 6).

turn, determines both production and borrowing. The maximization problem is given below in equation (13).

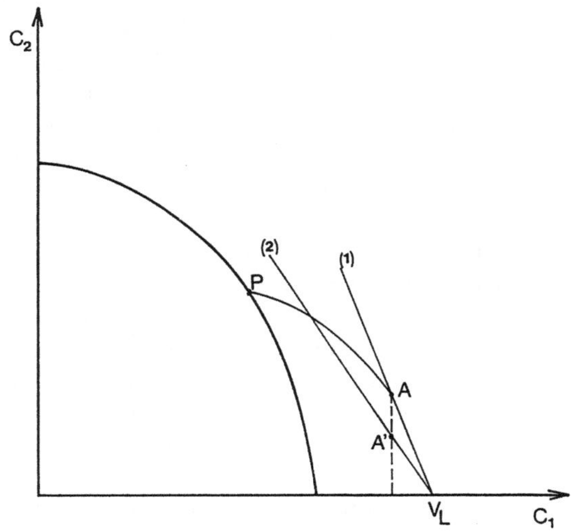

Figure 7

$$\max_{I,\alpha} V \equiv \left[W_0 - I + \frac{\alpha C_2(I)}{[1 + (1-T)r(C_2,\alpha)]} + \frac{(1-\alpha)C_2(I)}{[1 + K(C_2,\alpha)]} \right] . \qquad (13)$$

In order to simplify the maximization analysis we assume that the level of "operating" risk along the production frontier is constant, namely r and k do not depend on the level of C_2 which is selected on the production frontier. We also assume that $r'(\alpha)$ and $k'(\alpha)$ are positive. The first order conditions are:

$$\frac{\partial V}{\partial I} = -1 + \frac{C_2'(I)\alpha}{(1 + (1-T)r(\alpha))} + \frac{(1-\alpha)C_2'(I)}{(1 + K(\alpha))} = 0 \qquad (14)$$

$$\frac{\partial V}{\partial \alpha} = C_2(I) \quad \frac{(1 + (1-T)r(\alpha)) + r'(\alpha)(1-T)\alpha}{(1 + (1-T)r(\alpha))^2} - \frac{1 + k(\alpha) + (1-\alpha)K'(\alpha)}{1 + K(\alpha))^2}$$

$$= 0 \qquad (15)$$

From the first order condition (14) we obtain again

$$C_2'(I) = \frac{(1 + K(\alpha))(1 + (1-T)r(\alpha))}{\alpha(1 + K(\alpha)) + (1-\alpha)[1 + (1-T)r(\alpha)]} \tag{16}$$

The cut off rate in (16) is an extension of (12) where we have assumed that the corporate price of financial transformation of cashflows is equal to the personal one (r) and both are independent of α.

Let us analyze once again two extreme cases: (a) For $\alpha = 1$ we obtain $\bar{C}_2'(I) = [1 + (1-T)r(1)]$, which is equal to the after tax cost of borrowing. (b) For $\alpha = 0$ we obtain $C_2'(I) = 1 + K(0)$ which is equal to the cost of equity of unlevered corporation. In all other cases ($0 < \alpha < 1$) the cut off rate in (16) is once again the weighted average cost of capital. The crucial point is finding the optimal α^* (optimal capital structure) which simultaneously enables us to derive the average cost of capital which serves as a cut off rate for determining the optimal investment strategy. This optimum capital structure α^* can be solved from the first order condition (15).

$$\alpha^* = \frac{\dfrac{1 + K(\alpha) + K'(\alpha)}{(1 + K(\alpha))^2} - \dfrac{1}{1 + (1-T)r(\alpha)}}{\dfrac{(1-T)r'(\alpha)}{(1 + (1-T)r(\alpha))^2} + \dfrac{K'(\alpha)}{(1 + K(\alpha))^2}} \tag{17}$$

Though, in the most general case this is a complex term, it reduces in some specific cases to well-known results:

(1) If $r'(\alpha) = K'(\alpha) = 0$ and $(1-T)r(\alpha) < K(\alpha)$ then α^* approaches ∞ and, as expected, an extreme leverage is optimal.

(2) In general the specific solution of α^* depends on the forms of $K(\alpha)$ and tax rate T. If $r'(\alpha)$ is small enough then α^* increases with T. Namely, the risk of bankruptcy is relatively small, hence the saving due to corporate taxes is the dominating factor.

(3) Finally, Modigliani and Miller assumed (in the no-tax case) that $r'(\alpha) = 0$ and obtained that $V_L = V_U$ and $K(\alpha) = K(0) + [K(0)-r]B/S$. Similar results emerge as a specific case in our model. Let us look once again at the maximization problem and the value of the corporation as expressed in equation (13). According to (13) the value of unleveraged corporation when $T = 0$ is:

$$W_0 - I + \frac{\bar{C}_2}{1 + K(0)} \tag{18}$$

The value of the levered corporation is:

$$W_0 - I + B + \frac{\bar{C}_2 - B(1+r)}{1 + K(\alpha)} \tag{19}$$

where $B = \alpha\bar{C}_2/(1+r)$. If $V_L = V_U$ (as Modigliani and Miller claim) we obtain from (18) and (19):

$$W_0 - I + B + \frac{\bar{C}_2 - B(1+r)}{(1 + K(\alpha))} = W_0 - I + \frac{\bar{C}_2}{(1 + K(0))} \tag{20}$$

By rearranging terms in (20) we obtain

$$-\frac{B}{V_0} r + k(0) = K(\alpha)\left[1 - \frac{B}{V_0}\right]$$

However, $(1-B/V_0) = S/V_0$. Thus, we can find that $K(\alpha) = K(0) + [K(0) - r]B/S$, which is precisely the Modigliani and Miller result.

Concluding Remarks

Miller's presidential address has renewed an old debate with respect to the relationship between the value of the firm and its capital structure.

In this paper we employ Hirshliefer's investment-consumption framework to graphically obtain the following results:

1. Modigliani and Miller's results $V_L = V_U$ with no taxes and $V_L = V_U + TB$ with corporate taxes and production is held constant.
2. Arditti, Levy and Sarnat's result

$$V_L = V_U + B\left[1 - \frac{(1-T)(1-T_g)}{(1-T_p)}\right]$$

with personal and corporate taxes.

3. We demonstrate graphically Miller's claim that $V_L = V_U$ with corporate and personal taxes.

Then we show that with corporate taxes, but no personal taxes, the relationship $V_L = V_U + TB$ does not hold when we allow the firm to shift to the optimum production level. In equilibrium the following must hold, $V_L = V_U + TB + \delta$ when $\delta > 0$. Modigliani and Miller, analyzing the impact of corporate tax explicitly or implicitly assume that the firm does not change its net operating income. Hence, they compare two states where, in one state the firm adopts an optimum production plan while in the other state the firm does not execute projects with positive NPV, hence the firm is not at the optimum production point on its production plan. Thus, Modigliani and Miller, and most other studies which followed their work, ignore the interrelationship between the proportion of debt, cost of capital and optimum production.

Employing the certainty equivalent approach we find that the cost of equity is r and the cost of debt is $(1-T)r$. However, assuming no bankruptcy, the optimum capital structure is dictated by an extreme debt financing. In this case, the firm's cost of capital is $(1-T)r$.

Imposing an external constraint of the debt borrowing (e.g., due to regulation or agency cost), the firm's cost of capital is a weighted average of r and $(1-T)r$, when the proportion of debt and equity financing (B/V and S/V, respectively) serve as weights.

Finally, we analyze the case where risk and bankruptcy costs are explicitly taken into account. Assuming that the cost of borrowing $r(\alpha)$ and the cost of equity $K(\alpha)$ are increasing functions of the proportion of debt α, we found that the optimum capital structure may be an interior one. While this is not guaranteed in all cases, if $K(\alpha)$ increases sharply for high values α, it is almost certain that an interior solution would be obtained. The optimum capital structure is given by a complicated term which is a function of $k(\alpha)$, $r(\alpha)$, the tax value T, as well as the derivatives $K'(\alpha)$ and $r'(\alpha)$. If one assumes, like Modigliani and Miller that $r'(\alpha) = 0$, we obtain the well-known Modigliani and Miller results as a specific case of our general analyses.

In this paper we provide a theoretical framework for finding the optimum capital structure and the firm's cost of capital. Employing this model in practice is not an easy task and is involved with difficult measurement problems.

References

[1] Arditti, F.D., H. Levy, and M. Sarnat, "Taxes, Capital Structure and the Cost of Capital: Some Extensions," The Quarterly Review of Economics and Business 17, No. 2: 89-95.

[2] Ben Horim Moshe, "Comment on the Weighted Average Cost of Capital as a Cutoff Rate," Financial Management (Summer 1979): 18-21.

[3] Brennan, N.J. and E.S. Schwartz, "Optimal Financial Policy and Firm Valuation," Journal of Finance (July 1984): 593-609.

[4] DeAngelo, A. and R. Masulis, "Optimal Capital Structure Under Corporate and Personal Taxation," Journal of Financial Economics (1980): 3-29.

[5] Hirshliefer, J.H., "On the Theory of Optimal Investment Decision," Journal of Political Economy (August 1958): 329-352.

[6] Hite, G., "Leverage, Output Effects, and the M-M Theorem," Journal of Financial Economics (1977): 177-202.

[7] Kane, A., S. Marcus, and R.L. McDonald, "How Big is the Tax Advantage to Debt?" Journal of Finance (July 1984): 841-853.

[8] Kim, E.H., "Miller's Equilibrium, Shareholder Leverage Clientels, and Optimal Capital Structure," Journal of Finance (May 1982): 301-319.

[9] Masulis, R.W., "The Impact of Capital Structure Change on Firm Value: Some Estimates," Journal of Finance (March 1983): 107-126.

[10] Miller, M.H., "Debt and Taxes," Journal of Finance (May 1979): 261-275.

[11] Modigliani, F. and M. Miller, "The Cost of Capital, Corporation Finance, and the Theory of Investment," American Economic Review (June 1958): 162-197.

[12] Modigliani, F. and M. Miller, "The Cost of Capital, Corporation Finance, and the Theory of Investment," American Economic Review (June 1963): 433-443.

[13] Modigliani, F. and M. Miller, "Reply to Heins and Sprenkel," American Economic Review (September 1969): 592-595.

[14] Myers, S.C., "The Capital Structure Puzzle," Journal of Finance (May 1984): 575-592.

[15] Senbet, L.W. and R.A. Taggart, "Capital Structure Equilibrium Under Market Imperfection and Incompleteness," Journal of Finance (March 1984): 93-103.

[16] Schneller, M., "Taxes and the Optimal Capital Structure of the Firm," Journal of Finance (March 1980): 119-127.

[17] Trzsinka, C., "The Pricing of Tax-Exempt Bond and the Miller Hypothesis," Journal of Finance (September 1982): 907-923.

UTILITY FUNCTIONS, INTEREST RATES, AND THE DEMAND FOR BONDS

John W. Pratt*
Harvard University
Cambridge, MA 02138

1. Introduction

One riskless investment dominates any other with a lower interest rate in the simplest, most complete way one could hope for. Still, given the risky assets available, a lower riskless interest rate might lead a risk-averse expected-utility maximizer to (a) allocate more of his investment funds to riskless assets, or (b) allocate enough more to obtain greater riskless return including principal, or even (c) allocate enough more to obtain greater riskless income. One easy intuitive explanation is that, at a lower riskless interest rate, greater riskless investment may be needed to guarantee some minimum acceptable income or future wealth. Alternative characterizations of the three possibilities are that, for this individual, (a) demand for riskless future wealth has elasticity less than 1; (b) riskless future wealth is a Giffen good; (c) riskless income is a Giffen good.

From such individuals, the seller of a single-payment bond might (a) raise more capital at a lower interest rate, or (b) raise enough more capital to increase his future obligation, or even (c) raise enough more capital to result in greater total interest paid. Equivalently, a larger number of bonds could be sold to such individuals (a) at the same price with a lower face-plus-coupon (capital payment plus interest), or (b) at a higher price with the same face-plus-coupon, or even (c) at a higher price with the same discount from face-plus-coupon.

This paper determines necessary and sufficient conditions on an investor's utility function for these phenomena to be possible (or impossible) when the mix of risky assets is fixed, in the spirit well described and represented by Hadar and Russell (1974). The results are stated in the next section and proved thereafter. Fishburn and Porter (1976) note the possibility of phenomenon (a) and give

*I am grateful to Richard Zeckhauser for instigating and abetting this research, to Tae Kun Seo for comments, and to the Associates of the Harvard Business School for support.

sufficient conditions to preclude it, but those given here are easily seen to be weaker. They also give sufficient conditions for stochastically dominant improvement in the risky asset to increase investment in it, a question not considered here, and review related literature, which includes somewhat similar but not directly comparable work.

2. Statement of Results

Suppose that an investor with risk-averse von Neumann-Morgenstern utility function u defined on final wealth were required to divide his initial wealth between just two securities, one risky and the other riskless. Our questions, turned around, are: when could increasing the riskless interest rate reduce (a) the optimum amount allocated to the riskless security, or (b) the return derived from it including principal, or (c) the income derived from it?

Given initial capital w, if an amount θ is invested risklessly, with final value t per unit invested, and the remainder $\mu = w - \theta$ is invested in a risk with final value $\tilde{x}$ per unit invested, then final wealth is $\theta t + \mu\tilde{x} = \tilde{z}$, say. This has expected utility

$$U = Eu(\tilde{z}) = Eu(\theta t + \mu\tilde{x}), \quad (\mu = w - \theta). \tag{1}$$

Let $\hat{\theta}$ be the optimum riskless investment level. The corresponding return including principal is $\hat{\theta}t$ and the income is $\hat{\theta}t - \hat{\theta}$. For convenience, we shall say that u _responds strongly, normally, or weakly to interest_ if, respectively, $\hat{\theta}$, $\hat{\theta}t$, or $\hat{\theta}t - \hat{\theta}$ is a nondecreasing function of t for every w and every distribution of $\tilde{x}$. We define responsiveness _on the interval_ (w_1, w_2) similarly by requiring monotonicity if all possible outcomes are restricted to this interval, that is, if $t_1 < t < t_2$ and $P(t_1 < \tilde{x} < t_2) = 1$ where $t_i = w_i/w$. We assume throughout that $0 \le \theta \le w$ (no borrowing or short sales), $t \ge 0$ and $P(\tilde{x} \ge 0) = 1$ (no future investment obligation), and $0 \le w_1 < w_2 \le \infty$ (nonnegative wealth). For weak responsiveness, we assume that $t \ge 1$. Responsiveness on overlapping intervals obviously implies responsiveness on their union.

Clearly strong implies normal implies weak responsiveness by their definitions (or because they preclude (a), (b), and (c) respectively and (c) implies (b) implies (a)). It turns out that weak and normal are equivalent as they are defined, although fixing w or restricting its range would weaken weak responsiveness but not the other types. The reason that weak and normal responsiveness are nevertheless equivalent is essentially that income is very close to return including principal when the investment required to achieve a given income is very small (t is very large).

The necessary and sufficient conditions for (a) strong and (b) normal or weak responsiveness on an interval (w_1, w_2) can be expressed in terms of the risk aversion function $r = -u''/u'$ as

$$\text{(a)}\quad r(z_1) - \frac{1}{z_1 - w_1} \le r(z_2) + \frac{1}{w_2 - z_2} \quad \text{for} \quad w_1 < z_1 < z_2 < w_2,$$

$$\text{(b)}\quad M(w_1, z_1) \le M(w_2, z_2) \quad \text{for} \quad w_1 < z_1 < z_2 < w_2$$

where

$$M(w, z) = \begin{cases} wr(z) + w/(w - z) & \text{if} \quad (w-z)^2 \le z/r(z) \\ ([zr(z)]^{1/2} \pm 1)^2 & \text{if} \quad \pm (w - z) \ge [z/r(z)]^{1/2}. \end{cases}$$

In each case, "for" means "for all z_1, z_2 such that" and simplifications occur if $w_2 = \infty$. Condition (a) is equivalent to the existence of an increasing function g such that

$$\text{(a}'\text{)}\quad r(z) - \frac{1}{z - w_1} \le g(z) \le r(z) + \frac{1}{w_2 - z} \quad \text{for} \quad w_1 < z < w_2.$$

Condition (b) can be rewritten similarly. Fishburn and Porter's (1976) condition that $r(z)$ be either nondecreasing or $\le 1/z$ obviously implies (a) with $w_1 = 0$, $w_2 = \infty$ and hence strong responsiveness on $(0,\infty)$, their main result for the problem considered here.

Condition (a) with $w_2 = \infty$ and r nonincreasing implies that a decreasingly risk-averse utility function u responds strongly to interest on (w_1, ∞) iff

$$\text{(a}''\text{)}\quad r(z) \le r_\infty + \frac{1}{z - w_1} \quad \text{for } z > w_1$$

where $r_\infty = \lim r(z)$ as $z \to \infty$. Hyperbolic absolute risk aversion $r(z) = 1/(a + bz)$ satisfies (a") iff either $b = 0$ and $a > 0$ or $b \ge 1$ and $a \ge -bw_1$, that is, either risk aversion is a positive constant $1/a$ or relative risk aversion is a positive constant $1/b \le 1$ when wealth is measured from some origin $w_o = -a/b \le w_1$, corresponding to $u(z) = -e^{-z/a}$ or $\log(z - w_o)$ or $(z - w_o)^c$ for some $c \in (0,1)$ and $w_o < w_1$.

The normal responsiveness condition (b) with $w_2 = \infty$ is

$$\text{(b}'\text{)}\quad M(w_1, z_1) \le (\sqrt{R(z_2)} + 1)^2 \quad \text{for} \quad w_1 < z_1 < z_2$$

where $R(z) = zr(z)$ is the relative risk aversion function. Increasing relative risk aversion implies normal responsiveness on $(0, \infty)$ since the left-hand side of (b') is at most $R(z_1)$ and the right-hand side is at least $R(z_2)$. For decreasing relative risk aversion, normal responsiveness on (w_1, ∞) is equivalent to

$$\text{(b")} \quad M(w_1, z) = \max_{w_1<y<z} \; yr(z) - \frac{y}{z - y} \leq (\sqrt{R_\infty} + 1)^2 \text{ for } w_1 < z$$

where $R_\infty = \lim R(z)$ as $z \to \infty$.

Hyperbolic absolute risk aversion is normally responsive on $(0, \infty)$ if $w_o \leq 0$ $(a \geq 0)$, since it then has increasing relative risk aversion. It is normally responsive on the entire range of definition (w_o, ∞) if $w_o > 0$ and $b \geq 1$, since it is then strongly responsive as we have already seen. In the remaining case $w_o > 0$, $b < 1$, it is normally responsive on (w_1, ∞) iff $w_1 \geq w_o(1 + \sqrt{b})^2/4\sqrt{b}$, as can be shown by maximizing with respect to z before y in (b").

The following two theorems state our main results formally, the second adding some detail to the converse for strong and normal responsiveness.

<u>Theorem 1</u>: The utility function u responds strongly to interest on the interval (w_1, w_2) iff u satisfies condition (a). Normal and weak responsiveness are each equivalent to condition (b).

<u>Theorem 2</u>: If u does not satisfy (a), then there exist a final wealth v and risk $\tilde{y}$ in (w_1, w_2) such that, for any riskless rate t and initial wealth w with $wt = v$, the optimum riskless investment level for the risk $\tilde{x} = \tilde{y}/w$ has negative derivative at t and hence is strictly decreasing in a neighborhood of t. The same statement holds with (b) in place of (a) and return including principal in place of investment level.

3. Proof for Strong Responsiveness

Consider U, given by (1), as a function of θ and t for given w and $\tilde{x}$. Since U is concave in θ, for each t the optimum $\hat{\theta}(t)$ is determined when it is interior by

$$\frac{\partial U}{\partial \theta} = Eu'(\theta t + \mu\tilde{x})(t - \tilde{x})$$
$$= 0 \quad \text{at} \quad \hat{\theta}(t). \tag{2}$$

By implicit differentiation,

$$\hat{\theta}'(t) = - \frac{\partial^2 U}{\partial\theta\partial t} \bigg/ \frac{\partial^2 U}{\partial\theta^2} \quad \text{at} \quad \hat{\theta}(t). \tag{3}$$

Since $\partial^2 U/\partial\theta^2 < 0$ by concavity (see also below), $\hat{\theta}'(t)$ has the same sign as

$$\frac{\partial^2 U}{\partial\theta\partial t} = E[\theta u''(\tilde{z})(t - \tilde{x}) + u'(\tilde{z})$$

$$= \theta E u'(\tilde{z})(t - \tilde{x})\left(\frac{1}{\theta(t - \tilde{x})} - r(\tilde{z})\right) \tag{4}$$

where $\tilde{z} = \theta t + \mu\tilde{x}$. Suppose (a) holds and $0 < \theta < w$. For $t_1 < x < t$ we have $w_1 < wx < z = wx + \theta(t - x) < wt$ and hence, by (a'),

$$r(z) - \frac{1}{\theta(t - x)} = r(z) - \frac{1}{z - wx} \le r(z) - \frac{1}{z - w_1} \le g(wt). \tag{5}$$

For $t < x < t_2$ we have $w_2 > wx > z = wx + \theta(t - x) \ge wt$ and hence

$$r(z) - \frac{1}{\theta(t - x)} = r(z) + \frac{1}{wx - z} \ge r(z) + \frac{1}{w_2 - z} \ge g(wt). \tag{6}$$

Therefore, when $\hat{\theta}(t)$ is interior,

$$\frac{\partial^2 U}{\partial\theta\partial t} \ge \theta E u'(\tilde{z})(t - \tilde{x})g(wt) = 0 \quad \text{at} \quad \hat{\theta}(t), \tag{7}$$

whence $\hat{\theta}'(t) \ge 0$. Therefore u responds strongly to interest on (w_1, w_2).

For the converse, since the expected utility (1) depends only on wt, $w\tilde{x}$, and θ/w, we can assume without loss of generality that $w = 1$; then $t = v$ and $\tilde{x} = \tilde{y}$. If (a) does not hold, then there exist z_1, z_2, y_1, y_2 such that $w_1 < y_1 < z_1 < z_2 < y_2 < w_2$ and

$$r(z_1) - \frac{1}{z_1 - y_1} > r(z_2) + \frac{1}{y_2 - z_2}. \tag{8}$$

Choose v so that $z_1 < v < z_2$ and the spacing of y_1, z_1, v is proportional to that of y_2, z_2, v, that is

$$\frac{z_1 - y_1}{v - y_1} = \frac{y_2 - z_2}{y_2 - v} = \lambda, \tag{9}$$

say. Then $0 < \lambda < 1$. Let $\tilde{y}$ have possible values y_1 and y_2 with probabilities chosen so that $\partial U/\partial\theta = 0$ at $\theta = \lambda$, $t = v$. Then $\hat{\theta}(v) = \lambda$ by (2). Let g_o be a constant between the two sides of (8). Then by (9) and (4),

$$\frac{\partial^2 U}{\partial\theta\partial t} < \theta E u'(\tilde{z})(t - \tilde{x})g_o = 0 \quad \text{at} \quad \theta = \lambda,\ t = v. \tag{10}$$

Therefore $\hat{\theta}'(v) < 0$, whence $\hat{\theta}$ is strictly decreasing in a neighborhood of v.

4. Proof for Normal Responsiveness

The return $J(t) = t\hat{\theta}(t)$ has derivative $J'(t) = t\hat{\theta}'(t) + \hat{\theta}(t)$. Since

$$\frac{\partial^2 U}{\partial \theta^2} = Eu''(\tilde{z})(t - \tilde{x})^2 = -Eu'(\tilde{z})r(\tilde{z})(t - \tilde{x})^2, \tag{11}$$

which we see again is negative, $J'(t)$ has by (3) and (4) the same sign as

$$t\,\frac{\partial^2 U}{\partial \theta \partial t} - \theta\,\frac{\partial^2 U}{\partial \theta^2} = Eu'(\tilde{z})(t - \tilde{x})\left(\frac{t}{t - \tilde{x}} - \theta\tilde{x}r(\tilde{z})\right). \tag{12}$$

We may write the last factor as

$$1 + \frac{\tilde{x}}{t - \tilde{x}} - \theta\tilde{x}r(\tilde{z}) = 1 + \frac{\theta}{w}\left(\frac{\tilde{y}}{\tilde{z} - \tilde{y}} - \tilde{y}r(\tilde{z})\right) \tag{13}$$

where $\tilde{y} = w\tilde{x}$. As in Section 3, $J' \geq 0$ if the quantity (13) is larger for $\tilde{x} < t$ than for $\tilde{x} > t$, or equivalently if

$$\frac{y_1}{z_1 - y_1} - y_1 r(z_1) \geq \frac{y_2}{z_2 - y_2} - y_2 r(z_2)$$

$$\text{for} \quad w_1 < y_1 < z_1 < z_2 < y_2 < w_2. \tag{14}$$

Minimizing the left-hand side with respect to y_1 and maximizing the right-hand side with respect to y_2 gives (b), which therefore implies normal responsiveness.

If conversely (b) does not hold, then there exist y_i, z_i such that (14) holds with < in place of ≥, and the second sentence of Theorem 2 can be proved as the first was after (8).

5. Proof for Weak Responsiveness

The income $I(t) = t\hat{\theta}(t) - \hat{\theta}(t) = J(t) - \hat{\theta}(t)$ has derivative

$$I'(t) = (t - 1)\hat{\theta}'(t) + \hat{\theta}(t) = J'(t) - \hat{\theta}'(t). \tag{15}$$

Under condition (b), $J' \geq 0$ and hence $I' \geq 0$ (from the last expression if $\hat{\theta}'(t) \leq 0$ and the next-to-last if $\hat{\theta}'(t) \geq 0$).

If (b) does not hold, then $J'(t) < 0$ for some w, $\tilde{x}$, t. Since the optimum investment for aw, $\tilde{x}/a$, t/a is obviously a times the optimum for w, $\tilde{x}$, t, the corresponding return is the same and the income is

$$I_a(t/a) = J(t) - a\hat{\theta}(t). \tag{16}$$

Hence, for sufficiently small a, we have $I_a'(t/a) = a[J'(t) - a\hat{\theta}'(t)] < 0$ and $t/a > 1$, so weak responsiveness does not hold.

References

Fishburn, Peter C., and R. Burr Porter, "Optimal Portfolios with One Safe and One Risky Asset: Effects of Changes in Rate of Return and Risk." Management Science 22 (1976): 1064-73.

Hadar, Josef, and William Russell, "Stochastic Dominance in Choice Under Uncertainty." In Essays on Economic Behavior Under Uncertainty, ed. M. Balch, D. McFadden, and S. Wu, 82-92. North Holland, 1974.

MIX
Papier aus verantwortungsvollen Quellen
Paper from responsible sources
FSC® C105338

If you have any concerns about our products,
you can contact us on
ProductSafety@springernature.com

In case Publisher is established outside the EU,
the EU authorized representative is:
Springer Nature Customer Service Center GmbH
Europaplatz 3, 69115 Heidelberg, Germany

Printed by Libri Plureos GmbH
in Hamburg, Germany